RESEARCH AND PRACTICE IN PHYSICAL EDUCATION

Research findings in education can provide invaluable insight into how teaching practice can be improved, but research papers are often inaccessible and hard to digest. This innovative new text is designed to assist physical education pre-service teachers, practising teachers and teacher educators with learning how to read research and to apply it to practice in primary and secondary physical education. The text also provides insights and implications for those working with young people in physical activity and sport settings.

The book presents a clear, step-by-step guide on to how to read and interpret research, followed by a series of short and engaging introductions to contemporary research studies on key topics in physical education, from classroom management and programme design to assessment and social issues. Each study is discussed from the point of view of researcher, teacher educator and primary and post-primary teacher, providing the reader with invaluable insight into how to use research to generate new ideas and improve their teaching practice.

Research and Practice in Physical Education is the perfect companion to any course in research methods, current issues, learning and teaching, or pedagogy and curriculum in physical education.

Deborah Tannehill taught post-primary physical education for ten years in the USA. She is currently Senior Lecturer in the Department of Physical Education and Sport Sciences at University of Limerick, Ireland. She is Course Director for the Professional Diploma in Education: Physical Education, and Co-Director of Physical Education, Physical Activity and Youth Sport (PE-PAYS) Research Centre. Her research interests include physical education, teacher education, continuing professional development and communities of practice, and teaching physical education.

Ann MacPhail is Senior Lecturer and Head of Department in the Department of Physical Education and Sport Sciences at the University of Limerick, Ireland. Ann's main teaching and research interests revolve around physical education, teacher education, methodological issues in working with young people and school physical education.

Ger Halbert has taught post-primary physical education, civic, social and political education (CSPE) and social, personal and health education (SPHE) for the past 21 years in Ireland. She currently works as an education officer with National Council for Curriculum and Assessment in Ireland. She is part of a team that is supporting the introduction of the new junior cycle in second-level education.

Frances Murphy taught as a generalist primary teacher for 15 years. She is currently a Lecturer in Physical Education in the Education Department at St Patrick's College, Ireland. Her research interests include the development of appropriate after-school programmes for children to promote increased levels of physical activity, motor skill development and social development.

RESEARCH AND PRACTICE IN PHYSICAL EDUCATION

*Deborah Tannehill, Ann MacPhail,
Ger Halbert and Frances Murphy*

*With Lawrence F. Locke and
Dolly Lambdin*

Routledge
Taylor & Francis Group

LONDON AND NEW YORK

First published 2013
by Routledge
2 Park Square, Milton Park, Abingdon, Oxon OX14 4RN

Simultaneously published in the USA and Canada
by Routledge
711 Third Avenue, New York, NY 10017

Routledge is an imprint of the Taylor & Francis Group, an informa business

© 2013 Deborah Tannehill, Ann MacPhail, Ger Halbert and Frances Murphy

British Library Cataloguing in Publication Data
A catalogue record for this book is available from the British Library

Library of Congress Cataloging in Publication Data
MacPhail, Ann.
  Research and practice in physical education/Ann MacPhail . . . [*et al.*].
  p. cm.
  Includes bibliographical references.
  1. Physical education and training – Research. I. Title.
  GV361.M183 2013
  613.71072 – dc23
  2012026594

ISBN: 978-0-415-69863-4 (hbk)
ISBN: 978-0-415-69865-8 (pbk)
ISBN: 978-0-203-13692-8 (ebk)

Typeset in Goudy
by Florence Production Limited, Stoodleigh, Devon

MIX
Paper from
responsible sources
FSC® C004839

Printed and bound by CPI Group (UK) Ltd, Croydon, CR0 4YY

To Larry Locke and Dolly Lambdin for their initial rendition of this book and their considerable energy promoting and applying research for teachers.

To pre-service and practicing teachers who constantly strive to do better at providing a positive physical education and physical activity experience to young people.

CONTENTS

FIGURES

ABOUT THE AUTHORS

Deborah Tannehill is a Senior Lecturer in the Department of Physical Education and Sport Sciences at the University of Limerick. She is Course Director for the Graduate Diploma in Education – Physical Education and Co-Director of the Physical Education, Physical Activity and Youth Sport (PE-PAYS) Research Centre. Deborah earned her B.Sc. in physical education from Washington State University, her MA in guidance and counselling from Seattle University and her Ph.D. in sport pedagogy from the University of Idaho. Prior to joining the faculty at the University of Limerick, Deborah was Professor and Assistant Dean at Pacific Lutheran University (PLU) and Professor at The Ohio State University. She taught physical education at the middle school level for 10 years and coached athletics at the collegiate level and with disability sport (American Amputee Association) for six years. Deborah has been professionally active in both the USA and Ireland, having served on numerous committees and task forces for the National Association of Sport and Physical Education (NASPE). She is a member of the Physical Education Association of Ireland (PEAI) and works with physical education teachers through a national community of practice initiative and an urban schools project. In recognition of her professional service, Deborah has received several awards, including the 2009 NASPE Curriculum and Instruction Academy Honour Award, the Joy of Effort Award from NASPE, Research Fellow in the AAHPERD Research Consortium, NASPE Presidential Citation, and acknowledgment from PEAI for service rendered. In recognition of her teaching, Deborah received The Ohio State University Alumni Award for Distinguished Teaching and was nominated for the Shannon Consortium Award for Excellence in Higher Education Teaching. Deborah is past co-editor of the *Journal of Teaching in Physical Education*, served on the editorial board of *Quest*, and is currently a reviewer for the *Journal of Physical Education, Recreation, and Dance* and guest reviewer for a number of academic journals. She has conducted research on teaching and teacher education in physical education, and publishes frequently in both scholarly and applied journals with numerous individual or co-authored book chapters. She is co-author of three textbooks: *Developing teaching skills in physical education* with Daryl Siedentop and two editions of *Standards-based curriculum development in physical education* with Jackie Lund. Currently her work is focused on curriculum development, assessment and self-study of her own teaching practice. She can be contacted at deborah.tannehill@ul.ie.

Ann MacPhail is Senior Lecturer and Head of Department in the Department of Physical Education and Sport Sciences at the University of Limerick in Ireland. Ann has a B.Ed. (Honours) in physical education from Heriot-Watt University, Edinburgh, and a Ph.D. from the University of Glasgow. Ann's main teaching and research interests revolve around physical education teacher education, young people in sport, curriculum development in physical education, teaching, learning and assessment issues within school physical education, methodological issues in working with young people and ethnography. She has published in these areas in both scholarly and applied journals and in book chapters. Ann is a member of the Physical Education Association of Ireland Executive Committee and External Examiner for a number of physical education undergraduate and graduate programmes. Ann has been involved in a number of research projects as a member of the Physical Education, Physical Activity and Youth Sport Research Centre (PE-PAYS) at the University of Limerick. Ann is co-editor of *Young people's voices in physical education and sport* (2010) (Routledge) and is Associate Editor for the journal *Physical Education and Sport Pedagogy*, Associate Editor of *Revista Pedagogica ADAL/ADAL Pedagogy Journal* and a member of the Editorial Board for the *Journal of Teaching in Physical Education*. Ann enjoys eating copious amounts of chocolate and drinking buckets of Coke. She does like nuts, but not in chocolate.

Frances Murphy is a Lecturer in the Education Department of St Patrick's College, Dublin. She has shared responsibility within the Physical Education Unit for the preparation of primary teachers to teach physical education. After teaching as a classroom teacher at primary level Frances worked as part of a team on the development of the Primary Physical Education Curriculum that is currently implemented in Irish primary schools. This was followed by work on a programme to prepare tutors to support implementation of the curriculum in primary schools. She has supervised primary teachers who are pursuing work at masters level related to physical education. Her own research work has focused on initial teacher education and professional development. Frances coaches children and young people in school and club settings.

Ger Halbert is an Education Officer with the National Council for Curriculum and Assessment (NCCA) in Ireland. She graduated as a physical education and English teacher in 1979 and throughout her teaching career has been actively involved with her professional subject association attending conferences and continuing professional development (CPD) events in physical education. In 2002, she completed a Graduate Diploma in Health Education and Health Promotion and this led to a part-time role with NCCA with responsibility to support the development of a framework for Social, Personal and Health Education (SPHE) in senior cycle. She completed a M.Ed. in 2005, which involved an action research project into her own teaching of SPHE. Continuing to teach in a part-time capacity in a large all-girls secondary school, she acted as a part-time NCCA education officer, supporting the development of both the senior cycle physical education framework and the draft syllabus for physical education for those students who wished to study physical education for their Leaving Certificate examination. Ger now works as a full-time education officer and is part of a team supporting the introduction of the new junior cycle framework for junior cycle education in Ireland. Married to John, Ger has two adult children and enjoys travelling, being active and spending time with her family and friends. She can be contacted at gerhalbert@gmail.com.

INTRODUCTION TO READING RESEARCH

Deborah Tannehill, Ann MacPhail,
Ger Halbert and Frances Murphy

In 2003, Larry Locke and Dolly Lambdin published a gem of a book through Human Kinetics, *Putting research to work in elementary physical education: Conversations in the gym*. Whether working with pre-service, novice or veteran teachers at the primary/elementary or post-primary/secondary level we found this book invaluable for helping professionals learn to read, understand and appreciate research and its application to practice.

Like the first edition, *Research and practice in physical education*, now published by Routledge, is for physical educators. The audience we invite to read this book is similar to the audience for the first edition, including primary and post-primary physical educators, teacher educators and their pre-service teachers, novice researchers and those pursuing graduate study in sport pedagogy, programme administrators and coaches working with young people in physical activity and sport settings, and research scholars. So as not to confuse you, please note that we will refer to primary/elementary or post-primary/secondary interchangeably depending on the research report and the part of the world from which the researchers came. It is our intent to share, report and discuss research in ways that clarify the implications and applications for practice, assisting those interested in quality physical education and physical activity programmes in reading and understanding research in order to apply it in their own practice and subsequently contribute to their continuing professional development. This edition takes a similar format to the first, reflecting a conversation between researcher and veteran teachers, coaches and programme designers, although in our final reading of the text, we seem to take a more practitioner-oriented perspective.

Who are we . . . the authors?

We are four physical educators who have taught in schools at all levels, coached at primary, post-primary, collegiate and disability athletics, worked as a full-time research fellow, in curriculum development and teacher education, conducted research on teaching, coaching and teacher education, and supervised undergraduate, master's and doctoral research. One of us identifies most with her role as a primary teacher, while another values her research agenda and how it can inform practice. One of our final two authors is most committed to post-primary students and their engagement in physical activity and the other values her work in teacher education across initial and in-service education. Our collective teaching and research remits in education span over 125 years in three countries, the United States, the United Kingdom and Ireland. In describing ourselves we realise that many of our friends and colleagues call us 'nerds' because of our intense investment in our work and never missing an opportunity to discuss it even in social situations. When your work is enjoyable and a passion, can it really be considered work? We not only enjoy teaching, coaching and working with young people but value our discussions of pedagogy and interactions with colleagues in an attempt to improve what happens in the name of physical education and helping others choose a physically active lifestyle.

Who are you . . . the reader?

We often lament the fact that researchers tend to talk to researchers, and while their findings may indeed be intended to impact practice, the practitioners are not those with whom they share, discuss and build relationships around application. This text is intended to be accessible to a diverse group of readers, share an assortment of research studies that have relevance to teaching primary and secondary physical education internationally and will not require readers to possess a highly technical vocabulary, advanced scientific knowledge, or a detailed background concerning research methods. Rather than expect every research paper to have a companion pedagogical publication it is our hope that this work will assist the practitioner in reading and applying research to their own practice. Keep in mind that researchers do not publish in scholarly journals just to boost their egos but due to the requirements set by universities to maintain their positions, and to affect practice by informing colleagues of pertinent findings. One caution, however, we do not claim that our interpretations of the selected research are accurate from the original researchers' perspective, or even from how you will interpret it . . . these are our thoughts, which have resulted from our reading and extensive discussions, so use them as you may.

How the book is organised

The content of the selected 22 research papers are grouped into four categories:

1   student engagement and experiences;
2   instruction, learning and assessment;

3   curriculum models;
4   continuing professional development.

These categories are explained at the beginning of each section prior to presentation of the selected research papers. As with the first edition, each study is briefly described (from our viewpoint) and commented on from a research perspective. However, we then provide a response from a teacher educator, primary and post-primary teachers and, in some cases, a shared response, or only a shared response. With each of us coming from the varied backgrounds described above, development of our responses was collaborative and shared in most instances. On a few occasions you will see us use 'I' rather than 'we' and in those instances one or the other of us felt strongly about a particular issue or point and took it on from an individual perspective. We would read the paper, come together and discuss what it meant, problems we saw in the study design or interpretation, how it might inform practice in teacher education or when working with young people in schools, and then formulated an action plan for writing our perspective. One of us would be typing comprehensive notes during our discussions to guide all of us in framing and communicating our thoughts in the text.

Each chapter is broken down in a similar format with the following headings: **The study**, which provides a basic description of the research (purpose, participants, design and methods, and results), **Research perspective**, which tended to tackle our initial reactions to the research reported, and a **Teacher educator**, **Primary** and **Post-primary response** to the study and how it might be applied in practice. Which of us wrote each section of our response varied from study to study as, with our varied and overlapping experiences in teaching physical education, it was not clear cut who should take responsibility where. We drew on one another's ideas, squabbled in some cases and built our thoughts as a collective, bringing the response to fruition often using a final category of **Shared response**, or in some cases only providing a shared response, which allowed us to react as a collective when most appropriate. In the end, we read and re-read each other's writing, making constructive changes as we saw fit.

What fun we had reading selected papers, meeting for discussions, interpreting methods and findings, brainstorming ideas and applications, disagreeing on some issues and enthusiastically welcoming others. There were times when one of us would come into the day's discussion grumbling over an article that was a struggle to get through and suggesting it not be used when another of us would excitedly say, 'this was it . . . this article really rattled my cage, the best one we have read so far'. We cannot emphasise enough how much we learned from one another and our discussions of research and practice.

As our discussions evolved we found the different education hats we have each worn over the years affecting our understanding and interpretations of the research and how it might be applied to practice. Our diverse perspectives, developed in different countries, sometimes resulted in misunderstandings due to cultural nuances and language idiosyncrasies, yet we often found that once we interpreted one another we shared similar viewpoints. Don't misunderstand us . . . we did not always agree and you will see in some of our responses where we diverged. Our writing is personal, speaks from the heart and may or may not resonate with your own viewpoints at times. We invite you to learn from these chapters on how to read and interpret research, consider our perspective and interpretation of the studies shared and use what you can to have an impact on your own understanding and practice.

Scope of this book

To clarify what this book is and what it is not . . . let us explain. It does not aim to teach you how to design and conduct research, nor does it intend to provide you with 'how to' teach physical education or physical activity in various settings. It does not suggest programme design guidance or how to improve teaching based on research. What it does do is provide you with our insights on research and our discussions on what that research said to us, the implications we drew from each study for our own teaching practice and how you might read and interpret research to meet your own needs and those of your students. As noted previously, we tended to focus more on how the research caused us to think outside the box and make practitioner decisions on how to apply what we read. We hope that you can learn from the dialogue that took place between us and how we sorted through what we were able to draw from the various research papers. If you do get involved in your own discussion groups, enjoy them, draw as much as you can from each other and learn from one another's insights but most of all be open to what you can gain from research that has been conducted and published to inform our practice of teaching physical education.

Characteristics of research included in this book

As with the Locke and Lambdin edition, to be included as research in this book, each study required all of the following:

- Development of a question, which may have been as narrow as 'How frequently does that happen?' or as broad as 'What's going on here?'
- Explanation of how the question fit into what we already know (literature review) and why it was worth asking (rationale).
- Design of a carefully specified method for collecting accurate information (data) bearing on the question – information that may have been collected as numbers or words.
- Recording and preserving of data in a careful and systematic way.
- Analysing of the data in a manner that maintained its integrity while clarifying its meanings.

- Specification of exactly how the data related to the original question (findings).
- Presentation of the investigator's interpretation of what the findings may have meant when considered in light of the entire study (discussion and conclusions).
- Preparation and submission for review by other researchers (a procedure commonly called 'peer review') and subsequent publication of a reasonably complete account of each of the steps above (the research report).

Research tends to be messy, is not always linear and may portray the researcher in different ways from a participant observer to one who is in charge of interview transcriptions or statistical analysis of questionnaire data. No two research studies will look the same, from the context to the participants and from the research design to the results. In some cases the researchers may develop a set of recommendations for an extension of the conclusions into practical applications, or they may even include a discussion of alternative interpretations of the findings. Those, however, vary from study to study. As you read our descriptions of the studies you will find that we have made the decision on what to include and what to overlook . . . this is a decision we made that we believe will assist you in understanding the research reports we selected to share. Did we make the correct choices? Perhaps not, but we did the best we could on the task and we have used what we share to guide our discussions and interpretations.

By noting what we have included as research papers you should also be able to see what we have excluded. There were instances where we selected a research report, read it, learned from it and then, when we convened for discussion, one of us would remark, 'we can't use this as it does not meet our criteria'. While disappointed in some cases we stuck to the guidelines we drew in making our selections, which means we did not include popular journal articles, theoretical pieces by noted scholars or practitioner descriptions of teaching strategies or programme design. This is not a condemnation of these types of papers or in any way speaks to their quality or value – just that they did not fit the criteria for reading and applying evidence-based research to practice. As stated so well by Locke and Lambdin in the first edition:

> For our purpose, within this book, we focus entirely on assertions about teaching physical education that are supported by evidence from research. We made that choice precisely for the following reason: What researchers have to say in their reports differs substantially from the assertions of practicing teachers, authors, journalists, philosophers, and theoreticians. Unlike teachers, researchers are trained 'outsiders' who can step back from the buzzing confusion of a busy classroom, sometimes catching a clear glimpse of the whole forest, rather than the nearby trees. Unlike novelists, researchers are not constrained to tell a good yarn at the expense of describing the sometimes tedious nature of school life. Unlike journalists,

researchers do not have to meet deadlines and thereby rush past a part of the whole story. Unlike philosophers, researchers have to ground their descriptions in the hard stuff of actual observations, rather than on the foundations of persuasive logic. And, unlike theoreticians, researchers must deal with how things did happen, rather than with predictions of how they are likely to happen.

All the studies we selected for this text are examples of educational research that deal with pedagogy and with programmes in physical education and general education in one instance. Noting that each research study has undergone the peer review process, all represent reasonable levels of adherence to standards for careful planning, sound data collection, thoughtful analysis and appropriate conclusions. While this does not suggest that any of the studies or subsequent publications is without its limitations, we have judged the decisions of the review boards to be sound, and where we question some aspect of the research we note that in the 'Research perspective'. On the other hand, we found that in some cases, while we questioned aspects of the research itself, we found the reports compelling, thought provoking or that they prompted us to question our own understandings of research and its application to practice.

There have been frequent concerns over whether research on teaching can actually be conducted, at least through systematic and empirical methods of investigation. Others suggest that while research on teaching and learning in schools can be conducted using various research methodologies, interpreting the results and pointing to why something did or did not occur is problematic. We argue that there is much to be learned from varied research methodologies studying practicing teachers, perspectives of pupils, diverse teaching strategies and curricular innovations. Your task is to keep an open mind as you read research, drawing conclusions and applications that you can utilise in your own context with your diverse group of learners. Use the research to question, explore and grapple with your understanding of teaching and pupil learning. You may be surprised by what you take away from reading research.

Purpose for this book

In recent years there has been ongoing debate between practicing teachers and researchers about the relevance of pedagogical research for teaching young people in schools. As Locke and Lambdin (2003) originally noted, research findings in education do not provide assurance that something will always occur, in all settings and with all students, but they do provide insight into how things might be adapted or revised to improve practice. As we noted previously, research is not always reported in ways that clarify these implications and applications for teachers. As teacher educators we must help teaching professionals learn to read, understand and apply research findings to their teaching settings so that they might better impact and facilitate student learning. In other words, instead of separating theory from practice, we must help pre-service and practicing teachers see the connection between the two, interpret what research is telling us about practice, and find ways to adapt and revise it for our own practice. Like Locke and Lambdin, we anticipate that this textbook will assist pre-service teachers, practicing teachers and others working with children and youth in physical activity settings to value research and use it to improve practice and challenge learners in physical education.

GUIDELINES FOR READING RESEARCH

Lawrence F. Locke and Dolly Lambdin

The following 12 guidelines are intended to help you get started with the task of reading the annotated research reports that form the 22-chapter core of this book. They include simple advice about how to do it, what to look for and how to think about what you discover. There is no instruction about technical matters (none will be needed), and much that we have to say should closely match your own common-sense ideas about how to approach the task. The guidelines do, however, reflect a particular set of assumptions on our part, which in turn reflect our understanding of who the readers are likely to be and why they might find value in research.

We have assumed that our advice should be directed specifically to people who are seeking information and ideas that might illuminate the work of teaching elementary/primary and secondary/post-primary physical education. As you will see when reviewing the guidelines, our choice of the word *illuminate*, rather than *improve*, was deliberate, and it reflects one of the perspectives we urge you to adopt. Also, to the extent that the guidelines were devised to serve the needs and interests of a particular audience, the advice they contain differs in content and emphasis from what we might counsel for people with other backgrounds and needs.

We have tried to think about what you might find helpful. Please give the guidelines your close attention, read a few chapters, then make your own judgment about how well they have served your needs.

Guideline number 1: Take your time

Notice the small things, and wonder about the unexpected. Pause to reflect on your own experiences, and then compare them to the observations and assertions of the investigators. What is valuable in a study may lie as much in the thoughts it provokes as in the conclusions it asserts. We can't guarantee that you will encounter a career-altering revelation within the 22 annotations that follow, but an open mind is prepared ground. Who knows what amazing ideas might take root? None of that will be possible, however, if you turn the reading task into a race.

When you think you understand the contents of a chapter, you will more likely find those contents useful and retained in memory if you take the time to reflect on what you learned, how it fits with your experiences and where it might serve your own purposes. If it is possible to do so, give your new insight an informal trial run in one of your classes and by all means, share the study with others.

The same general caution applies to the pace at which you proceed through a series of studies. Try to limit yourself to one study per sitting. Ploughing through four or five chapters at a time will overload your memory, dull your sense of adventure and mush many important details and distinctions into a single amorphous heap. Like any substantial meal, a good research study requires time to consume – and digest.

Guideline number 2: Use the headings and proceed step by step

As arcane as they may seem at first, research reports are nothing more than elaborate stories – or, to be more precise, histories. As such, they must address a familiar set of questions: What? Why? Who? Where? How? and With what result? The headings inserted into each chapter mark the locations where you will find the answers.

  The study – the *what* and *why* of the study;

- *Participants* – *who* the subjects were and *where* the study was conducted;
- *Design and method* – *how* the study was designed and implemented;
- *Results* – *what* was found and reported in the results.

The remaining sections of each chapter consist of individual and joint comments on the story laid out in the annotation:

  Research perspective – Critical points that we as researchers found interesting in this study;

  Teacher educator response – Our thoughts on how this study might impact our practice in physical education teacher education;

  Primary response – Insights on how this study might impact practice in primary physical education;

  Post-primary response – Insights on how this study might impact practice in post primary physical education;

Shared response – Issues or insights drawn from this study that cross over teacher education, primary and post-primary physical education.

The headings used in the annotation actually represent an abbreviated version of a longer checklist that was designed for use in reading full reports in their original published form. If you are interested, that tool for reading and studying can be found in *Reading and understanding research* by Locke, Silverman and Spirduso (2010). As you will be reading only brief annotations here, however, the smaller set of basic headings should be sufficient to keep the unfolding story organised in your mind – provided you take things one step at a time and resist the temptation to try to comprehend too much, too quickly.

One by one, you can accumulate each part of the study's history. You need not be concerned about grasping the whole picture; it will become clear at the end. This is an instance in which part/whole learning is an effective strategy. After you have concluded a first tour through the annotation, if you sense that something is missing, just go back to the heading where it should be found. In most cases you can quickly track down what you missed. In some instances, however, you may not find the fugitive fact because of an editorial decision that the particular bit of information was not essential to the story – that is, it was simply left out (remember that annotations are by nature much abbreviated versions of longer stories).

Finally, please note that when preparing the annotations for this text, the story-like qualities of the original reports are emphasised. There was no attempt to write equal amounts of prose under each heading – some are paragraphs long and others consist only of a single sentence. Also, what the authors chose to write about often reflects their thoughts on what you would find interesting or useful, rather than what the researchers had elected to emphasise. Accordingly, the original was freely edited in an attempt to maintain both clarity and a good story.

Guideline number 3: Use your study skills

Whether in the form of an abstract, an annotation or a full report most accounts of research have to be studied, not just read. Perhaps one in a hundred readers can start at the title of an investigation and read straight through to the end – and really finish with a clear picture of the entire story. If you are not one of those lucky few, then you must be like the rest of us. You will actually have to study research, which means doing things such as initial skimming to get an overview of the study; skipping forward and back in the text to puzzle through difficult points; underscoring, highlighting and writing in margins to give emphasis to key points; and creating mental summaries as you go along. Most beginning readers quickly identify a number of such personal study strategies that improve efficiency and maximise comprehension. Those processes represent active studying, not just passive reading.

Reading research is often interesting, frequently provocative, sometimes satisfying and, on memorable occasions, even exhilarating. To be completely truthful, though, much of it is work – wholesome, respectable and productive – but work nonetheless. Even with carefully devised research summaries, nobody is promising you a stroll in the park. With a modest investment of time and effort, however, this is work you can learn how to do (and do probably far better than you expect).

Guideline number 4: Don't panic if you can't understand everything

It has been our experience that published research reports rarely contain defects that are absolutely fatal to the reader's understanding. That said, it also is true that failures to achieve complete clarity in the explanation of an investigation are fairly commonplace. Such problems are not surprising, given the complexity of a task that requires crafting a report that will be fully transparent with regard to every detail (to the eyes of every potential reader). The question here is, how are you going to feel when one of the annotations is not transparent to you? We have some firm advice on that matter.

When you find yourself confused, you will need to exercise some good mental hygiene. That healthy response begins with one simple rule – *Don't panic!*

Two valid reasons exist for not getting into a panic that will ultimately undermine your confidence. First, the problem may not be yours; it may be the authors' (or the annotator's). Key bits of a story do get lost, writers do make unfortunate word choices that mislead the reader, and complexity itself sometimes obscures prose that seemed perfectly lucid to authors, editors and annotators. What you have to remember is that *the person who is out of step may not be you!* Sometimes a report may be unintelligible for the simple reason that it is unintelligible and would be so to any reader. That is the way things are, and sometimes we truly do have to just live with it.

The second reason not to get into a panic is that you simply may lack some particular bit of background that is critical to understanding the material, or maybe you simply find this kind of reading more difficult than other intellectual tasks. It would be a surprise, in fact, if any of us failed to have problems when navigating in unfamiliar waters. If any of these are the case, believe us, it is neither the end of the world nor is it an indication that you will fail to glean something valuable out of what you have read. And it most certainly is not an indication that nobody can help you (they usually can) or that you won't be able to understand the next chapter perfectly well, even without assistance. Through all of this, our advice remains constant – *Don't panic!*

We have sound reason for persisting with such an injunction, and it comes from years of our own reading experiences in the research literature, as well as those of our students. The rule is simple: *missing a specific piece of a study almost never prevents grasping the more general whole.* Just be careful to identify what you don't understand, then set it aside and proceed. You will be surprised by how often the problematic point turns out not to have been essential to getting the main message. In sum, a valuable asset when practitioners read research is a capacity for ignoring troublesome details – technical jargon and statistical analysis included. So relax, give it your best shot, jot down a note about what puzzles you (the next guideline explains how to use that note) and move on.

Guideline number 5: Get help by having your own conversations

One of the best ways to get through (or around) unclear accounts of a research study is to share the confusion! Whether you put caution flags in the margins or make notecards to record points that puzzle you, don't keep them to yourself. The popular image of the lonely scholar sweating away in solitude over a giant stack of books and research journals is mostly fantasy. People who keep up with the research in their specialty do read, of course, but most of them also spend as much or more time talking about what they have read with others (such poor souls include hapless students, entrapped office mates and innocent secretaries).

Whether in doctoral-level seminars, research courses for undergraduates, in-service workshops, or our roles as physical educators, consultants and research advisors, we have found that conversation is the single most efficient agent for clarifying and enriching the consumption of research. Accordingly, our advice to you is to find a friend, form a club, corner a colleague or post an invitation on the Internet. In other words, somehow start a dialogue about the research you read – whether here or elsewhere. Sharing the confusion is an effective way of reducing confusion, and it is a lot more fun than struggling alone!

Guideline number 6: The main purpose of reading research is to help you understand your work

The primary purpose for reading research should be to help you think about your work in more sophisticated ways. We do not mean to disparage the idea of finding practical applications that change and improve what you do. This is simply a matter of what should be first priority when you read. In the end, beneficial changes may be inspired by ideas from research, but they have to come from you, from your understanding of your world. If you are looking for things that can help you get a better handle on what is happening in your classes and your programme (things that we call *valuables*), you will have the right priority when you read research.

Given that broad definition of what to look for in research, useful items will not always consist of specific instructions for how to teach. For example, you can collect valuables such as the following: new ways of thinking about particular problems, explanations that never occurred to you, clarification of complex relationships, precise language for describing things, potentially useful questions that you had never thought to ask, and lines of argument to support requests for change. Those are the sorts of particulars that add up to better understanding.

In the course of explaining what they did in their study, researchers can often complicate what you think and believe about your teaching. That is exactly the effect you should expect and welcome because teaching physical education is complicated work and demands complex thinking to match. No matter what the findings of the study were, all of those complicating ideas are there in the annotation or the full report, just for the taking. Snap them up, add to your fund of professional knowledge, and then look at your work in more sophisticated ways. If you deal with your own understandings first, concrete applications will come in their own time.

Guideline number 7: For many readers, the results are not the most useful product of research

The formal account of 'Results' produced by a study may turn out to be the least important item in the study for physical education teachers who want to learn more about their work. Such a rule applies just as much to the annotations in this book as to the original published reports. Studies are designed to find answers, but that singular purpose is only rarely achieved in any absolute sense. As in other areas of life, it is the journey, rather than the destination, that has the greater value.

Studies that are less than perfect as research or that fail in some respect to completely match your initial expectations may contain all manner of valuable materials. As you read your way toward the investigators' conclusions, pay attention to everything else you encounter. You can come out the winner even when the unfortunate researchers clearly lose their struggle to find completely satisfactory results.

Sometimes, of course, the results from a study truly are exciting, provocative or useful. When reading, however, resist skipping to the 'Results' heading in the annotations and then quitting (in full reports, results often are located in the section called 'Findings'). If you scan or even ignore the body of the study, you may miss some or all of what would have been valuable: provocative questions, identification of alternative explanations for student learning problems, leads to new ideas (and even to other studies), better ways to describe one of your teaching objectives, or improved tools for evaluating student progress – all of which can be scattered throughout the study and not mentioned at all in the concluding sections. When you read about an investigation in the gym, you have to keep your eyes and your mind open. For your purposes, the results may not be the only useful product of a study.

Guideline number 8: Expect to find valuables, not easy answers

The notion that you then immediately apply the results in your classes is naive. At the worst, a quest for prescriptions in research puts blinders on your eyes. At the best, however, you can adapt (not adopt) whatever findings and conclusions there are to the particular circumstances of your workplace – to your students, your programme, your gym, your school, your skills and your personal style. You can expect that it will require hard work, creative effort and at least some risk of failure. But have some fun with it. An attempt to implement a new application that results in failure is always more valuable than no attempt at all.

We all want to find things that make our programmes better and our teaching more effective. Most researchers sincerely want to discover things that help us accomplish exactly those objectives. It would be useful, however, if everybody could manage not to hold unreasonable expectations for what can be accomplished at a single stroke. Not all perfectly sound studies can generate explicit instructions for improving practice. You should always find new things to consider, but remember that the perfect prescription for all of your professional headaches is a rare and improbable find.

Guideline number 9: Remember that context controls, and it is your context that matters

Findings from educational research are always influenced by the context within which they were derived. What appeared to work with one teacher, class of students, school, measure of achievement or subject matter may not function perfectly at another place and time. Universally applicable truths are mighty hard to come by in physical education.

The familiar teacher complaint 'You just don't know my students (or school, principal, gym or teaching schedule)' is right on the money when it comes to research. The researcher does not (and cannot) know all of those things and thereby cannot possibly write a report that lays out every conceivable adaptation of the findings to fit every imaginable setting. In any case, figuring out exactly how to make use of a research finding in your gym is not the researcher's job. It is yours.

It is you, the reader, who must play the key role here. You have to stand between each study and the realities of your own workplace. You have to be there with all of your craft wisdom, creative skill, professional training and common sense. You must then think, 'What is here that might be useful to me, and how could I put it to work?' No researcher in the world can do that for you. There is no substitution in this game. If you want to play, you have to stand and deliver.

Guideline number 10: Scepticism is wise, but cynicism wastes your time

You already know that you can't believe everything you are told (and that you should only believe half of what you see). That rule of caution applies to research with equal cogency. As we all sometimes do, researchers do make mistakes and fall into embarrassing traps for the unwary. That is why a degree of scepticism is a healthy thing to have when you settle down to read about a study of teaching physical education.

That does not mean that you need to get all hung up over questions such as 'Is this good research?' and 'Was that the correct way to analyse the data?' Few experts can make those qualitative judgments with perfect reliability, and even with some training and practice, you might find yourself unable to decide. Instead, we urge you to simply post a yellow flag next to anything that sets off your common-sense alarm, then press on to the end and store the results under 'perhaps' in your mental file. Checking out those caution flags with someone who can evaluate the problem may later allay your suspicions – or it may not. Just keep those grains of sceptical salt handy, and remember that you can learn a great deal without believing everything you read.

Cynicism, on the other hand, is destructive for everyone! Healthy disbelief is one thing, but disrespect is quite another. If you truly believe that most researchers are pursuing only their own self-interest, promoting their pet notions about physical education, or just using their craft to recruit you to their personal ideology, then reading research certainly is not for you. Our view of the research enterprise in physical education and the people who work within it is far more positive.

We have known literally hundreds of physical educators who have made research a regular part of their professional careers, and the number we would suspect of serious and intentional academic sins are close to zero. The vast majority of research workers in physical education, as in other fields of inquiry, are honest scholars who receive scant reward other than personal satisfaction for their labours.

They also are people who hold their public reputations dear. Aside from personal integrity, there are truly draconian mechanisms within the research community that exert discipline by putting reputation at risk with every published report. A researcher gets caught cheating only once. There are no second chances.

As for bias, of course researchers root for certain outcomes as the study proceeds. Only a fool would not know the difference between findings that are congenial or hostile to a line of inquiry, and only the brain dead would not care. All the scholars we have known, however, could be counted on to let the chips fall where they might (however painful) and in their report tell you exactly how it happened. Anyone who tries to do that deserves your respect – not necessarily your agreement but always your respect. A wary reader is a smart reader, but cynical and disrespectful readers are only wasting their own time.

Guideline number 11: Don't toss out studies that produce conflicting results

It is understandable when newcomers to research make the assumption that if several different studies find conflicting results, the investigations must have been defective and should thereby be disregarded. That appealing logic, however, does not fit the realities of research and leads to the false conclusion that nothing can be learned when findings diverge. While the goal always is to achieve congruent and replicable findings across studies, divergent findings often represent valuable steps toward that objective.

It is a fact that such conflicts are not at all uncommon, particularly in the early stages of inquiry into a complex problem. Once you begin to read research, it will not take long to discover instances where the findings of two or more studies appear to be at least partly, if not wholly, discrepant. That, in turn, can lead to concerns about the truthfulness and dependability of research. How can two studies involving the same question produce different results and still make legitimate claims to validity?

In the majority of cases, the answer is disarmingly simple. The divergent results were produced by differences between or among the studies in terms of circumstances, procedures or participants. The research may have been perfectly competent, but the results reflected the study of apples in one case and oranges in the other.

Close inspection of reports with apparently conflicting results often reveals likely suspects for the source of divergence, and such comparisons can serve to further understanding of the variables involved. A learning curve exists for the design of research in any complex area of inquiry, but as studies accumulate so does sophistication. It is then that findings begin to converge.

Guideline number 12: Don't wait for the perfect study

Searching for the perfect study can be like Captain Ahab and the great white whale – long on waiting and short on satisfaction! As with the redoubtable Captain in *Moby Dick*, even if you do find your quarry, it may not make you all that happy. Think about this matter in terms of what makes perfection so difficult to achieve.

Even a modest study can be expensive in time, money and human resources; thus, getting a study done frequently involves trade-offs. The researcher often has to give up some ideal aspect of design or method here to reinforce something over there. Virtually all studies involve limitations resulting from imperfect conditions and the difficult choices they demand. Investigators have to work around the limitations as well as they can, then scrupulously plant caution flags in the report to warn the reader about consequent weak points in the evidence.

Those hard realities lead to an inescapable conclusion. If you insist on waiting for the perfect study before you invest any reading time, you may end up with a very long wait. Of course, there is a theoretical continuum of qualitative perfection on which every study must find its place. What we can tell you with certainty, however, is that the number of published studies falling at the extreme ends of that mythical line will be only a tiny fraction of the whole. So, don't insist on playing Captain Ahab! Do your best to find valuables in the studies annotated here and (if you go beyond them) from the thousands of solid, if sometimes imperfect, studies that are right at hand. White whales and perfect studies may not be extinct, but they certainly are on the list of rare creatures.

SECTION I

Student engagement and experience

Deborah Tannehill, Ann MacPhail,
Ger Halbert and Frances Murphy

The five papers in this section all acknowledge the importance of considering student perceptions and experiences in informing how best to strive towards the provision of a worthwhile, meaningful and relevant educational experience for young people.

Bevans, Fitzpatrick, Sanchez and Forrest (2010) examine the extent to which student characteristics and instructional factors affected engagement in physical education. Associations between perceived competence, body image and physical activity with engagement in physical education are reported, as are the proportion of class time devoted to developing physical skills and game play. The shared responses unpack the somewhat surprising findings that the development of physical skills was positively associated with physical education engagement while game play was negatively related to perceived competence in physical education, body image and student engagement in physical education.

Bevans, Fitzpatrick, Sanchez, Riley and Forrest (2010) evaluate resources that increase both physical education opportunities and levels of student activity during school physical education classes, finding that a lower student-to-physical education teacher ratio resulted in students having more physical education time, engaging in higher levels of physical activity during class time and a reduction in the time devoted to class management. The responses suggest ways to manage the available resources in a bid to reduce classroom management time in discussing the involvement of students in class management, teaching classroom routines, managing transitions and formulations and managing behaviour.

From the perspective of young people, Gorard and See (2011) examine what can be done to enhance the learning experience for young people during formal education. The authors list what students report as the determinants of enjoyment and the determinants of disengagement. Some of the determinants of enjoyment are explored in the responses to the paper through interacting with two teacher workshops focused on teaching personal and social responsibility. The responses also consider the extent to which past and current practice in physical education has tended to 'downplay' the importance of enjoyment as a main objective of the subject and challenge the extent to which we could and should prioritise enjoyment in physical education.

Krech, Kulinna and Cothran (2010) set out to design a shortened version of the Physical Education Classroom Instrument that addresses student misbehaviour patterns, anticipating that a shortened version would be more user-friendly for completion in school settings. The responses to the paper agree that the real experts on student (mis)behaviour are the students themselves and challenge you to consider the extent to which the same disruptive behaviours in different contexts perhaps warrant different responses. Both the post-primary and primary response to the paper focus on two essential elements of effective classroom management: (i) good teaching and learning and (ii) developing and maintaining positive relationships in the classroom.

Ruiz, Graupera, Moreno and Rico (2010) explore students' social interaction preferences for learning in physical education, focusing on three social organisations (cooperative, competitive and individualist) that encourage different relationships between the task to be performed and the intended student outcome. In reading the responses to the paper, you will be drawn to engage with how best to accommodate students' preferences in the teaching of physical education and challenged to consider how best to provide opportunities to expose students to a spectrum of social dimensions rather than relying on one.

1

INDIVIDUAL AND INSTRUCTIONAL DETERMINANTS OF STUDENT ENGAGEMENT IN PHYSICAL EDUCATION

 The study

Bevans, K., Fitzpatrick, L.A., Sanchez, B. and Forrest, C.B. (2010).
Journal of Teaching in Physical Education, 29, 399–416.

This study was concerned with student engagement in physical education, looking to examine the extent to which student characteristics and instructional factors had an impact on engagement, acknowledging that engagement in physical education is an important determinant of students' activity levels in school physical education. The authors hypothesise that:

1 perceived competence in physical education and body image would be positively associated with physical education engagement, which, in turn, would positively predict student physical activity levels;
2 student engagement would be positively influenced by frequent opportunities in a class for students to be actively involved in skill development through non-competitive play and practice;
3 game play would be positively/negatively associated with engagement among students with positive/negative perceived competence and body image.

Participants

Student participants included 2,018 students in grades 5–8 (10–14 years of age) who participated in a study, *Project healthy pathways*, that explored relations between child health and school performance. Participants were drawn from regular education classrooms in 11 elementary schools, 10 middle schools, and 1 school serving children in kindergarten through eighth grade in Maryland and

West Virginia. Teacher participants included all physical educators who taught in the school of students taking part in the study, with systematic observation of 31 lessons.

Design and method

Systematic observation of physical education lessons taught by physical education teachers was collected. Questionnaires that focused on health and physical education engagement were administered to children in elementary and middle school, ascertaining information on students' perceived competence in physical education, how they constructed their body image, their engagement in physical education and their participation in leisure-time physical activity.

Results

Statistically significant associations were found between (1) perceived competence and engagement in physical education, (2) body image and engagement in physical education and (3) engagement in physical education and physical activity. The proportion of class time devoted to developing physical skills was positively associated with physical education engagement. The amount of time devoted to game play was negatively related to perceived competence in physical education, body image and student engagement in physical education. Perceived competence was a more powerful predictor of student engagement in physical education than body image. The relation between perceived competence and engagement in physical education differed depending on the proportion of class time devoted to both inactive instruction and skill practice.

 ## Research perspective

We would challenge the authors' suggestion that further research is needed to identify facilitators of physical education engagement by stating that we already know what the facilitators are (e.g., increased perceived competence, feeling of success, opportunity to work in teams and contribute to the learning experiences, exposure to activities that students are interested in). We need to focus more on assisting teachers on the most effective way in which to encourage such facilitators through their curriculum and instructional strategies.

One interesting finding from the study was the development of physical skills being positively associated with physical education engagement, while game play was negatively related to perceived competence in physical education, body image and student engagement in physical education. This is perhaps surprising in the context of teaching physical education, where one would expect the preference for game play to that of skills practice. Such a finding could challenge the argument for teaching through games. It also encourages us, as teachers, to revisit how we incorporate games in physical education and how to incorporate curriculum models such as Teaching Games for Understanding (TGfU) and Sport Education (SE) effectively.

Game play in itself may not be the issue. While there is a concern in the study that an over-reliance on game play can have negative effects on student engagement in physical education, we would question the extent to which this is related to game play per se or the nature and context in which the game play is situated. The nature and context in which the game play is situated merits particular attention when the child is beginning to play games for the first time. Clearly, a positive experience of games at this point can lay a firm foundation for development within and through games. Hence, it is worthwhile considering the types of games that are offered in the physical education curriculum and the extent to which the promotion of the more traditional/familiar games favour those with an already higher level of perceived competence due to previous exposure to the traditional form of the game. Offering more novel game types in a differently structured physical education class may place students on a more common ground.

Learning in most games can be accommodated in the TGfU and SE curriculum models. Both of these models focus on students learning about how to play well, albeit in different ways. In TGfU, the students experience the game through developmentally appropriate modified games that use a multitude of modified games and equipment. The main aim is to develop students' tactical awareness and this is achieved through a series of small sided games focused on learning about a range of tactical principles. The teacher relies on focused questioning to allow the students to identify what it is that they have learned and where it is that they need to go next with the game.

SE on the other hand aims to provide students with an authentic experience of the game and to develop students as competent, literate and enthusiastic sports people. Students experience the sport in a very authentic way, as part of the same team, over a whole season. They learn to fulfil roles other than that of participant, thereby providing for students' fuller engagement in physical education class. When students participate in games in both of these contexts, they move way beyond simple game play. They develop their physical skills, their game skills and their understanding about how to play the game well. They also have a greater ownership of the whole experience.

A second interesting finding was the relationship between perceived competence and engagement in physical education differing depending on the proportion of class time devoted to both inactive instruction and skill practice. Students with greater perceived competence were more engaged in physical education and their levels of engagement were generally unchanged by class content. For students with lower perceived competence, inactive instruction was associated with reduced engagement and skill practice was associated with improved engagement. This encourages us to consider how best to offer learning experiences and associated instructional strategies (e.g., direct and constructive feedback) within a class that accommodates all levels of perceived competence. How do we keep those who are more confident, able and do not rely on teacher direction involved at the same time catering for students who are less confident and benefit from a high level of teacher direction?

 ## Shared response

As we discussed this research paper and its implications for practice, we found many similarities across both teacher education and various age groups in primary and post-primary physical education. With this in mind, we chose to address how teachers might have an impact on student engagement through application of various instructional strategies.

Games versus skill practice

While the authors' findings show game play negatively associated with student engagement in physical education this may seem a contradiction for those teachers at all levels whose students enter the gym saying, 'Do we get to play a game today?' We believe these same teachers will be equally surprised by the suggestion that increased skill practice was positively related to student engagement as we frequently hear about the difficulty teachers experience when attempting to implement skill practice. It is often reported that students find skill practice boring and unchallenging, which results in their resistance to taking part. We did question the extent to which the negative relationship between game play and engagement related to the type of game, the amount of time exposed to that game or the lack of any form of teacher interaction during game play, which might result in a negative student response. It prompted us to consider the teachers who merely turn the ball over to students and tell them to play without providing any teaching or supervision. This type of game play may easily result in some students losing confidence and therefore choosing not to engage. For these students skill practice might be more manageable and even allow them to gain confidence as their skills develop. Another possible scenario may develop within the primary physical education class where a teacher is unable to provide feedback at a 'teachable' moment as the teacher is managing a number of groups at once. Some children react very negatively when something very minor frustrates them in a game; where the teacher cannot spot this occurring (attention being focused elsewhere at this time) younger children can very quickly develop the sense that they are not competent and choose to drop out. In this instance, it might be wise for the teacher to structure a short skills practice time before re-starting the game. This requires considerable flexibility on the part of the teacher, an aspect of teaching that we should prepare student teachers to adopt. Perhaps we tend to advise them to adhere too stringently to what they have planned in advance.

Reading this paper confirmed many of our perceptions related to motivating young people to participate in physical education through well designed, appropriate and challenging skill practice that is 'game-like' in its realism and designed ultimately to improve game performance, and thus student confidence. In other words, 'game-like' might be the key for teacher consideration or perhaps 'game-like scrimmages'. A number of years ago, Mike Metzler (1990) published an article titled, 'Teaching during competitive games: Not just playin' around' in which he encouraged teachers to build lessons that focus on skill development and game-playing segments as it allows them to develop and apply new skills in realistic ways. He outlines seven strategies that range from a 'chalk-talk', a strategy we frequently see coaches employing to focus players on a particular game tactic, to 'you make the call', a strategy that requires students to identify a game-play violation and resulting consequence after the teacher blows the whistle on the said play. Using strategies such as those outlined by Metzler might be a pedagogical choice that has huge implications for student engagement and enjoyment.

Factors associated with students and their participation levels

As the authors note, increasing physical activity levels during physical education and in out-of-school settings requires pinpointing student and classroom-level factors that predict student activity engagement. They remind us that students' perceived competence levels are a key predictor of their engagement in all forms of physical activity in any setting. They encourage us to provide a mastery-orientated learning environment where students measure success through personal achievement rather than comparing themselves to others. As we discussed this issue, the pedagogical strategy of adapting learning experiences to meet the needs of all students came to mind. If tasks are appropriate to each learner's needs would this not increase the possibility that students would more easily develop confidence?

We began to explore ways to increase and decrease task complexity through such strategies as use of space, modifying equipment, amending time, varying rules, changing prompts and cues, increasing scoring options, altering actions, changing the number of participants and altering conditions, tactics or problems. While this may sound simplistic, these kinds of options are frequently overlooked as we plan and implement activities to promote learning. When a young child begins to play a game there are probably four key areas that we should focus on: the equipment used, the size of the play space, the numbers of children on teams and the rules of the game. The equipment needs to be checked regularly to ensure that it is the correct weight for the child and, particularly in the case of games involving striking, if the size of the bat or racket or stick is right for the child. This is a particularly challenging task for a primary teacher: it can be argued that support from any source – even children from older age groups – with this simple task should be a priority. So often the size of the play space determines the level of engagement of the child, and it should be remembered that the size may need to be altered at various points throughout the game. The size of the team should be determined to a large extent by consideration of the extent of involvement of the child in the game. The rules of games present further challenges for the young child. Often, the less skilled child is already at a disadvantage when her/his more skilled classmates are experienced players and rules are set in stone by the more dominant players. This can create a challenge for the teacher too, and the solution might be in offering more novel games placing children on a more common ground as discussed earlier.

Let's explore what this might look like in a badminton lesson focused on developing students' skill at creating space for attack by moving their opponent around the court (see Figure 1.1, below).

First, the space has been modified to use a long and narrow court. The serving player will use a large shuttle such as those designed for students with visual impairments. The server will also alter the serving action by using a dart style serve to start play.

If teachers were to use these types of adaptations to design a set of skill practice activities and consistently move students on as they progress we are convinced they would find young people being challenged more. We also encourage teachers to set the task and the follow through on what has been explained to students. For example, we question whether anyone would enjoy skill practice when the teacher indicates that you are to perform ten trials of an activity before you progress to the next task only to be left in the activity long after you have achieved the required ten trials. This does become boring.

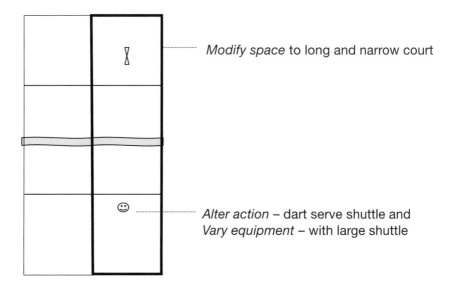

Modify space to long and narrow court

Alter action – dart serve shuttle and
Vary equipment – with large shuttle

FIGURE 1.1 Badminton

Within teacher education programmes the challenge is to endeavour to provide pre-service teachers (PSTs) with meaningful experience of children and young people engaging in these kinds of activities, where equipment *is* modified, where space *is* adjusted and where skill practices *are* constantly challenging. This may not often be possible for PSTs to experience 'live' and we may be challenged to provide recordings of these types of experiences in real settings where the process is illustrated for what it is: a process that requires perseverance on the part of the teacher to determine what is the best fit for a particular class.

Impact of instruction on physical activity

When considering instructional factors in physical education, the authors prompt us to consider mastery-orientated learning, engaging students in skill development experiences instead of competitive activities to enhance participation. They urge teachers to design innovative and appropriate ways to challenge young people through skill practice as opposed to overuse of game play situations. One idea that came to mind during our discussions goes beyond the notion of skill practice or game play. What we discussed was how much there is to be gained from involving students in negotiating their own physical education curriculum. Giving students the opportunity to share their voice, and having teachers actually listening to and responding to that voice, has implications for student engagement, enjoyment, meeting individual student needs and, ultimately, resulting in student skill development and the confidence that comes with that development. This involvement in curricular design might even allow students to reflect on and critique their physical activity experiences allowing them to determine what will and will not help them in becoming more physically engaged in activity. Student involvement in negotiating the curriculum will provide the physical educator with knowledge of what motivates young people, how to avoid barriers that deter students from participating, and gain ideas in what types of activities students find most engaging and relevant to their lives.

Teacher active supervision

It was interesting for us to read how inactive instruction was directly linked to lower levels of student physical activity as this supports much of what we communicate to prospective teachers about actively engaging with students throughout the learning process. The active teacher is one who:

1   develops a management system that helps students take personal responsibility;
2   plans and implements action-orientated, motivational lessons;
3   holds students accountable for learning;
4   provides a supportive and positive learning climate;

5   actively supervises student practice and learning experiences, responding frequently with feedback and prompts;
6   ensures a brisk lesson pace that matches student ability;
7   provides students with many learning opportunities where they experience high rates of success.

(Siedentop and Tannehill, 2000)

Of the qualities outlined, it is important to acknowledge that generalist primary teachers, for example, may be challenged to gain the content knowledge to provide the appropriate feedback and prompts as the child is engaging in an activity while creating a supportive and positive learning climate will present them with little difficulty. The important element is for each teacher to spend some time probing individual strengths (and sharing prompts with colleagues) while seeking support related to those elements that are challenging, perhaps from colleagues, from communities of practice with a physical education focus or by using appropriate resource materials. An active teacher is one who has developed a relationship with students and places them and their learning at the centre of education. We encourage teachers to reflect on an event, and collect data on how well they actively supervise the learning of their students in order to both improve performance and more effectively engage students in being physically active.

2

PHYSICAL EDUCATION RESOURCES, CLASS MANAGEMENT AND STUDENT PHYSICAL ACTIVITY LEVELS

A structure-process-outcome approach to evaluating physical education effectiveness

 The study

Bevans, K.B., Fitzpatrick, L.A., Sanchez, B.M., Riley, A.W. and Forrest, C. (2010). Journal of School Health, 8(12), pp. 573–580.

This study set out to evaluate resources that increase both physical education opportunities and levels of student activity during school physical education classes. A concern of the study was to evaluate the extent to which a structure-process-outcome approach to physical education quality could identify barriers and facilitators of programme quality. 'Structural indicators' of quality relate to the conditions under which physical education is provided and are listed as human (e.g., student-to-teacher ratio), curricular (e.g., lesson planning resources) and material (e.g., access to facilities and equipment). An indicator of 'process quality' is the content of the physical education lessons. Potential 'outcomes' are attributable to the availability of resources/structural indicators and how this affects the content of the lesson (e.g., student activity levels during physical education class). The authors hypothesise high levels of classroom management activities will be an outcome of inadequate resource availability and a contributor to reduced moderate-to-vigorous physical activity time in a physical education class.

Participants

Serving as the context for this study were 34 schools across elementary/middle/high school, serving a low socioeconomic and diverse population in three school districts in rural and small towns in Maryland and West Virginia. All 46 physical educators teaching in these schools agreed to participate in the research and represented an average of 9.5 years of experience, all with a B.Sc. degree and some with a master's, with most teaching other subjects besides physical education.

Design and method

Interviews were conducted with all 46 physical education teachers and data was collected through systematic observation of 184 physical education sessions in the 34 rural/small town schools. Teachers were asked questions related to human, curricular, equipment and facility resources, with respect to the provision of physical education in their school. Systematic observation assessed lesson length, student activity levels and the percentage of session time devoted to class management.

Results

The study found that students engaged in moderate-to-vigorous physical activity for 45 per cent of lesson time with 23 per cent of class time devoted to class management. A lower student-to-physical education teacher ratio resulted in students having more physical education time and engaging in higher levels of physical activity during class time. The reduced amount of time devoted to class management and the subsequent increase in physical activity levels was evident with the availability of a greater number of physical education teachers per student. Adequate physical education equipment and facilities also resulted in higher student activity levels.

 Research perspective

The paper verifies what one would suspect are common perceptions within physical education. That is, a lower student-to-physical education teacher ratio and adequate physical education equipment and facilities result in a reduced amount of time devoted to class management and higher student activity levels. However, the challenge remains for physical education teachers who are not in a low student-to-teacher position to identify the most effective way to manage the available equipment and facilities in a bid to reduce classroom management time. How this may be done is discussed in the sections below:

- Involving the student in class management
- Teaching classroom routines
- Managing transitions and formations
- Managing behaviour.

One reaction from reading about the time devoted to classroom management is that such time may be necessary in particular instances. There may be classes where in order to provide students with a worthwhile and meaningful physical education experience, the time devoted to classroom management may have to be high. The study also prompts us to consider the importance of preventative management strategies. Meeting with students for the first time or beginning a block of work should encourage us as teachers to introduce and emphasise preventative management strategies in the hope that these will become accepted and automatic strategies across the physical education classes. If the 'ground rules' are shared and agreed between student and teacher there would hopefully be a reduction of time devoted to classroom management as lessons progressed throughout the weeks.

The authors do acknowledge their focus on associating physical education effectiveness with moderate-to-vigorous physical activity levels as a limitation to the study. We would reiterate this admission and ask readers to consider the extent to which different curricula and instructional practices deliver other desirable physical education outcomes, such as socialising with peers and encouraging competency in movement.

 ## Shared response

We have chosen to provide a collective response to this article with a focus on management with applied examples in response to recommendations posed by the authors. We found that the paper prompts behaviours with which teacher educators and practicing teachers at all levels are already familiar but are less sure about how to change in practice. We have taken the authors' recommendations and provided our insights on how well they can be achieved in reality.

This paper focuses on increasing activity levels during physical education classes and hence prompts us to think about how a teacher of physical education can improve class management to maximise the amount of time that students spend engaging in physical activity. It is likely that improved class management can impact on the achievement of other physical education goals also, such as increasing a student's knowledge of skill acquisition or deepening their understanding of decision making within activities. The paper draws our attention to the impact of large class size and compels us to think about strategies that result in spending less time on management issues within physical education lessons. Attention needs to be directed to such strategies at pre-service/initial teacher education level where they may be frequently overlooked when there is a strong emphasis on exploration and treatment of *content* of physical education programmes. It is important to acknowledge, however, that as teachers gain experience of teaching physical education they are probably more likely to implement these strategies provided they are aware of the rationale for implementing them: the argument in this paper is focused on the outcome of increased physical activity.

Involving the student in class management

In the primary context it might be necessary to begin by exploring to what extent young children are able to help with management of lessons. Too often the beginning teacher is inclined towards practice that is driven by a desire to complete tasks quickly, and in the short term the primary teacher will probably distribute equipment more efficiently by taking on that responsibility. However, the management of lessons can ultimately be more efficient if the teacher takes the time initially to involve children in tasks such as setting out work/play stations with some help while gradually reducing the reliance on teacher support. Such an approach to class management is contributing to the implementation of Hellison's model of Teaching Personal and Social Responsibility (TPSR). For example, children are undertaking increasing amounts of decision-making and more responsibility is being shifted to them. The importance to the child of undertaking simple tasks such as setting out a line of red cones beside a classmate who is engaged in setting out a line of blue cones should not be underestimated.

At the post-primary level, when employing the Sport Education (SE) curriculum model, the teacher can assign the 'manager' role and have different teams responsible for set up and removal of equipment at the beginning and close of the lesson respectively. This ensures that at least one group of students are meaningfully engaged at the very start of class. In addition, the teacher can have materials arranged for students to access in performing their SE roles of captains, coaches, statisticians, such as a large bucket for each team with team jerseys, team handbooks (e.g., roles, responsibilities, game rules, a competition schedule), officials' whistles and penalty cards, warm-up guidelines and other related paraphernalia that will allow students to oversee much of the learning experience, relieving the teacher of these tasks.

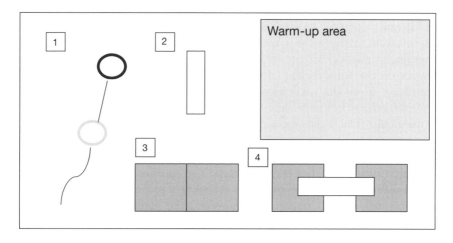

FIGURE 2.1 Equipment placement diagram

Large diagrams indicating equipment placement to allow students to assist in set up of the sports hall for class can be posted to guide student set up of the learning space.

Students can also be required to take turns in recording the attendance of their team at the start of class. Points can be awarded to teams whose attendance sheets are submitted shortly after the start of class and to the teams that are 'all present and correct' by an agreed start time. Such practices set the tone for a focused, worthwhile class. These practices can be taught during an SE block and can be continued into other programmes and activities. In post-primary, it is important that the teacher remain vigilant about their role in classroom management. Being punctual, having the learning activities set up, following up on students' involvement in the class management, acknowledging good work and noticing failure to take responsibility for tasks seem obvious but are so important for effective classroom management.

Teaching classroom routines

Classrooms that function effectively are typically framed by a set of routines that outline appropriate procedures for students to perform for frequently recurring behaviours. For instance, taking attendance, when to stop and/or start an activity, what to do when entering the gymnasium, how to transition from one station to another, and how to gain the teacher's attention are all tasks that occur many times throughout a lesson or set of lessons. If these routines are to assist the teacher in effectively managing the classroom, then they need to be specifically taught and practiced by the students while receiving prompts and feedback on their performance of them. In post-primary, students can be encouraged to take responsibility for classroom routines. This not only builds their leadership skills, but it also gives them a different perspective on managing people, and they may even empathise with the teacher and their role in managing the class. Below are several examples to clarify.

If children of any age are working in groups, could the groups be posted on the wall at the entrance to the play area for children to read, ensuring that no time is wasted as they move towards where their group is to begin warming up? Alternatively, students could be members of persisting teams throughout a unit and know that they are to complete their warm-up on their team court. With younger children, large diagrams might indicate where equipment is to be placed or teachers may have sets of equipment dispersed around the gym held within hula hoops for easy access (see diagram above). When grouping students for instruction or demonstrations, a poster might indicate where that is to happen or a set 'home' base might be used on a daily/weekly basis so students always know where they are to congregate. If it is necessary to take attendance at the beginning of a session can this be achieved in less than a minute? Perhaps if students are assigned a 'spot' at the beginning of each lesson for a warm-up routine, it is easy to spot who is absent by recording only the name linked to the vacant spot. Using cards to prompt quick recording of attendance is another possible option. Each of these routine ideas is just that, an idea. If teachers develop routines needed for their own classroom, teach them to students and then reinforce or correct their performance, the lesson will run more smoothly leaving more time for student participation and learning. If the teacher develops a routine of posting groupings or teams on the wall at the beginning of class, students will know to come in and look for it (see chart below).

Managing transitions and formations

Transition time in the classroom is that time when students are moving between activities (e.g., from station to station, from one activity to another, or teams changing courts) and can occur up to 20 times in one lesson. Add these transitions together and it can be a huge amount of time when students are neither practicing nor learning. Finding ways to manage these transitions can be essential if students are to find success in physical education.

Simple strategies using verbal and non-verbal encouragement, sometimes referred to as 'hustles', contribute to more effective transitions within lessons. The teacher could prompt, 'Let's go, move quickly', clap their hands to encourage hustling, counting down saying, 'You have 5 seconds, 5, 4, 3 . . .' Once students comply with this encouragement, ensure that you acknowledge that it was . . . 'Good . . . five seconds and we are ready to go'.

1. Megan 2. Pierre 3. Ian 4. Helen 5. Maria 6. Jack	1. Rebecca 2. Lucy 3. Daniel 4. Samuel 5. Ashraf 6. Jose
1. Abdul 2. Bjorn 3. Sophie 4. Heather 5. Gemma 6. Philip	1. William 2. Sarah 3. Johanna 4. Brian 5. Ross 6. Claire

FIGURE 2.2 Team colours, assignments and home courts posted on the wall

The strategy of setting up grids may be useful for facilitating effective use of time and space. Where the activity space is divided to provide areas for individual, pair or group activity children can move quickly to practise and explore activities. In other words, moving students from partners to a foursome or from lines into squares can be done easily if students know their place in the grid formation. Team games can also be played within the grids allowing for efficient transfer from playing one game to another, for using different equipment or for rotating players where a limited space needs to be shared. The strategy of setting up grids may be useful for teachers to transition students to a practice space; allow sets of equipment to be dispersed around the gym and using hula hoops to keep them in place. An example of an equipment and learning experience grid is pictured below.

Managing behaviour

Managing inappropriate behaviour is another critical preventative skill: to what extent can time on task be increased by initiating techniques to decrease inappropriate behaviour? First, it is important to draw the attention of the pre-service teacher to strategies for providing positive feedback and for promoting

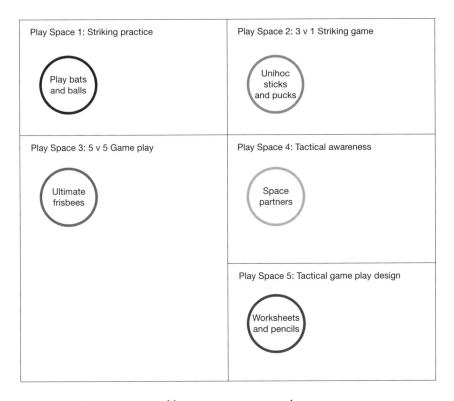

FIGURE 2.3 An equipment and learning experience grid

interaction between student and teacher. This is particularly important in post-primary where students can so easily become disengaged as they progress through the school. At post-primary, simple strategies such as getting to know students' names, checking in on their welfare if they have missed a session, commenting on their efforts to participate or when they perform well, can be significant in preventing discipline problems from building up and encroaching into physical education time. In planning physical education classes, include variety and ensure that all students can be meaningfully involved. Too often many of the activities can happen without the engagement of some students. Don't be afraid to include a non-playing role if that is what will keep a student on side. You can build on that positive engagement. The alternative is to demand their participation, and as we know, there will be only one winner there – the teenager! It is easy for young people to become disengaged and disaffected and to feel that this class is not about them or for them. Building positive relationships with students can allow you to get on with teaching physical education.

Managing the pace and variety of the lesson, how it flows, knowing when to intervene in an ongoing activity, allowing activities to reach a conclusion without interruption and providing opportunities for maximum participation are all important preventative measures in managing physical education classes (all elements identified as significant by Siedentop, 1991, over twenty years ago) and in increasing good behaviour.

Examining Hellison's (2011) instructional strategies can provide insight into how managing behaviour can increase opportunities for promoting physical activity levels as well as promoting personal and social responsibility. Initial teacher educators could prompt students to reflect on promoting awareness of

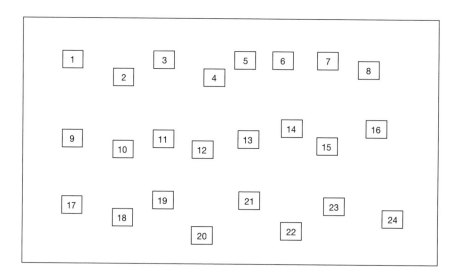

FIGURE 2.4 Classroom management techniques: assigning a 'spot'

the TPSR model, on providing opportunities for experiencing different levels of responsibility, on the role of choice within the model, on how problem solving is incorporated into the model, on the promotion of self-reflection as part of the model and on providing counselling time where the teacher and child can work through behavioural issues. This paper could prove useful in prompting teacher educators, pre-service and practicing teachers at all levels to monitor physical activity levels in their classes and to question what aspects of class management, including behaviour management, and what instructional practices would best support increased student activity levels. An example of a strategy that can be used to assist in managing the classroom can be viewed in the diagram on page 18. In this case, students are assigned a 'spot' for the beginning of each lesson to ease taking attendance and getting to know students' names, which is always helpful for managing the classroom.

3

HOW CAN WE ENHANCE ENJOYMENT OF SECONDARY SCHOOL? THE STUDENT VIEW

 The study

Gorard, S. and See, B.H. (2011). **British Educational Research Journal, *37(4), pp. 671–690.***

Encouraging enjoyment of learning in young people is a significant objective for teachers, and this study presents, from the perspective of young people, what might be done to enhance the learning experience for young people during formal education. The paper challenges a number of the given variables of teaching that are commonly believed to hinder the teaching-learning relationship but in effect are used by teachers as excuses, e.g., individual student background and working conditions of the school.

Participants

Participants were around three thousand 16- to 17- year-old students and associated adults working with them in England. The students were pulled from community schools, further education colleges, faith-based schools and academies, foundation schools, independent schools and referral units. Participants were geographically spread throughout England from various rural and urban settings.

Design and method

Data included combined individual student responses to a survey, the characteristics of each institution, the school student mix, an estimate from documents of the number of curriculum areas offered, school-level summaries of responses to the staff survey and transcriptions of a sub-sample of student and adult interviews. The analysis was based on a combined data file that linked variables that emerged from the varying data collection methods.

Results

The variation between those students who enjoy being at their school and those who do not enjoy being at their school, and whether students report lessons as interesting or whether they do not, is mostly attributed to individual experiences of education and not individual student background (personal and family) or school-level factors. Given the sampling of the participants noted above, this challenges generalising student responses related to their background or a particular school type. It also establishes that interest in lessons is not the disproportionate preserve of high attainers. The experiences of students at school that are related to enjoyment and those related to finding lessons interesting are very similar. These include being allowed to work at their own pace, sufficient opportunity to be involved in discussion and being encouraged to make their own decisions. The determinants of enjoyment included:

1   having friends and successful social relationships, with a particular focus on the social aspect of learning;
2   having a good relationship with teachers, with the notion of working in partnership with the teacher;
3   being exposed to a variety of delivery and activity approaches;
4   approachable teachers who provide assistance when sought.

The determinants of disengagements included:

1   disruptive behaviour of other students in the class;
2   a lack of engagement and rapport with teachers;
3   unimaginative lesson delivery.

 Research perspective

The research paper is part of a larger study that includes 45 case studies of institutions that had agreed to take part in the study for over five years in order to track changes in provision and attitudes for 14- to 19-year olds. In total almost 800 student and 300 adult interviews were conducted. All year-11 and year-12 students (16–18 years of age) who attended the chosen institutions were surveyed, totalling almost five thousand students. The sample size of the larger study and the number of variables that were examined in seeking to establish an accurate picture of students' self-reporting of enjoyment at school is significant. Such a level of data collection is complex, as is the associated analyses and discussion that arises from the numerous variables, and relationship between variables, that strives to present an all-embracing discussion on students' perspectives on enjoyment in formal education.

The paper conveys that all teachers are responsible for providing enjoyable learning experiences and provides weighting to the relationship between enjoyment and learning. Enjoyment is regularly noted by students and physical education teachers as a main objective for involvement in physical education. A number of people involved in the promotion of school physical education believe that to forefront enjoyment as the main objective of the subject limits the status of the subject and presents a reductionist view of all that physical education can offer. In fact, this study reports that none of the thousands of teachers taking part in the survey mentioned prioritising enjoyment for students as an objective when planning their teaching. This study challenges us to consider that there may be nothing wrong with prioritising enjoyment as a curriculum objective but rather focus on how to provide worthwhile, meaningful and enjoyable learning experiences that qualify the importance of enjoyment to learning for students.

 ## Shared response

From our perspective this was a powerful paper that has similar implications for each of us in our varied roles as physical education teacher education faculty, primary physical educators and post-primary physical educators. It is our contention that all subject areas are responsible for student enjoyment of education and learning and that the culture of schools can mitigate how we interact with students. In physical education it has been our experience that if the primary focus is merely the content of physical education then we risk losing student interest. However, we also see physical education teachers who are inclined to 'sell out' to giving young people downtime from academics with no focus on learning.

Learning should be fun for young people and they should come to physical education with the intent of actively participating in an enjoyable environment. However, teachers often hold a limited definition of fun that tends to get in the way of both learning and enjoyment. 'Enjoyment', 'interesting', and 'engaged' all may be considered the equivalent of fun. It is critical that we qualify what we interpret as fun while also understanding what children and young people consider fun. This paper gives credence to enjoyment of learning and suggests that this is the equivalent of fun!

Several issues are worth considering as we determine how to design experiences that focus on learning and enjoyment of that learning. If we are going to encourage young people to choose physical activity as a way of life it is imperative that we target each individual in our sports halls and on our fields. While we tend to teach groups of students in a classroom setting, we know that learning occurs within each individual student. This suggests that while we focus on learning we must also focus on the individual student, considering not only how we teach but the experiences that each individual has the opportunity to experience and explore. When considering this we must also recognise that both the context and culture of school might change along with the teacher/student relationship, yet the principles and determinants of enjoyment noted in this paper will remain the same.

We have chosen to respond to this article as a collective by interacting with and commenting on two teacher workshops (described below) focused on teaching personal and social responsibility (TPSR). These workshops were delivered by Melissa Parker (University of Northern Colorado) and Kevin Patton (California State University, Chico) to two groups of teachers, one primary and the other post-primary, on their 2011 visit to Ireland. We then intend to link the four determinants of enjoyment proposed in this research to ideas on how they might be applied in the physical education setting.

Annotated outline of teacher workshops

Responsibility, fitness and skills – disguised

Overview and closure for primary and post-primary workshops

1   With a small group write on a big piece of paper the things you want students to gain as a result of being in physical education. Share with all and hopefully reach the conclusion that responsibility is one of those goals.
2   Key points:
    - Responsibility is not learned by telling. Like motor skills, it must be taught and practiced with students receiving feedback.
    - Is Teaching Personal and Social Responsibility (TPSR) an instructional or curricular model? There is a slight but powerful difference:
        - Curricular in that it is the content you teach and physical activity is a medium; both must be taught as well.
        - Instructional in that physical activity and responsibility are the content and personal and social responsibility can be taught through various instructional strategies.
        - In all cases, both the physical activity content and the responsibility content must be taught well.
        - How you teach is important. You can't do this if you don't believe in it.
3   The Being: We will work on fitness, adventure, and sport. What do you want to happen today and what don't you want to happen today? . . . in small groups bring to one picture.
4   Set one goal for yourself and write it down. Have paper for this. They can fill out the achievement at the close of the workshop.

Goal Setting

Develop one goal for yourself in the next 90 minutes. What are you willing to commit to for this session?

_____

_____

Did you achieve your goal?

_____

_____

5   Five finger contract:
    The purpose of the five finger contract is to initiate and explore a full-value contract and establish norms. Each of the fingers is a reminder to us about points that will make this class a safe and respectful place for everybody.*

    Pinky: Safety – it's the smallest and most vulnerable finger; look out for the little guy.
    Ring finger: Commitment – willingness to let things go (and not hold grudges).
    Middle finger: Awareness of put downs and support.
    Pointer finger: Taking responsibility instead of pointing blame.
    Thumb: Agreement to try and do your best. Good job.

    Lastly, open up your hand to expose your PALM. Explain that this is a 'CHALLENGE BY CHOICE' activity and that no one can 'make' them participate . . . not adults, their friends, or you . . . the group leader.

    •   If they agree to the five finger contract, then sealing their approval to abide by the rules will happen when they 'HIGH FIVE' another person.

FIGURE 3.1 The five finger contract

*Once they've all agreed to accept this contract . . . begin the first activity.

(Pay close attention to the crowd . . . as shy or rebellious people will tend not to high five anyone . . . so make sure they do.)

- If you notice a 'FINGER' not being observed . . . feel free to remind the group loudly of which 'FINGER' was violated and how they can correct it.
- If the violation gets out of control (i.e., safety issues or negative words flying around), stop activity and go over the contract again as a reminder.

Activities for primary workshop

Fitness

Goals: Learn new and enjoyable ways to increase upper body/core strength. Try everything (at the intensity level of your choice . . . but make yourself work), support/help others as they learn.

Organisation: Participants will choose a partner or small group with whom they can be productive.

Part 1: Choose Your Intensity:

Task 1
Warm-up. Partners/small groups will rotate to a variety health related fitness stations. Each station will have three cards (red, white, blue). Red = most intense, White = medium intensity, Blue = least intense. The group will turn over all the cards. Each person can decide which activity s/he wants to perform. Participants can stick with one activity or change during the 1 minute time period. Stations will represent three health related fitness components (aerobic fitness, muscular fitness, flexibility).

Alternate task 1 (elementary). Cups, each with a fitness activity taped on the bottom, spread out, upside down, spread out around the space. The group travels in pairs, doing a movement (e.g., skipping, dribbling a ball, etc.), when the music stops they go to a cup and do the activity in the cup. When the music starts again they begin traveling and when it stops they find a new cup and do that activity.

Task 2
Create your own station activity. Something other than the three choices.

Part 2: Disguised core fitness:

Task 1
High Card. With a partner of your choice . . . while in plank position facing your partner play a card game. For proper plank position (critical elements) . . . be sure to have hands directly in front of shoulders, engage your abs, feet are in push up

position or you can try it on your knees. Card game 1 is high card. See if you can play for 10 seconds.

Task 2
Set a personal goal or partner goal . . . how long do you want to try to play? Students will set a goal and on the go signal try to reach the goal. Ready, go.

Task 3
Create your own card game (possible option . . . blackjack or a made-up game). Participants have 1 minute to think of a game and set a time for playing. Ready, go.

Reminder: Be sure you are trying new things and helping your partner succeed.

Part 3: More core fitness:

Task 1
Plank Hockey. New Game . . . same position but now push a small ball or yarn ball back a forth trying to get it between your partners arms . . . this is called plank hockey. See if you can play for 10 seconds . . . ready, go. This can also be a cooperative game.

Task 2
Players' Choice. New task . . . Students create a game/movement (that requires core or upper body strength/endurance). Cards, tennis balls and dice are available.

Task 3
Share your game/movement. Exchange games with another group/pair and play each.

Task 4
Create a routine. Pairs combine with another pair and create core a strength routine/sequence of moves (3–4 moves done as a group . . . not everybody has to do the same thing. Example . . . two people on the side might hold a side plank while the two people in the middle do two crunches. Be sure to help others do their best!

Closure/assessment

Completion of a written self-assessment:

1   Go back to your goal. Reflect in writing on the extent to which you accomplished it.
2   Group Reflection. Thumbs up or down on five finger contract.
3   One thing you learned.
4   What did we do – all that you can name that helped you practice responsibility? (Could be groups and share – or individuals.)

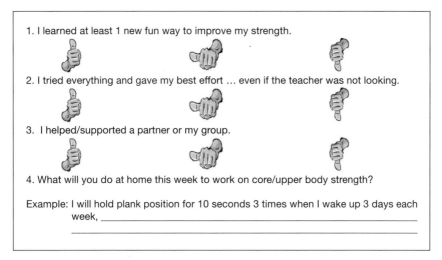

1. I learned at least 1 new fun way to improve my strength.

2. I tried everything and gave my best effort … even if the teacher was not looking.

3. I helped/supported a partner or my group.

4. What will you do at home this week to work on core/upper body strength?

Example: I will hold plank position for 10 seconds 3 times when I wake up 3 days each week, _____

FIGURE 3.2 Self-assessment

Activity for post-primary workshop

Skills

Goals: Explore various student-designed strategies for setting up to attack (score goal) in Ultimate; work cooperatively as a team.

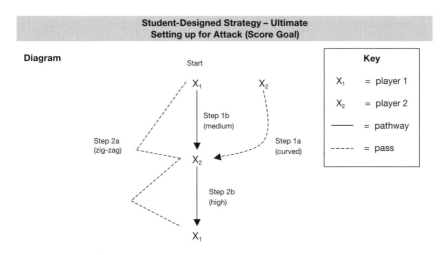

FIGURE 3.3A Student-designed strategy – Ultimate

Explanation/directions:

Note: this example involves two players; your task will be to design a strategy for three or more players.

Start	X_1 has the disc
Step 1a	X_2 travels in a curved pathway
Step 1b	X_1 throws disc at a medium level
	X_2 catches disc
Step 2a	X_1 runs a zig-zag pathway
Step 2b	X_2 throws the disc at a high level (around/over a defender)
Finish	X_1 catches disc and scores!

Warm up: Find a partner, select a disc and appropriate distance and begin practicing forehand/backhand throws, pancake and C catches.

Review cues: Throw cues (forehand: elbow to side, flat disc, snap towel; backhand: side to target, flat release, snap towel).

Peer Coaching Activity: In pairs decide which of you is the coach and which is the performer. After ten throws have a short debriefing session where coach provides feedback on cues (formal paper peer assessment?). Switch roles.

Student-designed strategy for Ultimate

Participants will choose a small group (3–4) with whom they can work productively.

1   Each group will design and record a strategy for setting up to attack in Ultimate (see below worksheet).
2   Each group will share their strategy with a new group. Pairs will provide feedback.
3   Groups will refine their strategy based on feedback.

Student-Designed Strategy for Ultimate

Designers: _____ ; _____ ; _____

                                               Key

Diagram:

Explanation/Directions:

FIGURE 3.3B Student-designed strategy – uncompleted worksheet

4   Groups will then identify themselves as a recreational, professional or 'just learning' team. Based on rating they will find a new group (with same rating) to play against.

If time allows ... play additional groups. Provide opportunity for groups to change their self-rating (if they choose).

Closure/assessment

Completion of a group self-assessment (several questions rating group on how well they: (a) worked productively as a group, (b) were engaged at a high level during practice and game times and you tried your best, (c) acted as a good sportsperson after we scored a goal/point and (d) acted as a good sportsperson after the game toward the other team).

Responsibility – team assessment

Names:
For each question check most appropriate box

Questions	1 (Never)	2 (Sometimes)	3 (Often)	4 (Always)
As a team, how well did your team address the following:				
1. *Safety* – We looked out for the little guy.				
2. *Commitment* – We were willing to let things go (and not hold grudges).				
3. *Awareness* – We were aware of put downs and support.				
4. *Taking responsibility* – Instead of pointing blame.				
5. *Agreement* – To try and do your best.				

 ## Shared response

Below we link the four determinants of enjoyment proposed in this research paper to ideas on how they might be applied in the physical education setting as informed by the workshop described above.

Having friends and successful social relationships, with a particular focus on the social aspect of learning

Young people have a social agenda when they come to physical education. Allowing them opportunities to work with their friends, share ideas and experiences, and provide one another with the lesson-focus and social conversation is critical. We as teachers need to determine how our lessons can accommodate both the students' social agenda and our learning agenda for them. The above example provides for both of those agendas and we challenge you to read our summary of the secondary Ultimate Frisbee activity and determine if you agree with the conclusion that these young people had the opportunity to progress in the social aspect of learning.

Visualise a lesson that has dual foci (as described in the secondary teacher workshop), one for young people to explore various student designed strategies for setting up to attack (score goal) in Ultimate Frisbee, and the second for these young people to work cooperatively as a team. The warm-up activity entailed students finding a partner with whom they can work, selecting a disc (from varied sizes/weights), setting up at a comfortable distance from each other and beginning to practice forehand/backhand throws and pancake/C catches. This was followed by the teacher reviewing cues for skill performance – forehand (elbow to side, flat disc/snap towel) and backhand (side to target, flat release, snap towel) – and then moving students into a peer coaching activity. Pairs decided who was coach and who was performer. After ten throws, the coach provided feedback on cues to the performer and the pairs switched roles. Finally, pairs were asked to join with another pair with whom they can work effectively. Groups of four designed and diagrammed a strategy for setting up to attack in Ultimate. Once it was designed and practiced, the group shared it with another group and gained feedback on how successful it might be in a game situation. Groups refined their strategy before deciding if they wanted to play professionally, recreationally, or as 'just learning' teams. Groups picked another group with the same chosen competitive level to challenge in a game. Class closed with a group self-assessment of how well they:

a worked productively as a team;
b were engaged during practice and game time;
c acted as fair players during game play;
d showed respect for all players regardless of competitive level, ability or who won the game.

Having a good relationship with teachers, with the notion of working in partnership with the teacher

From our perspective teaching is about relationships and helping young people feel valued and worthwhile in a teaching and learning setting. Teachers frequently set the stage in the classroom by reviewing their expectations for young people, the rules which will guide their classroom and the routines or protocols that will be employed to help manage the learning environment. While these strategies are in fact useful and assist in helping students to recognise what is appropriate and acceptable behaviour, why does it not play the other way? As a physical education teacher, we might start the year by asking the young people, 'What do you expect from me as your teacher?' Having recently tried this with students, it was interesting to hear them say similar points to those identified in this paper. They wanted the teacher to be knowledgeable, approachable, well organised, willing to listen to their concerns and perspectives, to treat them as individuals, and to hold the 'messers' accountable. We moved from that point into designing a full-value contract that reflected how they wanted the group to treat one another if they were going to be successful. This tactic has allowed the students to take responsibility for their learning.

In both the primary and post-primary teacher workshops described above, students were actively involved in the design of the lesson:

1   Creating learning experiences;
2   Setting their own goals;
3   Identifying what they were willing to commit to the lesson;
4   Assessing achievement of their goal.

Such opportunities reflect the students' voices being sought, valued and used to have an impact on their own learning. We suggest that this alone has a huge impact on the relationship that exists between and among students and the teacher, and in particular enhances the notion of students and teachers working in partnership.

Being exposed to a variety of delivery and activity approaches

One of the things we have come to believe is that learning and achievement are not just the purview of the skilled or those we think of as high achievers; if instruction is exciting, innovative and appropriately challenging, it can engage all learners. This thought contradicts some of the 'givens' we tend to hold true in education related to learner background, school context and those who are skilled and knowledgeable. The notion of 'challenge with choice' (students each choosing the level at which they feel comfortable beginning an activity) while first introduced in Adventure Education need not only be used in this context. Why not have challenges for all learning tasks that provide options for young people that reflect their level of comfort and confidence. Risk for some may be holding hands while for others it might be scuba diving. One student might feel exposed by performing a dance in front of peers while another is put off by intense competition. Would it not be preferable to have well thought-out choices for students to select from with none of the options being to opt out of activity? Perhaps by considering student feelings and needs we might be able to gain participation by all young people in ways that are beneficial to all.

In the fitness lesson described in the primary workshop above, we viewed strategies to expose students to a variety of delivery and activity approaches. The goal of the class was that students could learn new and enjoyable ways to increase upper body/core strength. The approach allowed for student choice according to their feelings (relevant perhaps just to this particular lesson) and needs. Partners or small groups rotated to a variety of health related fitness stations. Each station has three cards (red = most intensive, white = medium intensity, blue = least intensive) indicating an activity to be performed. The group or partners turned over all the cards and each person decided which activity they wanted to perform. Stations represented three different components (aerobic fitness, muscular fitness, flexibility). A slightly different approach perhaps most suited to a primary group involved fitness activities being taped to the underside of cones. Music was played as the children travelled in pairs skipping, jogging or dribbling a ball. When the music stopped, they went to a cone of choice and did the activity described. When the music commenced again they began travelling.

Indeed, there are links here also with literacy as children read each set of activities again implementing the principle of being exposed to a variety of delivery and activity approaches within a literacy context. A further link illustrating another delivery approach is where the teacher prompted each student to develop a goal for the particular physical education class that is to be taught, centred on identifying what the student is committed to for the class. The goal is written down. It might be that they will improve an aspect of a skill or take responsibility for working well with a partner or prompt a class member to stay on task. At the end of the class, they are asked to comment on the achievement of their goal. This activity might be undertaken sporadically and used to contribute to the variety of different approaches adopted by teachers in pursuit of the goal of enhancing enjoyment in lessons.

Approachable teachers who provide assistance when sought

Not all young people like receiving feedback or recognition in the same way. Think of the student who tends to shy away from giving demonstrations, sharing a game tactic they designed or having their name and score posted on the winners' ladder. Part of our role as teachers is to facilitate learning by designing ways for young people to gain feedback, set goals and monitor progress toward their development. However, how this is done must vary if it is to meet the needs of all young people. It may be that the teacher provides a variety of options from partner tasks to extrinsic feedback built into tasks, exposes students to numerous strategies from 'coaching' courts to group meetings, or even sets up ways for students to come to them for individual interactions. Key is finding out how young people want to be treated, how they are successful and what interactions will be most effective for each of them.

Along with these ideas for enhancing student enjoyment of physical education, it is critical to examine how we might be perpetuating student disengagement in our classrooms. From a lack of engagement with teachers to unimaginative lessons, and from disruptive students to lessons that are not enjoyable, young people are telling us what they need. This paper spoke of the concern young people had with the disruptive behaviour of other students in the class. After concluding the student-designed Ultimate Frisbee task described in the post-primary workshop above, as teachers we might reflect on how the pupils reacted and, considering our responses to them, might ask, 'Did I allow disruptive behaviour of students?' What are the consequences of misbehaviour? Who are the victims and what is the impact on them? These are questions that need to be considered and planned for so that all students are allowed to learn and enjoy taking part in the lesson.

4

DEVELOPMENT OF A SHORT-FORM VERSION OF THE PHYSICAL EDUCATION CLASSROOM INSTRUMENT

Measuring secondary pupils' disruptive behaviours in physical education

 The study

Krech, P.R., Kulinna, P.H. and Cothran, D.J. (2010).
Physical Education and Sport Pedagogy, 15, pp. 1–17.

The study set out to design a shortened version of the Physical Education Classroom Instrument (PECI) that addresses student misbehaviour patterns. It was anticipated that a shortened version would be easier for researchers and teachers to complete in school settings and that additional analysis work was required to retain the psychometric properties of the original instrument.

Participants

Previous data sets collected from 2,309 secondary school students and 303 teachers in three Midwestern states in the US were revisited to examine the extent to which a more concise instrument could be developed before recruiting a new sample of 422 secondary school students from two school districts in the south-western United States.

Design and method

Six subscales from the 59-item instrument had previously been identified as:

1   aggressive
2   low engagement or irresponsibility
3   fails to follow directions
4   illegal or harmful
5   distracts or disturbs others
6   poor self-management.

Statistical analysis of the 59-item instrument was conducted from the previous data set collected to determine which items to delete in a bid to shorten the instrument. Tests were also conducted to highlight any significant similarities or differences between student and teacher responses to the items. Using the new sample of secondary students, tests were run to assess the fit of the subscales arising from analysis of the previous data set.

Results

From re-examining the previously collected data the authors were able to reduce the instrument to 20 items, retaining five of the six subscales listed above that were highly supported as frequently occurring misbehaviours. The subscale 'illegal or harmful' was deleted. The new sample of secondary students supported the fit of the five subscales. The authors believe the subscales can identify representative disruptive student behaviours, providing insights into students' and teachers' days. Once in a position to identify behaviours occurring in the lesson, the authors encourage us to begin exploring why students are engaging in such behaviours.

 Research perspective

There is a tendency for us to use measurement instruments without being aware of how they have been constructed or validated. This paper explains the reconfiguration of an already established 59-item instrument to a more user-friendly version. There is, however, some confusion on who the reconfigured 20-item instrument is aimed at, with varying references throughout the paper. The paper states that the shortened version would be easier for researchers and teachers to complete in school settings (p. 211), that it can be used with secondary school students for identifying representative disruptive student behaviours, and that the project was not successful in developing a shorter form appropriate to teachers (p. 223). Regardless, the opportunity that the 20-item instrument provides for secondary school students to identify disruptive behaviours acknowledges the authors' earlier admittance that the real experts on student misbehaviour are the students themselves. Knowing more about what students define as misbehaviour, their consciousness in exercising certain behaviours and why they carry out certain types of disruptive behaviour may provide us with guidance on how to appropriately respond.

It is interesting that there is no definition or dialogue on what constitutes 'pupils' disruptive behaviours' or an acknowledgement that what is deemed to be disruptive behaviour from one group of young people in a particular school context is not necessarily identified as disruptive behaviour for another group of students in a different school context. The list of disruptive behaviours in the paper draws attention to the reality of not only identifying these in a lesson but also in being able to effectively address them. This also leads us to consider how teachers are best positioned to 'choose their battles' – that is, does it matter if students are talking if they are still on task? Does it matter if a student does not have the appropriate kit when they do not know how to treat other students? Regardless of what 'battles' teachers choose to fight, they need to be consistent in what they identify as disruptive behaviour and how they subsequently deal with it.

 ## Teacher educator response

Throughout our discussions of this paper, the primary and post-primary responses led the way as regards their thoughtful reactions with an abundance of examples to clarify their positions. The two responses below are prime examples of how teacher education can learn from practicing teachers. Read on and enjoy. Pre-service teachers could be assigned these responses as reading assignments prior to class discussions on teacher-student relationships, student behaviour and classroom management.

 ## Post-primary response

There is no doubt that 'effective classroom management is the cornerstone of successful teaching'. The question is, however, what underpins effective classroom management? We would suggest that there are two essential elements: (1) good teaching and learning, where students are interested and engaged and (2) developing and maintaining positive relationships in the classroom. Both are completely inter-related and both support students' positive experiences in the classroom.

This response will focus particularly on the centrality of teacher-student relationships in effective classroom management. We teach students, we teach students physical education and not the reverse of teaching physical education to students. They come to our classes, each with their individual history, unique personality and behaviours. We have no control over these attributes but we do have control over how we relate to our students, their behaviours and the next stages of their personal and social development.

The shortened PECI provides the teacher with a workable instrument to better understand and improve their practice by taking stock of the behaviour profile of any given class. When teachers have identified the particular misbehaviours in a class, they are in a better position to design specific management plans to address individual and group behaviour problems. However, relating to our students is a hugely subjective experience in which our personal and professional selves are implicated. Most of us have had the experience of finding it hard to relate to a particular student(s) while other teachers experience no problems with the same student. As teachers, our personal values and attitudes frame our interactions with our students. It is important therefore that we are aware of what particular behaviours trigger unhelpful responses in us and catch them before they further exacerbate the situation for ourselves and the students.

The first step in building our management skills in the classroom is to recognise our own triggers and their impact on how we respond in the classroom. The second step is to explore the multiple reasons why a student(s) might be exhibiting poor behaviours. No child sets out to have a bad experience and every child seeks positive regard. Many students, however, have learned that any attention is better than not being noticed, so if poor behaviour achieves this goal, then that is what they will exhibit. By responding respectfully, including stating the boundaries for acceptable behaviour clearly, we can contribute to students building the kinds of relationship skills that will serve them now and in the future.

One useful teaching strategy for helping young people to monitor their own behaviour is the full-value contract (FVC) associated primarily with Adventure Education. The intent of the FVC is for students and teacher to design a contract cooperatively that will identify appropriate behaviours to guide interactions in the class and allow all students to enjoy a positive and successful experience. Below is an example of a FVC designed by a teacher and her physical education students, posted on the gymnasium wall and referred to on a daily basis both to start the lesson and during closure when debriefing on what occurred.

An FVC provides one way for students to determine what they can and cannot tolerate in the classroom, how they like to be treated, how they are comfortable working with others and what peer behaviours they find encouraging or hurtful. It is also an effective way to gain an understanding of students' perceptions of misbehaviour. Knowing more about what students think about peer behaviour, how to deal with it effectively and how it makes them feel may provide guidance to teachers on how to deal with such issues. Do students understand what misbehaviour is? Why are they misbehaving? Perhaps having this discussion with them might bring it to their awareness. At the same time we need to be cognisant of the fact that some behaviours evolve as young people interact and develop.

At the same time, the FVC can provide the teacher a means of questioning her own understanding of misbehaviour, while helping pupils become aware of their misbehaviours and why they choose them. Teachers also need to consider what they are able to tolerate and how they are equipped to deal with misbehaviour. It might be useful for physical education departments or even total schools to discuss student misbehaviour, what types of student responses will be tolerated and how they might be dealt with by a school policy.

Full Value Contract

1 Put in best effort and encourage one another

2 Have confidence and never say, "I can't"

3 Listen to and include everyone

4 Be fair, and play fair

5 Respect each other and make group decisions

6 Enjoy yourself so learning is fun

FIGURE 4.1 Full-value contract

Hellison's (2011) Teaching Personal and Social and Responsibility (TPSR) model can provide the teacher with a framework for negotiating the next steps with the class. The TPSR model is designed to teach, through sports and physical activity, values and behaviour that can contribute to the positive development of students' lives. The teacher shares with the class what the PECI has identified as being the dominant misbehaviours in the class. Students can then be asked for their reaction and what they consider to be the main issues arising from the misbehaviour audit. Students can then be asked to identify the three or four misbehaviours that they will agree to work on over a period of time. Using the TPSR approach, students can be asked to identify the characteristics of the misbehaviours at their worst (Hellison's Level 0) and at each of Hellison's four subsequent behaviour levels right up to where students are taking complete responsibility for their improved behaviour.

Regardless of the strategies we choose to guide management of classroom behaviours, all teachers want students to relate respectively to their peers and to themselves. This suggests that we need to reflect on ourselves as well as on student behaviour. If students are misbehaving and all we are doing is providing game play then it might make sense that some students are choosing to misbehave. When we have a class setting where misbehaviour is frequent, we need to examine what we are doing and if we are meeting the needs of our students. If students' dressing in appropriate kit for physical education class is an important issue to us, we need to examine what it means to the students. In other words, uniform may be a minor concern for a young person who does not know how to treat other students – that is, the bully. Misbehaviour does not stand alone! It is critical we analyse student misbehaviour and select those we are going to tackle, and those which we must handle.

 Primary response

Acknowledging that while we don't have control over students' individual attributes we do have control over how we relate to students, let us focus in on setting up a positive climate for relating well to students. It is important that primary teachers set the scene for positive behaviour, especially in early years classes. The two essential elements of effective classroom management (good teaching and learning, and developing and maintaining positive relationships in the classroom) can provide a useful starting point for reflection. Is it possible that some of our teacher behaviour contributes to some of the behaviour problems that arise?

The importance of differentiating activities for young children, the importance of providing adequate time for individual play and the importance of planning for progression are arguably three key areas that will help promote positive behaviour.

Examining the issue of differentiation in a physical education class where there is a wide discrepancy in children's mastery of fundamental movement skills, it is crucial that work is planned to challenge the gifted child and that adequate support is provided to the child who is struggling to master a skill. Children in primary classes may be offered the same activities at the same level with little regard for their differences. Sometimes many activities within the same lesson emphasise competition between individuals or groups with a focus on winning; at an early age many young children have not developed the appropriate responses. Relay races, for example, within infant classes, while offering potential for learning and achievement, can challenge the maturity level of the child; can s/he wait in turn and accept the winning/losing element? Repeating relay activities at this age may not be a positive way of promoting desirable behaviour.

With reference to the second point above, does a relay race provide adequate time for individual play/practice? Often primary teachers struggle with the concept of maximum involvement of each child (can all children run at the same time?), fearing that the safety element is compromised (will children fall or bump?) and that their control of the class is lessened. However, it should be remembered that the more engaged the child is, the less behavioural issues will arise. The more energetic child who craves being active will be more likely to exhibit poor behaviour if queuing in a relay activity. The balance of activities within infant lessons is really important.

Finally, with reference to the third point above, where a child is offered progressively challenging tasks s/he is less likely to exhibit poor behaviours. Promotion of the 'I can' factor has to be balanced with offering some chances for a child to realise a weakness (maybe over rotation of the wrist in throwing a Frisbee) so that the child is progressively challenged. On further examination of the FVC outlined above, it would appear that while primary teachers are generally very concerned with all aspects of the agreement, point 2 has particular significance: 'I can'. Too often young children find themselves in situations where they are justified in saying 'I can't' . . . the task set by the teacher is not at an appropriate level or the equipment is not right (the uni-hoc stick is too long, the plastic ball rolls away each time). Would the beanbag be easier to manipulate or would the beach ball be easier to pat bounce? Could the play space be increased to allow room for error by the child who is struggling with mastery of the skill? Attention to class management 'details' or issues may prevent much of the misbehaviour that may arise simply because a child is experiencing frustration rather than achievement.

'Low engagement or responsibility', one of the subscale categories in the PECI, when related to a primary school child can often be prevented or at least lessened by effective class management by the teacher. Another PECI category, described as 'fails to follow directions', might cause the primary teacher to ask, are the directions clear, sufficient to prompt play yet not so tedious that the attention span of the child is tested? Or consider a further test item category, 'distracts or disturbs others' – has s/he sufficient space, equipment, direction and freedom to play? This research study can serve a particularly meaningful purpose if it prompts the primary teacher to reflect on specific misbehaviour in the class with a determination to adapt content and/or pedagogy so that young children avoid falling into patterns of misbehaviour.

5

SOCIAL PREFERENCES FOR LEARNING AMONG ADOLESCENTS IN SECONDARY PHYSICAL EDUCATION

 The study

Ruiz, L.M., Graupera, J.L., Moreno, J.A. and Rico, I. (2010).
Journal of Teaching in Physical Education, 29, pp. 3–20.

This study explored students' social interaction preferences for learning in physical education, focusing on three social organisations that encourage different relationships between the task to be performed and the intended student outcome. The first social structure of 'cooperative' is identified when students' objectives are deeply interconnected, with students achieving their objectives as part of a group. The 'competitive' social structure arises when students compete with other students in attempting to secure the best result for themselves. The main characteristic of the 'individualist' social structure is individual progress without worrying about the results of other members of the group. Team affiliation, where students construct a group identity, make group decisions and work towards common goals, is also introduced. Students conveyed a very high preference for cooperation, a high-moderate preference for competition and affiliation and a moderate-low preference for individualism. Girls were found to be less competitive and individualistic than boys and more cooperative and interested in peer affiliation.

Participants

Over six thousand 12- to 17-year-old students were drawn from urban and rural towns in two Spanish communities across 30 different public and private secondary schools. School participants experienced the same curriculum, which included physical education as a compulsory subject twice a week.

Design and method

All students completed a survey that explored the four learning preference dimensions of cooperation, competition, affiliation and individualism. Descriptive data were analysed with reference to gender and grade level.

Results

The study states that a main preference for learning in physical education does not exist, acknowledging that students may respond to a combination of the four social preferences in different contexts and with different objectives. Boys preferred more competition and individualism, while girls preferred cooperation and affiliation. Even with significant gender differences, boys and girls showed higher scores in the cooperative dimension and the lower scores for the individualist dimension. As in other studies, there is no analysis of any differences within gender groupings, failing to report or interact with any anomalies that arise from analysing boys' and girls' results. Rather than imply that teachers should develop integrated structures of learning that promote different objectives to suit boys and girls, the focus should perhaps be on individual students and not groups determined by gender.

 Research perspective

It is difficult to deny that understanding students' preferences in learning has important implications for teaching and learning. We are somewhat cautious in commenting on the effectiveness of the survey in identifying social preferences for learning as students can only respond to experiences to which they have had exposure. That is, if students have been exposed to one dimension more than another it is expected that their responses to the survey items connected to that dimension will be stronger. Students' preference for cooperative learning structures over competitive or individualistic ones encourages us to acknowledge the importance of peer relationships to young people and to consider how best to accommodate this preference in teaching physical education. The importance to students of both the cooperative and competitive dimensions challenges us to consider the most effective way in which to accommodate both preferences, rather than consign them to opposite dimensions of social preferences for learning.

 Shared response

We have chosen to tackle this paper by addressing both primary and post-primary for pre-service and practicing teachers simultaneously. First, we will discuss cooperative

learning (e.g., cooperation, affiliation) from a post-primary perspective followed by posing challenges to teachers in applying the concept in their own classes. Second, we pose an action research project idea in a primary setting, which we hope many of you will choose to undertake in your own contexts.

 ## Post-primary response

Description and benefits of cooperative learning

Reading this article, I am once again reminded that I teach young people, not content. Careful planning for teaching and learning in physical education can only be as successful as the extent to which physical education teachers take on board the importance of students' individual and group social preferences for learning. These preferences include cooperative, competitive, affiliate and individualistic learning styles. Each student in our physical education class has a particular preference but collectively, young people appear to place particular importance on cooperative learning followed by competitive and affiliate preferences with fewer students preferring individualistic learning. Each learning style has merit in physical education in post-primary school.

Cooperative learning tasks are designed so that each student's effort and success affects the whole group in a positive way. Cooperative tasks offer valuable opportunities to develop a range of personal and social skills including altruism, empathy and a positive regard for others. These skills are important for young people in their lives both in and beyond the classroom. Cooperative activities also provide opportunities for students to experience and build team affiliation, which was found to be one of the most attractive features of Sport Education for students.

Competitive learning experiences might be at risk of being judged harshly in this context. However, this ought not to be the case. While students' results showed that competitive tasks were not interconnected with others, competition can provide opportunities for students to cooperate and experience team affiliation in pursuit of a shared goal.

In individualistic tasks, each student can experience progress and success without needing to worry about the other students and the impact of their success or otherwise on their own outcome. These learning experiences free the student to take risks, to set personal challenges and to deal with failure without having to consider the impact on the group.

Different students prefer to learn in these different ways. However, it would be a mistake to tailor learning only to these preferred styles. These preferences do not simply develop, they are the result of a dynamic and complex interaction between the young person's natural dispositions and their past experiences as a human being and learner. For example, we all know the student who finds it difficult to contribute as part of a team. We know students who refuse to work on individual tasks. The gendered nature of young peoples' experiences may be such that they have not had the opportunity to assess the range of different learning experiences, which prompts us to consider how we might do so in physical education class.

Should we, as physical educators, plan for activities that require all students to contribute to the team effort? The challenge will be to ensure that this experience is a positive one and encourages further effort. The same can be said for 'the team players' who object to individual activities and reflection, for example. In physical education, we have the potential to provide meaningful opportunities for young people to develop a range of life skills through their learning.

We can build students' commitment and engagement in physical education by recognising that they have an overarching need to feel connected to the group and receive affirmation in what they are doing in physical education class. The Sippel scale provides a useful tool that might be used to critique professional practice in terms of what learning style preferences are being supported or to identify if the preferred conditions for learning and engagement in physical education prevail in physical education classes.

As teachers it is important that we are aware of our own learning style preferences. Consciously or subconsciously, we will tend to teach from this comfort zone, thereby perhaps failing to include a variety of learning experiences designed to appeal to, or facilitate the learning of, the greatest number of students.

Adolescence is a time where young people are engaged in forging a personal and social identity for themselves. It can be a challenging time for many young people and they rely on the support and affirmation of their peers to build their confidence and decision making. This reality presents both opportunities and threats to planning for teaching and learning in physical education. The opportunities come in the form of young peoples' positive disposition towards activities where they can engage in cooperative learning, work collaboratively with their peers and experience feelings of positive group affiliation.

The threat comes, however, where the group norm is one of general disengagement from learning and, in particular, towards physical education and participation in physical activity. The challenge for the physical education teacher is to include cooperative activities that are enjoyable, perhaps novel, thereby engaging the young people and helping to build more positive attitudes towards physical education. The key is to acknowledge the power of the adolescent group dynamic and that the young person's need to belong is stronger than the need to participate in physical education.

Sport Education provides one such context where every student has the opportunity to be involved in, and experience, connection/affiliation. Students undertake various roles, each one contributing towards the overall score awarded to a team when carried out correctly and efficiently. The composition of teams is designed to facilitate maximum participation and equality in the opportunity to be successful, thereby helping to provide a motivational experience for each team member.

The way I plan for teaching and learning facilitates a different kind of personal and social learning. Am I facilitating different learning preferences? Is there a balance, an in-balance? Are there opportunities for students to work alone, in cooperation with others or in competition, opportunities to enjoy learning differently than what they tend towards currently or opportunities for both sexes to develop pro-social behaviour?

As teachers, we need to become aware of our own understandings, biases and dispositions. What are the advantages and disadvantages of each type of learning? Students like being in groups, feeling they belong and have their peers' approval. Physical education is well placed to take advantage of these tendencies by designing and delivering a wide selection of student learning experiences that encourage varied learning preferences and styles.

 Primary response

Designing action research

The researchers used the Graupera/Ruiz Scale of Social Interaction Preferences in Physical Education Learning (GR-SIPPEL) to establish students' preferences for cooperative, competitive, affiliate and individualistic learning in physical education classes. It is interesting to note that it was developed with primary and post-primary students specifically for assessing peer social interaction preferences in learning in physical education classes. Reading this piece of research provoked me to think about my recent teaching of young children in a variety of subjects. They asked, Was I aware of the different learning styles in my group? Did I plan to meet the needs of the different types of learners? How might a typical class that I teach respond to learning situations that offered opportunities for a style of learning that they preferred or situations that offered few opportunities for learning in the way they prefer?

Perhaps it is time to audit our work with reference to the GR-SIPPEL items and four factors as outlined in the table below. A useful starting point might be to apply this to the next unit of work that we are planning to teach. In this instance, I can apply it to physical education but remembering that it could be applicable too in a mathematics unit of work or in a science lesson. I could examine a unit in outdoor activities. To what extent will my programme present opportunities for children to work cooperatively? You might find the table below a useful reference. It provides some guidance on conducting this audit of your work as a sample unit is worked through. In completing this audit you might find that many of the activities can be adapted to suit the individual learning styles of children. Note the overlap in column four! Stepping Stones for example can be undertaken as a team or as an individual, with an emphasis on competition or on completion of the task in a non-pressure situation. Use of the scale encourages me to think about whether I provide these choices for children.

TABLE 5.1 GR-SIPPEL 'Four Factors' adapted and applied to a unit of work in outdoor education for 6-year olds

Factor	Item Number	Item	Activity
Cooperation	2	I like to say and do things that help others.	Stepping Stones activity/ Cross the river.
	18	I like to help other classmates even if they do not help me.	Team Scavenger Hunt.
	26	I like to work in a group, even when the activity is difficult.	Find locations and record as many symbols as your team can in photo orienteering.
Competition	1	I like to do things better than the others.	Individual/Team Photo Star.
	9	I try to be the best in my class.	Orienteering where fastest group back is declared the winner.
	25	I work harder if I see that other classmates are doing better than me.	Crawl through the hula hut first in your group without knocking the hoops.
Affiliation	7	I need to participate in group work to feel well.	Team Scavenger Hunt.
	15	I like group games because my mistakes are hidden.	Team Scavenger Hunt. Team Relay: find the jigsaw pieces and make the jigsaw.
	27	The best way of learning in class is when I am accepted in a group.	Build the hula hut with your group.
Individualism	4	I like to work in my own way, without worrying about what others do.	Individual Scavenger Hunt: can I find 6 items to match those in the bag?
	8	My best way of doing things well is doing them alone.	Stepping Stones: Can I cross the river unaided?
	12	I wish that there were individual exercises for working alone.	Can I build and crawl through the hula hut?
	20	I love individual sports.	

Beginning by categorising the activity focus before moving on to examining how activities can be adapted to suit learning styles might be a simpler way to audit the unit of work. However, moving on to examine the activities through the lens of different children is an essential element of planning if we are to meet students' individual needs. That will of necessity mean that I examine how the activities I plan can be offered to all children simultaneously but with a different focus.

An action research challenge

The authors of the study describe social interaction learning structures to include cooperative, competitive, affiliation and individualistic. The implication that physical education researchers have chosen to narrow their focus to a comparison between cooperative versus competitive was somewhat worrying. While for some time we have been aware that competition in and of itself is not bad, but the manner in which it is used and the outcome are the issue of contention, similar concerns might be expressed about a sole focus on a cooperative or individualistic way of learning. Should young people not be given the opportunity to experience all learning structures in a well-developed and positively managed learning environment that allows them to learn from each experience?

We read that boys prefer games while girls preferences are linked to 'softer skills' than boys, perhaps suggesting an encouragement vs. competitiveness mind-set. We also learned that social interaction preferences vary for young people in post-primary school yet teachers do not always take advantage of these learner choices. In many instances these findings may encourage us as teachers to facilitate boys and girls to develop the skills and preferences that are typical for their sex, or offer activities that always encourage teamwork rather than individuality. However, we question whether we should propagate this or do we try to help both boys and girls enjoy and learning differently?

We encourage you to challenge these findings in your own practice. In other words, let's set about to contest the structure of physical education classes that advance cultural and gender differences; that is, challenge that boys should be competitive and girls should be compassionate. Ruiz *et al.* (2008) encourage teachers to design physical education lessons that allow students to undertake learning in a setting that has a place for both cooperative and competitive aspirations and participation. Their notion 'that teachers can develop integrated structures of learning that promote different objectives; social interactions, physical fitness, or social skills' (p. 15) is one worth investigating in our own individual settings.

With this in mind, our challenge to you is that you pay more attention to learning preferences and design an action research project that exposes all young people to different learning strategies and examine how they achieve and enjoy the experience. Perhaps you could teach with all social interaction learning structures and then ask young people which they enjoy, why they enjoyed them, whether and what they learned and why they believe they learned. This information would not only serve to assist young people in expanding their learning preferences but also allow them to enjoy learning through different and varied strategies.

SECTION II

Instruction, learning and assessment

Deborah Tannehill, Ann MacPhail,
Ger Halbert and Frances Murphy

The six papers in this section present a selection of instructional, learning and assessment practices that can be considered in striving to deliver worthwhile, meaningful and relevant physical education to all students. Each paper challenges the reader to reflect on their current practices. The reader is also prompted to consider the extent to which our dispositions, values and beliefs are enacted in the physical education provision we provide and subsequently heighten or limit the student physical education experience.

Casey and Hastie (2011) report the teacher's and students' responses to a student-designed games unit to illustrate how games-making provoked change in understanding students' knowledge, actions and construction of concepts with regard to games. The teaching experiment framework in which the researchers frame the exploration of practices in physical education lessons is likely to be interesting to practitioners and is considered further in the responses to the paper. The responses are presented from the perspective of teacher education, primary and post-primary, with each concerned with considering how best to facilitate learning through the provision of different instructional strategies and content.

Hay and Macdonald (2010) challenge the concept of 'ability'. They explore the potential ways in which ability is constructed in order to suggest how to maximise the benefits of physical education and optimise physical education for all students. One of the most powerful findings from the study is that teachers appear to be the most influential factor in the gendered nature of ability construction. This finding directs the responses to focus on the preconceived notions of what will work and what will not work in physical education, our understanding of 'ability' in physical education and the extent to which this understanding socially constructs and transmits the value of ability in physical education lessons.

James. Griffin and Dodds (2009) examine teachers' and students' perceptions of assessment tasks through the content that is taught in physical education (instructional task), the behavioural and organisational aspects of physical education (managerial task) and the social intentions students have for interacting during physical education (social). The focus of the study on assessment that takes place at the end of a unit of work may have contributed to the negative reactions shared with respect to the assessment tasks. Subsequently, the teacher education, primary and post-primary responses consider how best to incorporate meaningful, worthwhile and enjoyable assessment tasks into physical education lessons.

Larson (2006) set out to identify what students perceived to be caring teaching in physical education. The teacher education response considers how we help novice teachers to realise that a caring teacher is not one that steps aside and is permissive with students but rather plans, challenges, poses problems, leads, probes, coaxes, pushes and perhaps even coerces. The primary and post-primary response each revisit what students identified as caring teaching behaviour – recognise me, help me learn and trust/respect me – and the opportunities available through physical education to foster a caring relationship with students.

Redelius and Hay (2009) examine what students learn about the purpose, practice and possible consequences of summative assessment. The responses to the paper support the importance of examining assessment along with pedagogy and curriculum and focus particularly on four discussion points: (i) assessment does not serve the very students we want to serve, (ii) provide students with task specific statements as well as an explanation of the content and assessment practices, (iii) educate teachers on the use of assessment in physical education and (iv) the implication that if it is not assessed, it is not valued.

The practice-based research reported by MacPhail and Halbert (2010) involved the refinement and evaluation of a post-primary physical education assessment for learning (AfL) planning framework with the implementation of associated assessment instruments. The responses provide the reader with three insights related to the focus of the paper. The first is further consideration of what the authors introduce as a 'rich task' – that is, a way of integrating learning experiences that represent learning outcomes in a practical environment. The second insight focuses on teacher progression in learning to assess and the third focuses on alternative ways for students to demonstrate achievement.

6

STUDENTS AND TEACHER RESPONSES TO A UNIT OF STUDENT-DESIGNED GAMES

 The study

Casey, A. and Hastie, P.A. (2011). **Physical Education and Sport Pedagogy,** *16(3), pp. 295–312.*

Student-designed games encourage students to design their own games within teacher-set parameters. This paper explores the use of student-designed games with two groups of secondary school boys and reports the teacher's and students' responses to a student-designed games unit. The purpose of the study was to illustrate how games-making provoked change in the researchers' understanding of students' knowledge, actions and construction of concepts with regard to games.

Participants

Participants were 28 boys (between 14 and 16 years of age) from a state-supported selective school in England. The students had significant prior experience of co-operative learning and Teaching Games for Understanding (TGfU). The teacher contributed to the study in the role of 'teacher-as-researcher' and the school's librarian and media specialist provided technical support as wikis were developed to document the students' games. An external expert, who was also the second author, contributed to, and communicated through, electronic wikis and mail.

Design and methods

The teaching experiment design encompassed the inclusion of a description of the unit of work being studied, an analysis of the events that occurred and systematic reflection. In addition, the voices of the teacher-researcher, the students and the school's librarian and media specialist were included. Data were collected from post-teaching reflections, analysis of wikis, interviews and observation. Data analysis was ongoing throughout the study to allow for the planning of future activities in the investigation. The analysis allowed for the identification of commonalities across and unique components within games.

Results

Students invested in the process of games-making, reporting that having to think of new and creative ways to play, as well as playing these newly designed games, resulted in experiencing more fun and challenge than regular physical education. Students excluded problematic skills from the games-making process, including only those skills that allowed them to experience success. Students also engaged in being innovative, sharing their ideas and experiences, working as teams and learning with their peers. The only frustration appeared to arise when games-making became game-playing and other teams did not fully understand the game. The paper concludes that it is possible to gain an insight into the processes by which students apply their knowledge about physical education by trusting pupils and supporting them to be creative in the games that they play.

 ### Research perspective

An attraction of student-designed games is that the approach appears to free students from prior learning (where appropriate) or exclude learning experiences not favoured in previous physical activity opportunities. This allows students to begin their experience in games-making from a collective starting point, with similar challenges, standards and discipline around rules and demands expected from all.

The researchers use a teaching experiment framework in which to frame exploration of practices in physical education lessons. They explain that a teaching experiment allows teachers to examine and draw inferences about student learning through the examination of teaching episodes. We suggest that since the students had built a relationship over a number of years with the teacher, and the students had been exposed to, and receptive of, innovative teaching, contributed to the teaching experiment framework resulting in useful information. Subsequently, the use of a teaching experiment framework is perhaps something that is most likely to succeed once a positive relationship has been established between the teacher and students. However, that is not to say that games-making is not something you can do with all students and not necessarily a practice that requires specific prerequisite requirements. The level of accountability intrinsic to the task set through games-making has the potential for students to take responsibility for their own, and peer, learning as we learned from Rovegno and Bandhauer (1994).

The use of technology in the form of a wiki is likely to be an attraction to students, providing a new way in which to communicate with each other and with those external to the school. However, the extent to which the wiki was essential to the teaching experiment is not clear and leaves us to consider to what extent it contributed to a discussion forum for the games-making process. Are there other discussion forums that would allow for student, teacher, researcher-professor and librarian interaction? That is, the use or not of a wiki should not be a stumbling block to pursuing games-making.

 ## Teacher educator response

Most of the physical education curriculum models being delivered in schools, whether Sport Education, Adventure Education, Teaching Games for Understanding or Teaching Personal and Social Responsibility, are student centred. When children and young people are allowed to work in these 'differently' structured complex learning environments it allows them to be creative, to learn from their own mistakes, and to take responsibility for their own learning. The question becomes, how do we as teachers facilitate learning in these environments? Or perhaps, how do we as teacher educators prepare teachers to effectively facilitate learning?

Facilitation is not a new teaching strategy. It is, however, a strategy that beginning teachers often have difficulty implementing. It requires teachers to plan in innovative ways, challenge young people with problems to solve or solutions to find, and in some cases causes us to re-examine the type of expectations we have for learners. Teachers using the 'pedagogy of facilitation' (Poekert, 2011) place students in a position to broker their own learning. The teacher sets this situation up for students, offers them the opportunity to be challenged with individual choices, and allows them to question, explore and innovate as they come up with their own responses to a problem. The pedagogy of facilitation asks us to consider in what ways can we, as teachers, be helped to effectively implement new practices in the classroom? It encourages us to question how facilitation can influence student learning in a context of a student-centred environment. Content knowledge, including appropriately designed learning progressions, are key facilitator skills and influence students' learning.

Experiential learning lies at the heart of facilitation. It suggests that learning is achieved through hands-on personal involvement in a learning experience. We know that creating an experiential learner-centred environment can be challenging for teachers who have been taught through traditional classroom techniques. Developing activities that allow learners to understand and interpret concepts can be a new and challenging experience for both teacher and student. Teachers need to be creative to engage students, immerse them in an experience, and facilitate learning and discovery with their peers. Effective facilitators are able to stimulate students' imaginations and keep them hooked on the experience when they recognise that facilitation is more about listening and asking the right questions than it is about giving the right answers.

 Primary response

The authors point out that the relationship built over a number of years between teacher and students was significant in paving the way for facilitation of learning. This involves trusting students and supporting them, in this instance, to be creative in the games that they play.

It is worthwhile considering this type of teaching and learning in a primary context. Facilitation of learning, by its nature, takes time to enact. The effective classroom teacher in primary schools can 'buy' time for this type of teaching over the course of a day. In terms of building relationships with children, the primary teacher has an entire school day and indeed an entire school year to build the relationship that is described in this research paper. The existence of this strong relationship can ease the pressure within physical education classes. The relationship doesn't necessarily only begin as the physical education lesson begins, nor does it end as the physical education lesson concludes. Typically, primary teachers can begin facilitation of work in the classroom. For example, they can pose the problem or set the challenge in the 'dialogic space' beside the interactive whiteboard before the children leave the classroom setting. They can then allow the children to work on the challenge (in this case creating games) within the physical education class and bring the lesson to a conclusion again in the classroom. Throughout this process, the teacher can encompass aspects of literacy development for example as s/he facilitates learning in an almost incidental way. The benefits for the child can be enormous with the learning of the child being significantly enhanced provided we trust and support the child to be creative in the games that they play. We can then claim to be truly facilitating the learning of the child.

 Post-primary response

Despite what we have come to know about what works and what does not work in post-primary physical education, some of us are still guilty of an over reliance on traditional team sports to the detriment of many students' active engagement and participation in physical education. As physical education teachers, we can often rely on those activities with which we are most familiar and have been successful in. Therein lies a problem, however. By the time many students enter post-primary education, their prior learning in, and poor experience of, many traditional games has started a process of disengagement that can often be difficult to counteract. Opportunities for students to engage in games-making in physical education as outlined in this paper has much to offer in addressing this problem.

Students are challenged to design a game, within given parameters, that is fun, sufficiently challenging and, yet, in which everybody can potentially experience success. Students are given access to any equipment available in the equipment room. Alternatively, they can be assigned a 'random set of equipment', they can choose to make their own or they can acquire equipment at reasonable expense. Students are given some knowledge on game design and issues about health and safety are discussed so that the new game can be developed in a safe and equitable manner.

The potential for deep learning with this approach is immense. Working in their teams, students are required to work together negotiating the creation of the new game. Automatically, differentiated learning is happening. The game will, of necessity, reflect the ability level of the group including appropriate levels of skill and strategy challenges. Students work continuously to refine the game. They will practice and re-practice, all the time reflecting on what provides the most enjoyable and engaging game play. Students are free to make mistakes as they are the sole arbitrators of what the game is to be. They are not intimidated by their perception of performance excellence, which might be the case in their engagement with more traditional games. All of the students are starting at a common level and are not favoured by their previous playing experiences. Students are able to define what level of competition is appropriate and how it is to be managed. This approach encourages students to problem solve, to negotiate, to listen to each other and to draw on their prior knowledge and understanding of game play as they construct this new game.

The use of web-based wiki as a platform for recording the game and all its various editions, in the developmental process, was inspiring. In the post-primary setting, the use of wikis provides an effective interface between the world of technology where our students are the 'digital natives' and learning in physical education. It provides the possibility for our students to be accountable for their learning in physical education as they compile and update a history of their games-making process. It allows each team to review what other teams are doing, to try other student designed games and to critique them by providing feedback on how they might be improved and made more challenging and/or enjoyable. For older students, the use of wikis could help ensure that teams engaged seriously in the games-making process and continue to challenge themselves to refine and improve their game. The element of competition – where the class is encouraged to select the most enjoyable game – is also a worthwhile practice. Each team will have to ensure that their final game 'product' is clearly articulated on the wiki and/or demonstrated to their peers to ensure it will be a serious contender for 'best game' accolade. The potential to introduce other categories in this competition are worth exploring, for example, best use of equipment, clearly articulated rules, appeal to different age groups.

The potential of student-designed games to actively engage more students in physical education and to enhance their understanding of the components of game play – that is, skills and strategies – is exciting. It requires that we, as post-primary physical education teachers, reflect on what we consider to be valuable knowledge and learning in physical education. Where there is an over reliance on traditional games playing, we risk further alienating many students. Student designed games making would appear, from this research, to support the active and enjoyable engagement of a wide range of students with differing abilities and levels of motivation. Given the creativity that is evident in the ever changing world of adult physical activity participation – for example, roller hockey, mixed tag rugby – it is worthwhile that we encourage students to engage in activities that are different, but nonetheless enjoyable and worthwhile. The role of the teacher in a student designed games-making is concerned with facilitating learning and using questioning to challenge and guide students' active and enjoyable creation of their unique game.

7

THE GENDERING OF ABILITIES IN SENIOR PE

 The study

Hay, P.J. and Macdonald, D. (2010). **Physical Education and Sport Pedagogy,** *15(3), pp. 271–285.*

The paper challenges the conception of 'ability' and explores the potential ways in which ability is constructed in order to suggest how to maximise the benefits of physical education and optimise physical education for all students. Understanding the impact that a student's belief of their ability has on their (perceived) access to a movement culture allows physical educators to reconfigure the most effective way to encourage sustained involvement in such a culture beyond school physical education.

Participants

One teacher and six year 11 (ages 15 to 16 years) students from two Queensland secondary schools – one a low socioeconomic, government school and the other an 'elite', co-educational private school – took part. Both the teachers and students were involved in senior school physical education.

Design and method

Teachers and students were interviewed five times and observed weekly by the first author across 20 weeks of the school year.

Results

The teachers and students consistently perceived differences in the nature of female and male abilities in physical education. It appears that traditional and popular conceptions of ability continue to contribute to the gender inequalities in physical education. Even when the students' physical performances were to be given the same weighting as the written performances, teachers and students consistently prioritised the physical over the written component as being fundamental to ability in physical education. Consequently, females remained at an educational disadvantage as the expectation was that they would be less physically able, even though the female students were more able in the written work.

 ## Research perspective

One of the most powerful findings from the study is that teachers appear to be the most influential factor in the gendered nature of ability construction. There is concern that teachers are not conscious of the extent to which their values and expectations shape physical education practices and by association their relationships with students and their judgment of students' abilities. However, it was disappointing that the paper did not provide more of an insight into the two teachers' values, beliefs and expectations, as this has implications on the findings. It would have also allowed the authors to subsequently examine the extent to which both teachers were conscious of how such characteristics played out in their enforcement of the gendered nature of ability. There is a definite message that, as teachers and teacher educators, we need to be able to identify and understand how our own beliefs and dispositions inform the design of the curriculum/ programme and, by association, the potential engagement of all students.

The paper provides a nice example of the value of triangulating data collected from a mixed-methods approach, in this instance interviews and observations. One example is when the first author observes the manner in which Mark's practice consolidated the relationship between the physical and the gendered nature of ability during the 800 metres event. In this instance Mark, the teacher, appears to equate the boys' faster time than the girls in completing the event as the boys working hard, although the first author observes that the girls worked as hard as the boys but were not as fast. The second example concerns Chantel being portrayed by Anthony, the second teacher, as unmotivated and not proactive in engaging with the class. However, the first author's observations note that Chantel was involved in every lesson but, due to spending most of the lesson playing on a make-shift court at the side of the hall, lacked the opportunity to have Anthony recognise her ability.

The concepts of 'ability', 'habitus' and 'fields' may be new and daunting to physical educators interested in learning more about the gendering of abilities and may result in teachers choosing not to read the paper. One way in which the same piece of work could potentially reach more practitioners would be to reconfigure the paper for a professional journal. To enhance the readability and understanding of such concepts for those who do choose to access this paper, there are opportunities for the reader to take particular interview or observational data from the paper and attempt to locate them within elements of the appropriate concept(s). This would encourage the reader to appreciate the way in which theoretical constructs can enhance our understanding and critique of physical education practices.

Teacher educator response

Reading this paper and discussing it with our team brought some interesting insights to light relative to the expectations we as teacher educators hold for ourselves and those that our pre-service teachers hold for students, content and their own teaching performance. In fact, it is not just about the pre-service teacher's expectations or how they are a manifestation of teaching ability but how students view the teacher's ability to teach as well. In other words, it is not one dimensional.

We often see pre-service teachers who hold preconceived notions of what will work and what won't, so they end up not trying a pedagogical strategy, movement form, or activity with one group of students for one reason or another (age, gender, socioeconomic background, behaviour). For example, one second-year teacher chose not to implement a full-value contract (FVC) during her adventure education unit despite its success during her own teacher education course (Dillon, 2012). She felt that the students would perceive this teaching tool as childish and cause them to refuse to participate or even question her ability to teach as a result. She failed to recognise that the FVC concept might be new to the students and cause initial discomfort as change is difficult for all of us. By not giving up and revisiting the FVC over a number of lessons, students may realise its benefits and recognise that it is giving them a voice in their own learning and responsibility for an important aspect of the class. As a result of his not enjoying dance in post-primary school himself, another student teacher decided that the boys he was teaching would not either. As a result, and following discussion with his cooperating teacher, he chose not to include dance as part of his fourth-year teaching practice as it was more appropriately intended for girls, and after all they were only a part of his class. During weekly seminar when several of his peers discussed the success of teaching street dance using YouTube as a teaching and motivational tool he continued to question whether it would work for him. His teaching peers spent considerable time sharing student responses to the dance lessons and provided video of some of the moves they had choreographed, indicating that it had become one of their most enjoyable schemes to deliver. This novice teacher did not have the confidence to step outside of his comfort zone and try something he had learned to teach but did not enjoy so continued to assume his own students would not either.

As teacher educators, we need to challenge pre-service teachers on these views or they will not move on, develop as professionals and give all children the same opportunities for success and enjoyment. If we can help pre-service teachers to appreciate teaching practice as just that, practice then perhaps we can assist them in taking a risk in an environment where they have support and encouragement. They need to persevere in their effort to become competent and effective teachers and recognise that if they are not willing to take a risk and try something new they are limiting opportunities for both themselves and the young people whose interests and needs they are striving to meet.

 Primary response

This research paper suggests that the influence of the teacher on gendering of abilities is highly significant. While much has been written about teacher beliefs and their influence on the practice of teachers, reading this paper prompted me to look at where this influence has its roots. As a female, I began to reflect on my primary and secondary school experience, both in an all-girls context. What were the prevailing beliefs in those settings?

From a physical activity perspective, my primary school play space was limited, hence running at break times was prohibited. Abiding memories for me are dodging among the crowds of girls gathered in the school playground playing a game of chasing that was dominated by walking but interspersed with short dashes for cover. However, in terms of physical education there appeared to be a more positive experience for children in this school. A particular memory of a senior class teacher stands out for me. Although not 'sporty', she taught physical education in earnest, providing it status as a subject and ensuring that 11- and 12-year-old girls were exposed to activities such as gymnastics. Class size was not a deterrent – there were more than 40 in the class. Did this attitude influence my thinking at the time? I believe it did . . . in terms of my recognition of my own ability within the field of physical education, I began to understand where my strengths and the strengths of others lay. Within my secondary experience of physical education, I received recognition for achievements and reflect now on whether this affirmation would have been as positive if I were in a mixed school. Would I have been within that group of girls in a class described in the Hay and McDonald paper who, although investing significant effort, were not recognised by the teacher as the performance of the boys was deemed better?

However, while the focus of research in this paper was on investigation of how two teachers influenced gendering of abilities, the researcher perspective above has questioned widening the focus of the investigation of gender to include perhaps examination of some other influences on gendering of abilities. In my case, boys (three) and girls (four) in my family were equally supported in terms of our engagement in sports from a very early age. I believe this was a strong influence on the forming of beliefs by both boys and girls in the family . . . we were influenced by the values, beliefs and expectations prevailing in the 'field' (which probably was both school and home contexts). We received significant support from our parents regardless of the inherent ability displayed by the individual. Such support informed by parents' values I believe has contributed to the continuing participation of all boys and girls in the family in sport and physical activity, all confident about their abilities. Perhaps the support of female sport by the male members of the family as they coach females in sport is particularly significant.

The gendering of abilities remains a puzzling theme: can teachers work to construct abilities in a more supportive manner? Coaches, parents and others may be just as significant in this field. I believe that awareness of values and beliefs must be raised if we are to truly provide opportunities for girls to judge their abilities in a more positive light. It is likely that there are many teachers whose values and beliefs inform their practice and whose classes provide such opportunities. Such settings need to be documented and practice shared.

 ## Post-primary response

Having read this article, I have found myself reflecting on my understanding of 'ability' in physical education and the impact that this has on the ways in which I relate to students and my expectations for different students' capacity to be successful in physical education. I realise now that my perspectives about the nature of ability and in turn my expectations about the educability and achievement potential of students in physical education has been outside my conscious awareness. Yet it has had a profound impact on how I have carried out my role as a physical education teacher.

As a young girl, I played many different sports. I loved swimming and water-based activities, and I enjoyed being in the outdoors. I was never an elite performer. My experience of competitive sport was at an inter-school level and we were never highly rated but I loved being active and participating. In my youth, I was seen to have ability by my physical education teacher and it was encouraged. I brought this cultural understanding of the nature of ability to my pre-service teacher education. Some of my fellow aspiring physical education teachers were of similar backgrounds. Others were excellent performers in a range of disciplines or had been part of a system that understood the nature of ability in physical activity mainly in terms of how it contributed to sporting success. The importance of these formative experiences in physical activity and sport is they later become transformed into our values as we get older. Pre-service education has, therefore, I would contend, an important role in facilitating becoming teachers to reflect on their formative experiences in physical education and in turn their perspectives on the nature of ability.

When I decided to become a physical education teacher, it was largely because I got so much out of being active that I wanted to encourage as many students as possible to get involved. From where I was positioned, physical activity and sport belonged to everybody, all abilities, shapes and sizes and not just the excellent performers. Success came in many guises including meeting one's own goals no matter how modest.

I can appreciate now that as physical education teachers, we each bring our different perspectives about the nature of ability into our own professional lives. These perspectives would appear to have been hugely influenced by one's personal cultural and social experiences in physical education and sport. In turn, these perspectives influence what we deem to be worthwhile in physical education. They underpin what we decide to emphasise in our programmes, the students we enable and expect to thrive and those that we may not cater for. We may deem some students to have little or no ability because they do not fit with what we recognise as ability worth developing in physical education.

For many pre-service and beginning physical education teachers, the range of abilities present in a given classroom may come as something of a shock, coming as they do, from backgrounds where personal commitment, ability and achievement in physical activity and sport are the norm and in accordance with what was defined as having ability. With experience, many physical education teachers learn to broaden their perspective of ability when they witness how students can demonstrate a range of abilities when given different opportunities in physical education, for example, sport education, adventure education.

It is essential that as professionals, we reflect our own perspectives about the nature of ability and the impact this has on our practice in physical education.

- Who are the students that I consider to have ability in physical education? Describe them.
- How does my programme, my pedagogical approaches and assessment practices support those students in developing this ability?
- What percentage of my students fit into this category?
- What about the rest? What is the nature of their ability?
- How does my programme, my pedagogical approaches and assessment practices support their learning or not?
- What would be worthwhile about addressing this, for myself, for my students?

While the primary focus of this research article has been on the gendering of abilities in senior physical education and its impact on teacher engagement with students in the classroom and in assessment practices, it has highlighted broader issues for me about the inevitable impact of how we, as physical education teachers, perceive ability in our students. I recognise that there are gender inequities, but there are other more subtle inequities that occur as a consequence of one's perspectives about the nature of ability. Consciously and unconsciously, we are always making judgements about our students, their ability and their potential to improve. For example, if I position the male athletic body as the normal body, what is the impact of this on how I see and relate to my students in physical education? Do I expect more of those students who have some of these athletic attributes and see others as being deficient and unlikely to have or to develop any particular athletic ability?

When we teach a class for the first time, we very quickly make decisions about students' ability based on initial impressions judged against our criteria about what constitutes ability in physical education. We often have different expectations, for example, for boys versus girls, tall versus small students, athletic looking versus thin/frail students, lively versus serious, team players versus performance sports people, academically able versus not so able. The categories are endless but we bring our perspective of the nature of ability to each of them and this in turn impacts on how we relate to these students and what our expectations are for these students' engagement in physical education.

Brown and Rich (2002: 80) argue that physical education teachers are the 'key intermediaries in the social construction and transmission about what counts as "gender legitimate" knowledge, dispositions and practices'. I believe physical education teachers legitimise knowledge, dispositions and practices based on even wider categories as discussed above. This has important and serious consequences for how young people experience and thrive in physical education. I encourage the reader to reflect on their personal perspectives about the nature of ability and to tease out the implications for their practice in physical education.

8

PERCEPTIONS OF MIDDLE SCHOOL ASSESSMENT

An ecological view

 The study

James, A.R., Griffin, L. and Dodds, P. (2009). **Physical Education and Sport Pedagogy, 14(3), pp. 323–334.**

The study examines teachers' and students' perceptions of assessment tasks through an ecologic lens. An ecologic model provides a framework for understanding the dynamics of physical education classes. The ecology of physical education comprises three task systems. The instructional task system is related to the content that is taught in physical education, for example, game play, skills and drills, appropriate sporting behaviour. The managerial task system includes tasks related to the behavioural and organisational aspects of physical education, for example, assignment of groupings and collecting and returning equipment. The social system relates to the social intentions students have for interacting during physical education, for example, having fun with a peer.

Participants

This study was conducted in the US with an intact class of 36 12-year-old students and their teacher. The school was located in an affluent area where high-stakes test scores were among the highest in the state of Massachusetts.

Design and method

Data collection began with the researcher visiting the school on a number of occasions to build a rapport with the teacher and students before introduction of the study and subsequent instruction. Observations of two units of instruction (fitness activities and volleyball) were conducted for 50 minutes twice a week over 12 weeks. Assessments used within the units were peer- and teacher-directed assessments, including checklists and quizzes. Each lesson was videotaped and the researcher completed field notes after each class. Interviews were conducted with the students and teacher. Interview and field notes were analysed by identifying common categories and themes that arose within these categories.

Results

There are three main results. First, assessment tasks presented to the students appeared ambiguous, with students not receiving information on how best to judge their performance or how such assessment could improve their performance. This resulted in students being confused about the assessment task as well as what was being assessed. Although the assessment tasks were ambiguous the amount of risk for the student in not understanding the tasks was diminished as students were not held accountable for completing them. It appeared that the teacher's preference for not judging students on their physical abilities and lack of planning for the assessment tasks contributed to the ambiguity and limited risk students associated with them. The limited accountability that the assessment task promoted contributed to the second result. It was obvious to students that the teacher did not use assessments as an accountability technique. The teacher preferred to use assessments as a tool to motivate students and demonstrate their improvement than as an effective way in which to hold students accountable for learning in physical education. Third, it was clear that students conveyed a preference for authentic assessments. That is, assessments appropriate to the context and in this case, the game of volleyball. When assessment did not meet the student agenda of socialising and having fun, assessment tasks became ineffective and time-consuming. One way of accommodating the student socialising agenda was through the introduction of peer assessments.

 ## Research perspective

The paper encourages us to recognise the dynamics of individual class context by considering how the interaction of the instructional task, managerial task and social systems informed students' and the teacher's perceptions of assessment in physical education. The relatively young age of the students involved in this study also prompts us to consider the importance of students' early experiences with assessment and how this can inform their future dispositions towards assessment in physical education.

While the results of the study convey the teacher's and students' negative reactions to the assessment tasks, we are prompted to consider how best to incorporate meaningful, worthwhile and enjoyable assessment tasks in physical education lessons. First, it is clear that for assessments to be meaningful they need to be authentic – that is, assessments that are implemented in the context of the activity. Assessments need to challenge students otherwise they become disengaged and resent the assessment tasks being included, or detracting from, their participation in the physical education class. Second, assessments need to accommodate students' agendas of socialising and peer and group assessment should be encouraged where appropriate. Third, there needs to be a degree of accountability tied to the assessment so that it is evident to students that the task will affect student performance or learning. The teacher needs to share the intention of the assessment tasks with the students as well as the criteria by which they are to be assessed by a peer, the teacher or self.

It is disappointing that the study focuses only on 'high stakes' assessment (assessment that takes place at the end of a unit of work) as a means by which to encourage students to engage with the importance of assessment tasks. There are many ways in which assessment tasks can continually enhance both teaching and learning (commonly referred to as formative assessment/assessment for learning) throughout a unit of work and subsequently contribute towards a final assessment of a student's overall profile for an activity area. Formative assessments do not need to contribute solely to grades but rather be used to inform students of how to improve their performance and learning in specific tasks.

 Teacher educator response

As teacher educators, the paper prompted our thinking on several key assessment issues that have implications for the education of pre-service teachers (PSTs). For example, when the authors proposed the idea of the three task systems (instructional, management, social) interacting to create a programme in which the teachers and learners design and embed activities, we were prompted to consider how the idea of the 'rich task' might be introduced to PSTs. A 'rich task', based on the work of several Australian scholars (Macdonald, Hunter and Tinning, 2007) is characterised by presenting learners with real and meaningful problems that they must resolve as they experience and interact with a particular unit of work. For any unit, a task would be considered 'rich' if it was both realistic to the learners and in line with the learning outcomes set forth for learner achievement during the unit.

The 'rich task' might be an appropriate starting point for PSTs to begin to understand the importance of designing instructionally aligned lessons where learning outcomes, assessments that provide evidence of learners achieving those outcomes, and the instructional practices that allow learners to achieve success are aligned. PSTs considering how learners might become part of designing appropriate and challenging assessments that meet the outcomes outlined by the teacher, or even selecting outcomes and assessments to meet their own needs might be useful. This practice would support learners' social agenda providing them with a choice in the design and/or selection of assessments that are more realistic and also accommodate their desire for taking part in physical activity with their friends in an enjoyable social setting.

A second issue that has implications for our work with PSTs relates to the notion of ambiguity, which the authors suggest is a critical component of the ecological framework. Like Doyle (1983), they indicate that, 'ambiguity is a result of gaps in information about performance expectations' (p. 325), resulting in learner confusion or questions on what and why they are doing a particular task. In other words, an assessment task is ambiguous if the learner is not told how they will be assessed, on what they will be evaluated, or the outcome of the task. Discussion throughout the paper brought to mind the literature on assessment for learning (AfL) that has its focus on facilitating learners to become critical thinkers involved in their own learning. AfL proposes that assessment is an ongoing part of the teaching and learning process where information gained from ongoing assessment informs and shapes the learning process. Another paper to which we have responded in this book identifies key principles of AfL as (1) sharing learning intentions with students, (2) sharing success criteria, (3) involving students in assessing their own learning and (4) providing feedback (MacPhail and Halbert, 2010).

In line with AfL, it is our contention that the practice of sharing a teacher's assessment philosophy with learners, the purpose of assessment, how assessment is designed, and the learners' role in assessment sets the stage for its importance. This 'best' practice helps learners identify and appreciate what is meaningful and worthwhile for their learning, which has connotations for the quality of their learning and subsequent planning by teachers. It is worth noting that if a teacher does not appreciate assessment in the learning process then it is unlikely the learner will take it seriously and use assessment as a means for their own growth and development.

 Primary response

This article prompted me to think about teaching and assessment within an ecological framework as described by the paper. To help me apply the research I began to frame my thinking around a lesson that I have taught and observed others teaching on numerous occasions. I have attempted to describe a typical scene from a part of a lesson I observed:

> Seven-year-old Tom is asked to link three balances that illustrate different levels as he explores movement. The teacher observes Tom performing and records that he has shown a really good understanding of level while also demonstrating good control moving from the first balance to the next. ('You have held that first low balance very well and moved really smoothly as you stretched up high for your next balance. Well done Tom! That last balance is a little difficult to move into but you've made a really good effort

to hold it again at a low level. Try it again . . . can you move a little bit more steadily into it?') As the teacher provides this feedback she prompts him to work a little more on controlling his movement from the second to the third balance. Tom is then asked to describe the balances that David his partner has selected.

When we attempt to examine the managerial and instructional systems discussed within the ecological framework, we can conclude that within the class described they are probably implicit within the task. The teacher is likely to be ensuring that appropriate behaviour is established and maintained if children are learning to perform sequences of movement (managerial element) while she is concerned too with the content that is being taught (instructional). The interaction of Tom and David as they engage in peer assessment is representative of the social system (are the boys on task throughout? Are they treating each other with respect? It would seem that the three systems are creating a programme of action represented by the children's engagement with the task.

The researchers in this study concluded that assessment needs to be meaningful, ambiguity needs to be addressed and students need to be challenged by tasks. They found that students wished to work with their friends so that tasks were more fun and assessment needed to be implemented in the context of the activity.

In the vignette presented above we get a glimpse of how these principles are applied in teaching young children. The teacher has set a task that has challenged the child (he has further work to improve his performance) and he has received meaningful feedback that has provided guidance for him to improve his work. There is a hint that he is working with a friend, too, each being prompted to comment on the work of each other. Finally, the assessment is being carried out in the context of a typical class where children are being asked to undertake tasks that are part of their normal activity within gymnastics lessons.

Although the focus was on children in middle school, it seems very likely that primary school teachers working with even the youngest children can apply these basic principles to their physical education lessons too. The researchers have provided a blueprint for effective assessment. The potential for beginning good assessment practice at primary level is within the grasp of primary practitioners. Primary teachers regularly conference with young children about achievement in a gymnastics lesson, for example, and this can provide opportunities for meaningful assessment in the context of the activity itself. Young children can work very well with a partner, although learning to work well may have to be taught, it is not always 'caught'. The opportunity to work with a friend may provide children with a good starting point as they begin to apply those principles that make peer assessment work in practice. How much more effective could assessment be if undertaken by middle school teachers and teachers at post-primary level if children already had positive experiences from their physical education lessons in primary school?

Post-primary response

If we are honest, for many of us in post-primary education, planning for assessment, either formative (for learning) or summative (of learning), is often low on the list of our planning priorities. Instead the focus is more likely to be on providing a range of teaching and learning experiences designed to maximise the students' learning and engagement in the particular physical activity. Somehow, we don't seem to believe that assessment has a role to play in this. The extent to which the students engage and appear to improve in the activity is all the feedback we need to make a subjective assessment of the learning that is taking place. The difficulty with this, however, is that the student is rarely given the opportunity to consider their individual performance and their contribution to the overall performance in the context of a group/team activity. In this paper, the authors take us through a review of assessment practice in physical education in a different way.

The notion that every physical education class has a unique ecology prompts us to think more deeply about our planning in physical education and specifically in the development of assessment approaches. Many physical education teachers have had the experience of teaching the same physical education class to different class groups and eliciting a very different response. This paper has prompted me to bring this intuitive awareness to the foreground. Each physical education class has its own unique ecology comprising the interaction of what is being taught, how it is being taught and who is being taught. Planning for teaching, learning and assessment in physical education could be improved by considering not only what and how I will teach but also to consider more carefully the individuals and the class involved in the learning. Perhaps, planning templates and reflective practice approaches would serve us better if they encouraged the teacher to consider the three systems that impact on how we experience teaching and how students' experience physical education.

The authors' particular focus on the student social system provides valuable insights into what makes for an enjoyable and worthwhile assessment experience in physical education. Students like to know why they are doing the assessment task, and what counts as an excellent, good, fair or poor performance. In other words, students prefer to have a clear picture of what they are aiming for including clear descriptions. Hellison's (2011) Personal and Social Responsibility model is one example of where students have a clear picture of what they will be doing at each of the different levels. It would appear that knowing the criteria for success supports a fuller engagement in the assessment task. Students enjoy tasks that are sufficiently demanding and where they have something specific toward which to aim.

How often have we designed individual teaching, learning and assessment tasks with due consideration of the students? This research reminds us that students have an agenda in the classroom and their agenda is what we see as they interact with each other in the student social system. The wise thing we can do as teachers is to be aware of the social system and design tasks that are supported by this social system. Students like to be involved with each other in the activity so the assessment task should, if at all possible, be part of the game or activity in which the students are engaged. The fun and enjoyment should not stop when assessment becomes the focus. Students enjoy peer assessment tasks. They are more likely to try to do better having made mistakes when working with a peer as they do not feel as exposed as they might if they were being assessed by the teacher. Once the task is clearly outlined, students will try to perform as best they can in a peer assessment situation.

The learning therefore for me has been to acknowledge the powerful influence of the student social system in my physical education class. This research piece has highlighted a number of principles worth observing in the design of assessment tasks:

- Be clear about why you are doing the task.
- Explain this clearly to the students including what the different assessment levels are and what they will look like.
- Design assessment tasks that are part of the activity and that do not detract from the fun and enjoyment that learners are having.
- Let students work in pairs and/or groups using clearly outlined assessment tasks.

9

STUDENT PERCEPTION OF CARING TEACHING IN PHYSICAL EDUCATION

 The study

Larson, A. (2006). **Sport, Education and Society,** *11(4), pp. 337–352.*

In an attempt to identify what physical education students perceived to be caring teaching, critical incident techniques were used to describe the teaching behaviours these students suggested.

Participants

Subjects were recruited through contact with eight physical education teachers from a large urban city located on the west coast of the US. These teachers, representing primary, junior high school and high school from various school contexts, understood the purpose of the study as identifying characteristics of caring teachers from students' perspectives. The sample included 518 students (108 primary, 295 junior high school, 115 high school) whose school district and principal gave permission for the study to ensue.

Design and method

Participants were asked to complete a critical incident form that asked them to describe one time when your physical education teacher was caring. Before being asked to complete the critical incident form, the researchers spent time explaining the intent of the research and that participation was voluntary. In an attempt not to bias the students or elicit certain responses, the researchers were cautious not to provide examples of caring behaviour. Data were analysed using a systematic process that first involved separating forms by those that were appropriate or inappropriate. Appropriate responses were those that met the criteria of identifying a specific teacher behaviour as opposed to a teacher personality characteristic. Using Strauss and Corbin (1998) to guide analysis, critical incident forms were read and re-read in order to identify caring behaviours. Key behaviours were identified along with any narrative describing the behaviour before being interpreted and assigned a label. These labelled behaviours were then grouped by clusters for further examination. Finally, in order to develop a theory to describe a caring teacher as experienced by the students, the original data and emergent categories were further examined. As a result, a main category evolved along with descriptors that linked each category to the main theme.

Results

There were 389 reported incidents of caring out of the total 518 responses. Of note, 98 per cent of these occurred in class, with 56 per cent being content-related and 42 per cent non-content related. The authors provided an overview of the caring behaviour clusters, frequency with which they were noted and an example to clarify. Clusters included (with the frequency noted in brackets):

- showed how to do a skill (82)
- honoured my request (67)
- gave me a compliment (52)
- confronted my behaviour (36)
- inquired about my health (29)
- attended to me when I was injured (29)
- allowed me to re-do my test (22)
- motivated me (22)
- played/participated with me during class (22)
- persuaded me (14)
- showed concern for my future health (14).

The three subcategories were described as were the main category. Clusters were further broken down into three subcategories of caring teaching behaviour and included (1) recognise me, (2) help me learn and (3) trust/respect me. The authors conclude that not only do physical education teachers have the chance to exhibit caring behaviour but that students notice and appreciate this attention when given.

 Research perspective

Use of critical incidents to collect descriptions of caring behaviour seem an appropriate choice as they allow examination of what participants have actually experienced rather than merely their impressions. The actual events described in the critical incidents were analysed to reveal a set of behaviours that suggest the importance of building a relationship between the teacher and his/her students. A strong case can be made that effective classroom management is the foundation for a positive learning environment. Research over the past three decades indicates that classroom management is one of the critical ingredients of effective teaching. Three questions we might ask:

- Are effective classroom managers born, or can you become one if you are not one already?
- Can caring teachers be created?
- Can teachers be taught to build relationships with students?

Marzano (2003) argues that in all three cases teachers that show these qualities are made. These teachers understand and use specific techniques that they have become aware of and taught to use, which in turn change student behaviour and ultimately impact student achievement. The teacher and student relationship is key to classroom management as seen when teachers interact with, and learn more about, their students. Teachers build and maintain a positive relationship with their students by communicating with them and providing frequent and appropriate feedback to them. Teacher educators can help pre-service teachers move away from a focus on self to recognise how the relationship built with young people can impact their own confidence.

 ## Teacher educator response

Interesting to us was that these young people identified a caring teacher as one who sets expectations for student behaviour and learning while holding them accountable for their performance and achievement of these expectations. In other words, a teacher cares enough to demand and acknowledge standards of behaviour. Often, beginning teachers struggle with classroom management and holding pupils accountable for their behaviour. One pre-service teacher might suggest that enforcing consequences will result in pupils perceiving them as a mean teacher. The alternative is of course the teacher who does not smile until Christmas thinking that by being stern the pupils will come to know who is to be in charge. How do we help novice teachers come to realise that a caring teacher is not one that steps aside, is permissive with pupils, or 'does it to them' rather than inviting them to learn? A caring teacher plans, challenges, poses problems, leads, probes, coaxes, pushes and perhaps even coerces. All of these teacher behaviours demonstrate to pupils that we care enough to challenge them to learn and let them know we are there to facilitate that growth and learning.

Recently, while attending a professional conference for pre-service teachers in the final year of initial teacher education across subject areas at our university, the keynote speaker, Dr Patrick Ryan, caught everyone's attention with the title of his session, 'Teenagers: X-bored, X-rated but Wii still need to kinect360 with them'. He spoke about how teenager statistics with which we are bombarded in the media impact how we respond to, and interact with, young people. We were challenged to consider how to create a space for youth to learn, how to stimulate curiosity, and how to build on the strengths of young people. Discussion revolved around the idea of 'curiosity' as the heart of teaching and acknowledged that curiosity can frequently result in student confusion. Often as teachers, we see confusion, misinterpret it and attempt to remove it by giving students the answer. Patrick encouraged us to be patient, allow confusion to remain, and permit students to grapple and subsequently learn. He indicated that if we give away the answer then teaching may be taking place but learning is halted.

Teachers can learn to be caring. It is an attitude that can be fostered and even practiced. Connecting with students is key to caring and essential if young people are to learn. Part of our role as teachers is facilitating student learning. If we are to facilitate the learning of all students we need to focus on each of them as individuals, considering what might be inhibiting their learning and how you, as the teacher, might be reinforcing these inhibitions. In order to read the cues that every one of us portrays, we must get to know the pupils; know them beyond where they are from. Know their strengths, their joys and their passions, know how they prefer being treated and what they expect from you, know what is meaningful to them and what causes them to be anxious, know their goals and their dreams so that you might determine how to assist them in best achieving them.

 Primary response

While teacher educators (above) are concerned with the ability of teachers to learn to be caring and contend that it is an attitude that can be fostered and even practiced, this research can prompt primary teachers to reflect on the significance of their caring role within physical education classes. What teaching behaviours outlined by the students in this study does the primary teacher exhibit? From my experience as a primary teacher and from my observations of primary teachers teaching physical education, I have witnessed many behaviours of primary teachers that match the three subcategories of caring teacher behaviour (recognise me, help me learn, trust/respect me). I believe that primary teachers within physical education lessons frequently exhibit behaviours that would lead children to acknowledge that they are recognised, trusted and respected. However, the traditional emphasis in many physical education programmes at primary level on having fun might suggest that the 'help me learn' subcategory is not as strongly represented. This research provides some concrete examples of learning that led students to comment on this aspect of caring. It is worth considering the clusters of behaviours that form this subcategory (help me learn). To what extend do I as a primary teacher motivate children to learn? Persuade them? Show them how to do a skill? Allow a child to do a re-test/confront a child's behaviour? Show concern for the future health of a child? Clarify directions? Join in with children on occasion when executing content (motor skill and fitness)? Show a child how to interact more positively with another child? While the paper article prompts reflection on many aspects of caring, the hub of the issue is centred on providing individualised feedback, recognising achievement, noticing when something is different and acknowledging preferences. Perhaps it is timely for a primary teacher to recognise, as the teacher educators do, that caring is an attitude that can be fostered and practised and that it is never too late to do so.

 ## Post-primary response

Physical education teachers have many opportunities to foster a caring relationship with their students. We are reminded hereof the importance of the teacher-student relationship in physical education and its impact on both the extent to which students engage in physical education and their motivation to do so. Students' perceptions about caring physical education teaching matter, therefore, because of the impact of this on students' willingness to engage in physical education class.

What do students perceive as caring teaching in physical education? It matters to students that their teacher knows their name, compliments them where appropriate and enquires after their wellbeing, for example, when they are unwell or injured. It matters that the teacher supports individual student's learning, taking the time to encourage them as they learn to participate and perform.

There are numerous opportunities for physical education teachers to exhibit these caring behaviours in class. However, this is more likely to happen if the teacher has a personal conviction about the importance of forging a personal connection with individual students. Most teachers enter the profession because they want to make a difference in young people's lives. Physical education teachers believe that physical education can make that difference to young people's enjoyment, development and wellbeing now and in the future. While this conviction about the value of physical education is important, it is not enough. Students are more likely to be convinced about the value of physical education if they experience it through a caring relationship with their teacher. We know from the research that teaching behaviours influence students' positive or negative attitudes to physical education. Noddings (2002: p. 144) suggests that 'it matters whether or not students like their teacher and teachers like their students'. Students are more likely to be convinced about the value of physical education if they experience empathy, respect and positive regard from their physical education teacher.

Physical education class provides many opportunities for quality interpersonal interaction with students. While the potential is there, the reality of teaching physical education can also be challenging in this regard. Students normally have physical education once a week. Unlike classroom based subjects, students are moving around, constantly changing groups and partners as they engage in different activities. They are communicating with each other for the most part so it can be challenging for the teacher to get to know students' names and to build up an individual rapport with different students. A student is sometimes more likely to be recognised because they are (a) he is off task regularly or (b) exceptionally able. There is a middle group in each class who can often remain largely anonymous. Given the significance of caring teaching for students' interest, performance and motivation in physical education, it would appear to be worthwhile to reflect alone or with a peer on the extent to which different caring behaviours are present in one's teaching with a particular class group. The following questions might be used in support of such a reflection:

Recognise me . . .

- How many students can I name in this class?
- How many students did I interact with directly with today? – compliment, encourage, ask after?
- Did I notice anything peculiar about any student in this class?

Help me to learn . . .

- To what extent did I encourage individual students to participate?
- To what extent did I support individual students in learning a skill or technique?
- Did I explain a tactic or approach to performance to an individual student?
- Did I participate/play in class today? Which groups did I participate with and why? What do I believe was the benefit of my participation for my students?
- Did I confront poor behaviour? Did I put in place clear, agreed and achievable goals for improved behaviour with my student? How do I feel toward this student now?

Trust/respect me . . .

- How did I respond to students today when they suggested we do another activity/task?
- How did I respond to students when they want to take the lead in the activity?
- Did I allow/encourage students when they asked to use equipment/facility?
- Did I check in with students about how they were experiencing the learning?

Empathy, understanding and responsiveness are at the heart of caring teaching (McCroskey, 1992). As teachers, when we affirm and encourage, we allow students to experience 'a better self and encourage its development' (Noddings, 1992: 25). As physical educators, we have many opportunities to exhibit caring in support of optimum student engagement. It is in reflection that we can become aware of the extent to which we engage in caring. It is in planning that we can ensure that 'caring teaching' behaviours are considered alongside other pedagogical considerations.

10

DEFINING, ACQUIRING AND TRANSACTING CULTURAL CAPITAL THROUGH ASSESSMENT IN PHYSICAL EDUCATION

 The study

Redelius, K. and Hay, P. (2009). **European Physical Education Review,** *15(3), pp. 275–294.*

A large-scale study, the School-Sport-Health project, commenced in Sweden in 2001. This paper reports on findings drawn from the follow-up phase of the study. In Sweden, Physical Education and Health (PEH) is a mandatory subject in the post-primary years of schooling. Generally students are offered two lessons, each lasting 100 minutes, of PEH every week. The syllabus is not detailed but provides significant opportunity for teachers to select their own content, materials and working methods as long as students meet the stated learning outcomes. The latest national evaluation of the subject reports that ball games are the most common activity together with gymnastics, fitness training and track and field. Drawing on these experiences the focus in this paper is on what students learn about the purpose, practice and possible consequences of summative assessment.

Participants

There were 355 16-year-old students (189 boys and 166 girls) who participated. They attended 28 different schools in Sweden and had achieved a Pass grade (36 per cent), a Pass with Distinction (44 per cent) or a Pass with Special Distinction (20 per cent).

Design and method

All the students answered an extensive questionnaire that included general questions about their views of PEH as well as questions specifically related to assessment and grading. Twenty-three focus group interviews involving 73 students were conducted, probing participants' views on the criteria used for assessment, the characteristics of students with the highest grades and factors that determine a high grade. Both the open-ended question from the questionnaire and the focus group interviews were analysed by identifying patterns of content and assembling categories or themes.

Results

The function of grades was overwhelmingly the provision or communication of information, with grades pointing to potential for future educational paths. Assessment was viewed as a marker of a valued element of the curriculum, motivating students to engage. With reference to criteria for assessment, the dispositions, attitudes and interactions of students as well as appearances ('looking fit') and displays of physicality were consistently identified as the most important criteria for high grades. However, the dispositions and attitudes discussed indicated that doing your best was highly valued compared with other subjects. Assuming leadership roles was identified as a significant high grade factor also. There was an inconsistency between the student views of the criteria for assessment and the official criteria. Irrespective of this, students readily identified key values in terms of dispositions, appearances and histories in obtaining achievement success in PEH.

 Research perspective

There appears to be a disconnect between the use of 'assessment' and assigning of 'grades'. The paper supports the importance of examining assessment along with pedagogy and curriculum, reporting the oversight of previous physical education literature in examining pedagogy and curriculum at the expense of exploring assessment procedures and their related outcomes. Indeed, considering effective instructionally aligned physical education entails the inclusion of curriculum, assessment and instruction. It appears that the initial concern with the importance of the assessment process is somewhat lost when the focus on assessment appears only to be concerned with the assessment outcome – that is, the grade(s).

It is difficult to appreciate the relevance of the authors' interest in the recontextualising field – that is, where state and local authorities determine the syllabus and its conditions for implementation, and the secondary field, where the syllabus is reproduced in and through the relationships between teachers and learners. While it is clear that the mediation between the two fields influences the enactment of the syllabus in the secondary field, the paper focuses on establishing students' perceptions on grades rather than the pedagogical relationships between teachers and learners in reproducing the syllabus.

The authors introduce us to the Swedish grading system and grading criteria but do not revisit this in the paper. It appears that the system and criteria had not been shared with the students but rather that they had been asked to respond to their perceptions of criteria for receiving the highest grade in PEH. It is therefore difficult to appreciate the necessity for the inclusion of the grading system and grading criteria in the paper when neither appeared to be used as a framework in eliciting students' perceptions of assessment criteria. The study appeared to be more interested in establishing students' perceptions on (i) what they believed were the functions of grades, (ii) the means of acquiring high grades in PEH and (iii) descriptions of the criteria for achieving high grades in PEH, rather than in having students contribute to interrogating the Swedish grading system and grading criteria. An alternative research design that would have accommodated the Swedish grading system and grading criteria would have been what the authors allude to in the conclusion. That is, providing students with task-specific statements guided by the PEH 'Goals to attain', allowing students to be conscious of what goals they were striving towards, the criteria that would deem them successful as well as exposure to the formative assessment processes that would enhance their learning.

 ## Shared response

We have chosen to respond to this paper as a collective (teacher educator, primary and post-primary physical educators), focusing on four points that surfaced in our discussions of this research.

Assessment does not serve the very students we want it to serve

One of the most upsetting findings from the study is that the students for whom physical education may be of most benefit can potentially be marginalised through the perceived meanings and consequences of assessment outcomes – that is, what the authors term 'the possible pedagogical consequences of assessment processes'. That is, those students who are already marginalised in a physical education setting can be further disenfranchised through assessment procedures and associated outcomes in physical education and consequently their place within the institutional culture of schools.

Considering students' cultural capital appears to have potential in informing us as physical education teachers on integrating more suitable and effective assessment procedures for students. While the patterns of cultural capital exposed in a particular school may convey similar attributes, it is likely that cultural capital will differ between schools and across countries. In this study, the embodiment of cultural capital that conveyed dispositions, attitudes and interactions of students, as well as their appearances and displays of physicality, was consistently identified by students as the most important elements of the criteria that resulted in high grades. That is, the appearances and performances of bodies were clearly important to the achievement of high grades. This implies that in the case of students who do not possess cultural capital that manifests itself in what is deemed (by teachers and students) as appropriate appearance and performance for achievement in physical education, they are excluded from opportunities in physical education and the school that would encourage such dispositions. Alternatively, physical education could provide them with opportunities that accommodated their present state of cultural capital and perhaps allowed them to address appearance and performance dispositions if they so wished. Otherwise the cultural resources that students bring to school only have capital worth if they are recognised by the teachers. What is recognised by the teachers very quickly sends messages to the student about preferred characteristics and behaviours of students. These messages tend only to be heightened through assessment processes. The exposure of the body is probably more prominent in physical education than any other school subject and it is therefore important that we consider the most effective way to assess individual student's physicality. That is, the physical attributes/characteristics that a student brings to the class and how such attributes can positively contribute to their experience in physical education.

Provide students with task-specific statements as well as an explanation of the content and assessment practices

Assessment is the tail that wags the dog. The dog in this case represents everything that happens in the physical education classroom in supporting students' success in their assessments, particularly when the outcomes of the assessment are high stakes and contribute to the next stages of students' lives. In designing assessment approaches, therefore, the challenge is to ensure that the resultant pedagogical experiences that students have in physical education should support the kinds of learning that we aspire to in the aims of the subject, including students developing a lifelong interest and commitment to physical activity and sport.

This paper focuses on what students learn about the purpose, practice and possible consequences of summative assessment in physical education. By studying their beliefs and perceptions about what they need to know and be able to do to get a high grade in physical education, the authors were able to understand better what students learn about what is important in physical education.

Assessments are designed to ascertain what students know and are able to do as they learn or complete a course in physical education. However, what we choose to assess is not a neutral activity. Assessment provides a powerful 'message system' about what we value in physical education, and according to Broadfoot (1996: 87), 'assessment procedures are so closely bound up with the legitimisation of particular educational practices'. The messages come not only from those who are responsible for designing the assessments but also from the teachers who mediate the message in the classroom.

Reay and Williams (1999), quoted in the paper, report that assessment outcomes had quite powerful influences on students' perceptions of their capacities and the capacities of others, as well as their likely futures. It is important, therefore, that we reflect on the design and implementation of assessments in physical education. The following questions might be useful in reflecting on the design of assessment approaches:

- What do the assessment arrangements in physical education in my setting tell my students about what is valued in the subject?
- Having completed the assessment, will the students have demonstrated the knowledge and skills that are most valued in physical education?
- How do we ensure that the resultant experience of assessment in physical education can maximise students' positive perception of their place in the physical culture?
- Will they understand where their grade comes from, what they are good at and how they might improve?
- Are there clear assessment criteria in the form of rubrics that students can refer to?
- Are the assessment arrangements equitable or do they advantage particular students?
- For example, are students who have had opportunities to engage/excel in different activities beyond the school at an advantage in the assessments?
- Will students' experience of the assessment motivate students continued commitment to self-directed and lifelong learning in physical education?

As physical educators, assessment is a central part of our role in physical education. Generally speaking, what is assessed is valued in education and this in no less true in physical education. Not everything can be assessed and the teacher gives a legitimacy to what is assessed and how it is assessed by virtue of their 'pedagogic authority'. Opportunities for students to be recognised by the teacher were seen to be important in this paper. Do I provide all of my students with equal opportunity to excel in the assessment? Do I give preference to particular students, who perhaps are very involved in sport in or beyond the school? Do I explain clearly what the criteria for success are? Do I facilitate/support students in improving their grade? Do I explain to students the basis for their grade? Do I ask students about how they have experienced the assessment and what they have learned about themselves having completed it?

When assessments are well designed, they will form a central part of teaching and learning throughout the physical education course. The first time a student engages in the assessment should not be a 'once off', for grading purposes. By providing students with opportunities to engage with similar assessments, they can build up their capacity to excel and their motivation to do so in the assessment.

This paper confirms the potential of assessment to affirm and embed those values and outcomes that we hold dear in physical education. In this paper, the students were found to have learned, through the process and outcomes of assessment, the valued characteristics and behaviours for what was required to achieve high grades. The challenge therefore, is to design and carry out assessments that reward evidence of those values and characteristics that we aspire to for our students when they have completed their study in physical education.

Educate teachers on the use of assessment in physical education

A key concern in terms of assessment is the professional development (PD) that is required for assessment to be effective. It is important that professional development initiatives are informed by studies such as that of Redelius and Hay. Their recommendations are wide-ranging. They suggest that grading schemes are task-specific and that PD should focus on the writing of these task-specific statements. Furthermore, they argue that the PD should focus on standards statements and how they can be used to promote a shared understanding of valued learning. They suggest that PD should emphasise collecting defensible assessment evidence. A strong rationale for such focussed PD is that these grades have high-stakes implications and that they provide students with direction related to possible futures in areas related to physical education. One clear message that can be drawn from the paper is getting assessment right is important.

If as we argue above the challenge is to design and carry out assessments that reward evidence of those values and characteristics that we aspire to for our students when they have completed their study in physical education, we need to turn our attention to how teachers can undertake this work effectively. Establishing those values and characteristics must be at the centre of any PD work. Using all of the best guidance that is available on effective initial teacher education and professional development it would appear wise to begin with some debate at each level (initial teacher education and PD) on the why, what and how of assessment. While Redelius and Hay argue that assessment related to physical education is a requisite element of practice, in most western education settings it is still unclear in many settings what is really valued in physical education.

Professional development may often need to 'begin again'. Many physical educators need to begin with a key question, why assess in physical education. The most compelling argument (and there are many) is that assessment, particularly formative assessment enhances teaching and learning in physical education. Teachers and pre-service teachers need time to work with assessment in physical education, to identify what they might assess if assessment is to be used to enhance their teaching and lead to better learning by their pupils. A useful emphasis in this phase of work is for teachers to read the work of researchers such as Black *et al.* (2003) who present strong arguments for assessment in the wider educational context and then to examine the research undertaken by Rink and Mitchell (2003) and MacPhail and Halbert (2010), the latter discussed elsewhere in this publication. This paper could be a really powerful starting point for ITE or PD related to physical education providing a rationale for assessment in general and then offering an argument that is specific to physical education.

However, it may not be necessary to look any further than the article of Redelius and Hay if teachers were trying to work out *what* to assess. Some questions are raised below that could help teachers work out the values and characteristics that might define *what* may be assessed. It could prompt a really useful discussion on those values and characteristics that we aspire to for our students when they have completed their study in physical education. The questions considered above might keep such discussions grounded – that is, what really needs to be assessed and what is important for students to learn but may not be possible to be assessed.

Once these values and characteristics have been identified, a focus for teachers' PD might be on the tools of assessment: *how* to assess. Teachers are generally discussing how instructional techniques, for example, questioning, can help assessment, how rubrics can help record evidence of learning, how assessment wheels may help students self and peer-assess and how instructional technology can help the process of assessment. Physical education teachers need to continue to explore these issues in the context of their subject, and classroom teachers who are teaching physical education are beginning to explore these assessment tools for use in primary classrooms. Projects that are exploring student use of digital technology in physical education by pupils are good examples of how students and teachers can work collaboratively to ensure that assessment is a shared responsibility. Some projects are examining how teachers can collate information in a manageable way to help with both formative and summative assessment. Professional development must continue to be informed by such research work. It is an ongoing process for all teachers that can only be enhanced by working through the issues raised by, among others, those researchers who are examining current practices and making recommendations based on their findings.

Implication is that if it is not assessed it is not valued

This paper implies that if learning is not assessed it is not valued. We have heard this argument made in education frequently and as physical educators we have seen our content being marginalised and under-valued when it is not part of the accountability system. While we do consider assessment separate from 'grading', we do appreciate the importance of assessment for learning as a means of helping young people recognise how they are doing, whether they are successful, and how they might improve performance. However, to our surprise, we are challenging the idea that if something is not assessed it is not valued. In fact, this paper caused us to question our own beliefs about assessment and what we have been teaching pre-service teachers; perhaps it is just semantics but it needs to be considered. When introducing instructional alignment and the relationship between learning goals, assessment and instruction we have always said, 'If it isn't assessed, it isn't worth teaching'.

Unfortunately, this has become true to the point where we have reduced some content areas to only what is on the exam. We have eliminated the notion of learning for enjoyment and simple pleasure, and we have reinforced that every movement form or physical activity area must be assessed if it is going to be taught. If this is the case, then we may see young people who do not perform well in a physical activity receive the message that he or she need not attempt to choose a physically active lifestyle as they will not be successful in doing so as they get older. As noted in an earlier section, this has huge implications for young people who may need physical activity and health the most yet also for those who are not highly skilled but enjoy taking part in physical activity. In this instance, the idea of doing your best rather than being the best is crucial when considering what we learn in physical education. We are not suggesting teachers 'grade' on effort and participation but we do suggest that teachers acknowledge the enjoyment that young people gain from taking part in activity for the sake of activity. Trying and doing your best seems to contradict other content areas where students can fail. If we want to be physically active there are benefits of doing well yet the message that not doing well has major consequences for lifetime choices might be too severe.

11

'WE HAD TO DO INTELLIGENT THINKING DURING RECENT PE'

Students' and teachers' experiences of assessment for learning in post-primary physical education

 The study

MacPhail, A. and Halbert, J. (2010). Assessment in Education: Principles, Policy & Practice, 17(1), pp. 23–39.

This study was initiated in response to a perceived need for additional teacher support for assessment in physical education in Ireland. It involved the refinement and evaluation of a post-primary physical education assessment for learning (AfL) planning framework, with the implementation of associated assessment instruments by teachers.

Participants

The project involved 20 post-primary schools, with each school nominating one physical education teacher to be involved in the year-long project. Criteria for school selection included a geographical spread, differing school type, the nominated teacher being a qualified physical education teacher and a range of teaching experience. Initial contact was made with schools by identifying teachers who had previously been supportive of learning of ways in which to improve their practice.

Design and method

Teachers were asked to focus on one area of study in physical education, and to incorporate project materials into this class through planning, teaching and learning experiences. Each teacher was to use a 'rich task' framework in planning for lessons, share planning and content related issues with other teachers and accommodate an evaluation visit. An initial teacher seminar was held where all teachers were brought together to discuss suggestions on how best to use the prepared project materials. Fourteen schools were visited to offer support in the work of the project. Teacher network meetings allowed teachers to meet three or four times during the project to report on progress or discuss issues. The facilitator at each school visit and teacher network meeting recorded discussions and these were added to other data sources such as prompt sheets, teacher interviews and student focus groups. Prompt sheets were sent to students and teachers to help identify views on AfL in the context of physical education.

Two case study schools were identified as contrasting examples presenting the possibilities of working with AfL, irrespective of previous teaching and learning preferences. One teacher from each school was interviewed on completion of each phase of the project. Two student focus groups were conducted in each school at the same times. The study involved teachers and students in trialling materials in the school setting, supporting teachers' involvement in an action research approach. Data were analysed by coding with reference to the main components of AfL, for example, sharing the learning intention, criteria for success and offering feedback. Further categories were constructed on the incidences of particular words and phrases, and these categories formed the basis for discussion of the findings reported below.

Results

A planning framework was provided for teachers by the research team. Its focus was on:

a   outlining syllabus learning outcomes and matching learning experiences, including challenge, and content to the outcomes;
b   outlining assessment approaches and instruments;
c   identifying the equipment needed for the unit.

This was found to be useful and teachers reported that it helped them develop a structured, organised unit of work and lessons with a clear focus on learning, teaching methods and outcomes. Teachers reported that students took on a level of ownership of the lessons, which students acknowledged in their feedback. Students were positive about the shared learning intentions and having a task to complete by the end of a unit of work. An assessment wheel instrument was viewed as easy to understand and its use did not intrude on physical activity levels within the class, with students believing it helped monitor their progress. While the terminology 'rich task' was not used frequently, students were generally positive about the concept as a culminating event or process.

In terms of the focus on learning, students were conscious of learning differently and learning more in AfL lessons, while teachers suggested that learning in physical education had become more meaningful for students. Some students perceived that the focus on learning resulted in less physical activity and more 'class work'. Questioning and feedback were two elements that were identified by many teachers as increasing students' involvement in lessons. Both teachers and students believed that the quality of student learning (referred to by students as 'intelligent thinking') had improved as a result of engaging in AfL.

 ## Research perspective

This study represents important and valuable practice-based research informing the growing body of research on formative assessment and AfL in physical education. As noted by the researchers, this paper emphasises the perceived learning noted by students rather than providing evidence of the actual learning that may have occurred. The teachers involved in these case studies reported the benefits of using the assessment wheel as allowing students to note their individual progress and provide a means to assess their learning. The researchers discuss helping teachers to reconfigure learning experiences so that they are also assessments, which would change the emphasis to recognising both perceived and actual learning. Ideally, this study would be strengthened if it included an actual assessment component reflecting if students' perceived learning matched the actual learning.

Noteworthy was these teachers' recognition that the time involved to collect student learning evidence during assessment is problematic. Since this study involved a group of committed and exceptional teachers, they may not have felt this issue to some extent as other physical educators in different settings might. These teachers were part of a project where accountability may have influenced this attitude and they were provided with a network of teachers and researchers with whom they could share and discuss issues and problems as they arose. They seemed positively disposed to the study and felt the outcomes were worth their time and effort. When given time to reflect on the experience, they were able to recognise the worth of assessment suggesting that it was the whole package of engagement of teaching, learning and assessment and not assessment as an 'add on'.

 ## Shared response

This paper prompted extensive rich discussion of formative assessment and the practice of AfL. As a result, and rather than tackle a response from a teacher educator, primary and post-primary perspective we chose to discuss three aspects that were most intriguing to us; the rich task as a focus, a progression for teachers in learning to assess and

alternative ways for students to demonstrate achievement of learning. It is hoped that these insights will cause each of our readers to think differently about the assessment process.

The rich task as focus

The 'rich task' shared in the paper conveys integrated learning experiences that represent learning outcomes in a practical environment. It is important to consider further the extent to which an effective rich task serves as more than an assessment but rather as informing the weekly teaching and learning as students work towards the end of unit challenge. The rich task focuses particularly on AfL, in particular the impact of formative assessment (the example used in the paper is an assessment wheel) on student learning. In this particular study, students appreciated being given more responsibility for their own learning and teachers believed that the use of questioning and feedback increased the number of students positively engaged in the physical education class. While it could be stated that the rich task is in essence a way of teaching toward the assessment, it is intended to be done in a way that allows all students to learn differently and demonstrate learning in ways that allow them to provide evidence of success. Consequently, this places each entire lesson in the learning journey as moving toward an ultimate end of unit goal as opposed to only concerning the link between one lesson and the next. The former links every learning outcome to the concluding assessment. Subsequently, a rich task could be considered as the generation of a physical education assessment-planning framework with various assessment instruments deemed to be 'authentic assessments' for use by teachers and students in association with the physical education syllabus. For this to be effective, teachers would need to pre-define learning for each week, taking into consideration feedback from students on how they have responded to previous learning experiences related to the task.

A meaningful and coherent physical education programme reflects an alignment between learning goals, assessments that determine if students reach those goals, and the instructional practices that provide students the opportunity to achieve success. The rich task denotes the three elements of instructional alignment. The first piece of the instructional alignment triad is reflected in the teachers' goals for student achievement – that is, what it is students will learn in physical education. In this study, this is noted as the 'Challenge' and the associated 'Learning outcomes' in the planning framework. The second piece of the alignment is assessment – that is, assessments are properly aligned to the learning experiences that, on achievement of each, will lead to the successful completion of the 'Challenge'. A clever way for teachers to align assessments is to be able to reconfigure learning experiences so that they also act as formative assessments. That is, in providing an opportunity for students to undertake a particular learning experience, is there a way that you and the student can gather evidence from the outcome of that experience that informs the extent to which students have been successful and subsequently informs the next learning experience? The final piece of alignment is instruction and how teachers design student learning experiences and instruction to facilitate learning. Choice of instructional strategies and learning experiences need to be active, worthwhile and challenging if we are to engage young people in meaningful and enduring ways. Aligning learning as noted above may assist physical educators in offering what Ennis (2003) describes as a 'coherent curriculum', where learning is connected and realistic.

Teacher progression in learning to assess

This paper reminds us of the richness that well thought-out AfL approaches can offer to our practice in physical education. While assessment in physical education has generally tended to be a neglected area, this paper serves to re-energise our enthusiasm about, and commitment to, the role of AfL in quality physical education.

So how might we go about convincing more physical education teachers to give greater consideration to the place of AfL in their teaching? How might you, the reader, become more convinced, if you are not already? What is in it for you as a teacher and for your students? In other words, why does AfL really matter in physical education? In our opinion, it really matters because it impacts on both the teacher's and the student's experience of physical education requiring both to be more involved in the learning.

There are a number of non-negotiables in adopting an AfL approach, but none of them need be particularly onerous for the teacher and/or the student. In each lesson, the teacher is required to share the learning outcomes with the class. This requires that we identify what constitutes knowledge and learning for this lesson. The next task is to identify exactly what the criteria for success will be for these learning outcomes. How will we know that our students have learned what we have set out as being worthwhile? By generating the criteria for success in collaboration with the students, not only is the teacher clearer about what a successful outcome will look like but so too are the students. We are working in partnership with them. Too often in physical education, our students are engaged in meaningful activities but they may be in the dark about the purpose of the activity and its significance in the greater learning journey.

The final non-negotiable, we would suggest, is to plan to provide focused feedback in some way in the lesson. This feedback does not have to be to every child in every lesson and neither are you, as the teacher, the only source of feedback. The assessment wheel provides an excellent manageable approach to self, peer and teacher/student assessment. It can be used in a multiple ways and it does not always involve the teacher as the source of feedback. This requires that the teacher is prepared to trust students in assessing their own learning and to have confidence that this will be a worthwhile engagement. Whatever the approach to feedback and whoever is the source, it must always be referenced to the criteria for success and involve identifying next steps in meeting these criteria.

Adopting AfL approaches does involve a different way of doing business in physical education. It does take time. It does require careful planning. It does mean a different way of working with students, trusting them to take more responsibility for their own learning. But the dividends are significant.

As teachers, we can be clearer about what we are about in each lesson. Sharing the learning outcomes and criteria for success at the outset of each lesson commits us to that. We become more accountable. This may be challenging for us initially. We may promise too much at the beginning of each class and we may have to learn to scale back and be more realistic in our expectations. We may also have to compromise on the criteria for success, taking on board what the students define as success in conjunction with how we might define it. Initially, we may find working in such a collaborative way with our students more challenging. However, in working this way, we are modelling positive relationships skills such as respect and active listening.

By engaging in AfL practices, we are regularly reminded about what students are learning or not learning in our classes. It allows us to refine our teaching in response to these insights. At another level, the feedback we receive from AfL practices can affirm our practice, confirming that students are indeed learning and are progressing towards an end goal. It allows us to speak with greater conviction about our practice both with colleagues but also in the wider school context. It can, we suggest, help to sustain our confidence and commitment to physical education.

The benefits for our students are important. They experience a more respectful collaborative learning environment. They are clearer about the learning outcomes and how they might achieve them. This can help to sustain their engagement in physical education because they can see clearly the stepping stones that will be required to succeed in each learning outcome. Not all students are expected to achieve in the same way. They can see clearly that their learning needs are being taken into account as difficulties and challenges uncovered by the AfL practices are addressed in subsequent lessons. Students are given more responsibility for their learning and for supporting others in their learning. Physical education can become a more worthwhile and authentic experience for them.

The way forward for more teachers to engage in AfL practices is to start slowly. Start by identifying and sharing the learning outcomes for one lesson with one class. The next step requires that the criteria for success are identified and teachers should be prepared for this to be a challenging step. Encourage students to get involved and aim to build the detail of the criteria slowly.

Don't expect to include focused feedback for every student in every class. They will tire of this as will you, so perhaps aim for every third lesson and then don't always be the one responsible for giving the feedback. Encourage students to self and peer assess. Be open to the unexpected learning and the realisation that you will need to be prepared to adapt your teaching plan in light of the feedback received. You will also have to encourage your students to identify their next steps in light of the feedback they have received.

As you embark on your AfL journey, seek out a fellow traveller – a colleague even from a different subject area – so that you can reflect individually and together on how the process is unfolding. Celebrate your successes and plan to overcome your challenges. Check in with your students about how they are experiencing the process and be prepared to be surprised and to feel validated for your efforts.

Alternative ways for students to demonstrate achievement

Whether using a rich task format or merely aligning learning goals, instruction and assessment, the idea of providing alternative ways for students to demonstrate achievement is critical. We know that students do not all learn in the same way, they are taught through differentiated instruction that gives them various opportunities to interact with content in individual ways, yet often as teachers we design one assessment tool to allow all students to demonstrate learning. This study used Adventure Education, specifically orienteering to provide an example of the planning framework for pedagogy and assessment and included a set of worthwhile and meaningful learning outcomes for students to achieve. In addition to technical competence, safety and a respect for outdoors, one of these outcomes

---

Rich task: Students will prepare for and take part in a day of hill walking, navigating their course using map and compass.

Preparation: Along with the skills necessary for taking part in an orienteering event (e.g., thumbing, symbol recognition, country codes) students will have been taught appropriate selection of clothing (e.g., layering, shoe selection) for variable and changing weather conditions that may be encountered when on a day hill walk.

Formative assessment/Learning experience: A learning experience designed for the week prior to the actual rich task event will involve navigating an orienteering event and/or serving as the assessors of the event.

Working as a hill walking team, students will initially:

- Select appropriate clothing (for one walker) for the hill walk.
- Navigate the 5-control point course.
- When arriving at each control point, dress your hiker for the weather noted on the posted task card.
- When arriving at the next control point one of the assessment team will assess the choice of clothing decisions made.

Through a final debrief of the lesson clothing, success in navigating the course and safety procedure decisions will guide where learning is still needed.

was student appreciation of appropriate personal equipment. In line with suggestions from the authors that assessment also be a learning experience, contain more than one learning outcome, and involve 'acquiring, applying and evaluating knowledge', we propose a complimentary assessment that could also serve as a rich task.

SECTION III

Curriculum and instruction models

Deborah Tannehill, Ann MacPhail,
Ger Halbert and Frances Murphy

The six papers in this section provide an insight into the Adventure Education Model, Fitness Model, Game/Sport Model, Personal and Social Responsibility, Skill-theme Model, Sport Education, and Teaching Games for Understanding. It will be noticeable to the reader that the importance of (i) teaching 'in the moment' – that is, being able to respond to what happens in an actual activity rather than relying on what you had previously intended the outcome to be, (ii) as physical education teachers we teach students physical education rather than teach physical education to students and (iii) the distinction between curriculum and instructional models, are three observations that are revisited in the responses to the papers in this section.

Brock, Rovegno and Oliver (2009) examine students' social interactions during a Sport Education season and their perceptions of this experience, with the intent to examine whether there was any influence of student status on group interactions, decision making, responsibility or perceptions during a SE season. The shared response to this paper revolves around addressing taking a closer look at group work, characteristics that determine status in a physical education context and resignation of minimal involvement with peers.

Hastie and Curtner-Smith (2006) present a hybrid Sport Education–Teaching Games for Understanding unit with an interest in identifying innovative ways of teaching and learning that may arise in collating the two models. The responses to the paper include discussion on the distinction between curriculum and instructional models (suggesting that both Sport Education and Teaching Games for Understanding are curriculum and instructional models), the potential of such a unit to increase cross-curricular links in primary schools (particularly in the area of literacy) and the possible learning opportunities students are exposed to through such a hybrid unit.

Li, Wright, Rukavina and Pickering (2008) focus their attention on testing the validity and reliability of a Personal and Social Responsibility Questionnaire, seeking to examine the relationship between perceptions of personal and social responsibility and intrinsic motivation in physical education. The responses to the paper focus on discussion on the teaching pedagogies, especially those prompted in the Teaching Personal and Social Responsibility model, which might be employed to affect student motivation to participate.

Culpepper, Tarr and Killion (2011) investigate the impact of the Fitness Model, Game/Sport Model and Skill-theme Model on physical activity by measuring the amount of total steps accumulated during physical education lessons. The responses to the paper clearly make the case that it is not necessarily a particular curriculum and/or instructional model that increases physical activity levels in a physical education class but rather the instructional strategies through which the model is delivered and how best the time allocated to the physical education lesson is utilised.

Stran and Curtner-Smith (2009) examine how two pre-service teachers interpret and deliver Sport Education during their student teaching placement and determine factors that led to their interpretation and delivery of Sport Education. The responses focus on the appropriateness of the delivery of Sport Education being 'labelled' as either a 'full', 'watered down' or 'cafeteria' version and the importance of encouraging those teaching physical education to acknowledge how 'occupational socialisation' leads us to appreciate and understand the different dispositions and values that are evident in the delivery of physical education.

Sutherland, Ressler and Stuhr (2011) explore how pre-service teachers learned to incorporate a meaningful debrief in a five-day Adventure-Based Learning unit. The responses to the paper explore the application of the Experiential Learning Cycle to a teacher education, primary and post-primary physical education context. That is, the guiding 'What?' questions, the reflection encouraged by the 'So what?' questions and the transference of learning prompted by the 'Now what?' questions.

12

THE INFLUENCE OF STUDENT STATUS ON STUDENT INTERACTIONS AND EXPERIENCES DURING A SPORT EDUCATION UNIT

 The study

Brock, S.J., Rovegno, I. and Oliver, K.L. (2009). **Physical Education and Sport Pedagogy, 14(4), pp. 355–375.**

This study drew from the general education literature reporting the role of status in group work and the increase of curriculum models in physical education that encourage social interaction among students facilitated through group work. The authors examined students' social interactions during a Sport Education (SE) season and their perceptions of this experience with the intent to examine whether there was any influence of student status on group interactions, decision making, responsibility or perceptions during a SE season. Researchers' assumed that skill level and gender were characteristics students would associate with high and low status in a physical education context.

Participants

This study took place in a primary school located in a rural middle class community in the US. The physical education teacher worked closely with the university supervising student teachers. He was recognised for the quality of his instructional programme and experience teaching SE. Students in this mixed-ethnic school of approximately 465 students received daily physical education delivered by grade level, thus each class included from 70–100 students with one physical education teacher and two instructional aides. The researchers sought to examine students' social interactions at a micro-level (focus on individuals and their interactions) across an entire SE season. To achieve this, they chose one team of five boys and five girls aged 11–12 years from a physical education class of 80 students, all of whom had experienced at least one previous SE season. Teams were assigned by the teacher dividing pupils into eight equitable and mixed-sex teams of ten based on a timed soccer dribble test. The team that represented the most diversity relative to race and economic level was chosen as the focus team for the study.

Design and method

The SE season consisted of 27 lessons taught three days per week for nine weeks by the physical education teacher and focused on modified soccer. As is usual for SE, teams met to select team names, colours, co-captains, and rules committee member, and to design team posters, a league bulletin board, practice routines and game strategies. The season was divided into a pre-season (warm-up, team practice, strategy development, inter-squad scrimmages, rules test, team photos, referee selection), a regular season (game play combined with team/captain meetings, whole class discussions, a round-robin tournament where teams earned game play and sport behaviour points) and a post-season (double-elimination competition and awards ceremony).

Qualitative research methods were utilised to examine students' experiences and perceptions while working in teams over the season. Data was collected from multiple sources including a student demographic questionnaire; video of all lessons to show playing time and points scored; lesson plans and student artefacts; focus group and individual team member interviews highlighting group interactions, behaviours and detail on other data; teacher interviews following every lesson to discuss season progress and issues of concern; informal classroom teacher interviews to understand expectations for students; student journals to allow an avenue to communicate thoughts and perceptions; and a researcher journal reflecting concepts, issues, themes and questions that emerged from daily analysis of audio, video and student journal analyses. Data was initially transcribed, labelled and copied. Patton's methods of content analysis were applied with the coding and categorisation of data patterns resulting in more comprehensive themes.

Results

Students in this setting specifically defined status based on four characteristics: economic level, attractiveness, athletic involvement and personality. It was evident that status influenced students' social interactions during group work in terms of whose opinions were acknowledged and which students were silenced. Student status had an impact on the decisions made about playing time during the SE season based on skill level and gender of the students. As is evident from this study, it is important to understand the role status plays during group work, how to recognise the negative impact of status, and how to prevent these problems when students are working in groups. Also, we should note that status is specific to the environment and defined by the student culture in which the group work is taking place. Curriculum models such as SE provide us with a medium for addressing the influence of status during group work, as long as we recognise it and value its importance.

 ## Research perspective

This was an important study linking group work that is frequently used as a pedagogical strategy in physical education with student social interactions and each student's place within the team and classroom setting. With the current thrust in some countries toward framing our content within main theme curriculum models, and the frequency with which sport is taught in our school settings, SE as the framework for this investigation is appropriate. It was unsettling reading however. As physical education teachers we acknowledge the variability in our classrooms and the many student differences that exist. We also recognise that while bullying does happen, and probably even in our own classes, we don't always think of it when designing teaching strategies and organising team and group activities. Reading prompted visions of young people on teams where their voices were not sought, or heard, when they did share, their participation levels were low being hampered by the choices of their peers, and situations where some youth were made to feel less than valuable as team members. The authors cause us, as teachers, to understand how status influences and impacts young people as they experience physical education and to consider how we might better design and implement effective group strategies to address status concerns of young people.

As researchers we were impressed with the multi-method design, the depth with which the first author collected data (in-school lessons and out of school events) using a variety of tools (video, observation, questionnaire, individual and focus group interviews, student journals, researcher field notes, lesson plans and artefacts) and the organising system employed for data analysis that seemed to leave no stone unturned. However, a number of questions related to the methodology employed to study students' social interactions and their perspectives on what happened during a SE season did emerge.

The rationale used by the authors to assign teams somewhat contradicts the SE student-ownership philosophy of helping young people learn to take responsibility for their sport experience. While in early SE experiences the teacher will not hand everything over to the students, as this was at least the second season for each of these students, including them in the design and selection of teams may have been appropriate. As it was, the assigned teams were almost 'sterile' in that they represented similar skill levels and gender and the final team chosen to study also reflected a mixture of race and socioeconomic background. In other words, the researchers chose the characteristics they assumed students would associate with status. We wondered if there were other characteristics that had an impact on status from the students' perspectives, which the teacher and researcher did not recognise, such as children who had close friendships, who lived in the same neighbourhood, whose parents were socially involved, or who shared a common interest in an activity outside of school.

Another question that came to mind was the length of time the researchers remained in the research setting. We felt that the reality of student status suggests that, in this case, the researchers may have only gained a snapshot of what occurred. As the SE season unfolded, student status and their perceptions of how they were treated would also be influenced by the teacher response to peers' actions and behaviours toward team members. This reinforces the nature and value of longitudinal data that in this case might provide a broader view of how student status develops, changes and impacts children and youth.

 Shared response

We have chosen to respond to this paper as a collective of educators focusing on three issues that surfaced in our discussions and have implications at all levels. The three issues are (1) taking a closer look at group work, (2) characteristics that determine status in a physical education context and (3) resignation of minimal involvement with peers.

Issue 1: Taking a closer look at group work

This study prompted us to take a closer look at group work, which is a key instructional pedagogy within the SE classes described in the study. It is not clear to what extent students in this study were prepared for the level of group work involved in engagement with the SE model. Indeed, it could be argued that SE itself could form part of that preparation. However, given the significance of the student status that emerged within this study, it is worth examining what other elements of preparation are necessary for group work to be effective and to provide a voice for children or young people without a voice. Where group work is undertaken in a range of subjects at either primary or post-primary level, it underlines further the importance of preparing children and young people to engage with this kind of learning.

The aim of reflection and discussion among teachers related to group work is to prevent the problems highlighted in this study (where student status is based on characteristics related to economic level, attractiveness, athletic involvement and personality) when students are working in groups. First, should teachers consider discussing in groups with students, in advance of the grouping, what happens when working using the SE model? It is important in such work to examine how groups function best and to debate issues such as effective listening (what effective listening 'sounds like', e.g., speaking politely, and 'looks like', e.g., making eye contact with the speaker). Follow-on work could be based on building in what effective listening 'feels like'. Other group strategies that could be taught to students could include round robin activities where each student in turn has to verbally give their opinion before decisions are made. Use of role play, or examination of scenarios related to group members' roles could be useful to emphasise the importance of working well as a group.

However, arguably of even greater importance within physical education is the size of the teams or groups. In this study, each team consisted of ten members. For children in primary schools in particular, having ten members in any group presents additional challenges as children are only developing the ability to work in groups. Where possible, teams could be selected that contain no more than five members for the same reasons that small-sided games are more appropriate for the young child. Within these smaller groups there is also scope for 'pair share' work ensuring that the less dominant voices become heard within a safer environment at some stages of the process. These amendments to practice could prove worthwhile and contribute to the lessening of the impact of social status within physical education lessons.

Issue 2: Characteristics that determine status in physical education context

This research has prompted us to look again at how and why we include group work in physical education and to acknowledge that the inclusion of group work per se, without some means of critiquing how different students experience and learn through it, needs particular consideration. Over the past number of years, SE had become one of more popular curriculum and instruction models. Physical education teachers believe that it allows every student to be meaningfully involved and to experience physical activity in an authentic way. SE relies on students working together toward a common goal with each student's level of engagement and 'buy in' potentially impacting on a final successful outcome for their team. On the journey toward the culminating event, students assume different roles, all as participants but also undertaking non-playing roles that require them to work with and for their team. What then is the problem?

This research supports the well-established findings of classroom research that various aspects of students status influence what happens during group work (Cohen, 1994). Status matters in group work because students who have higher status have higher social interactions during group work, participate more in the learning, have more playing time and in turn, have a more positive experience in physical education. What constitutes status varies from group to group. It is influenced by the individuals within the group, the culture of the group and what is most valuable to the group in that particular space and time. In physical education, students who have high athletic ability often occupy high status positions and are often more likely to be male. In addition, this research found that students' perceptions about which students had high status in their group was based on (in order of importance) economic level or 'being rich', being attractive, being athletically able and having a good personality. Students bring these qualities to the group and, more than likely, have had positive prior experiences of group work. This allows them to 'hit the ground running', as it were, and to assume proactive and leadership positions. Students who are accorded lower status positions react to how they are perceived by the dominant people in the group and often assume a more 'back seat' role. One's status in the group fundamentally affects the extent to which students will be actively involved and in turn will affect their learning.

So what can be done to address this issue? In the first instance, we believe it is important that as part of pre-service teacher training, beginning teachers should have opportunities to observe and reflect upon how one's status impacts how we experience group tasks and how this, in turn, affects how we learn. It is possible to provide experiential learning opportunities where pre-service teachers engage in tasks where they are attributed a particular status that dictates the ways in which they can or cannot participate in the group. For example, one could be the student who cannot play badminton, who does not have 'the right gear', and who is not part of the 'in group'. For the beginning teacher, to actually experience what this is like for such a student can be a powerful learning experience and can help them to empathise with students who find themselves in these circumstances. Others in the group can also reflect on how it feels to be in a dominant position and what they might do to be more inclusive in their behaviour.

Given that all groups have some status hierarchy, it would be interesting for pre-service teachers to observe physical education class noting whose are the dominant voices and what appears to be the experience of the less dominant students in a SE class. They could test the validity of their observations by conducting a small number of short 'post class' interviews with selected students to check what they think they have observed.

In planning for teaching and learning, physical education teachers could consider the following two approaches in SE and more generally if possible. When students are either assigned or select roles, they are provided with a clear outline of the kinds of tasks that their role entails. Encourage students to reflect at regular intervals on the tasks that they are successfully completing and why. Make sure that the list of tasks are such that every student should be able to experience success at some level, irrespective of whether the full role is demanding, for example, being a captain. If students can identify some task that is manageable for them, they are more likely to be able to participate even in the company of higher status individuals as they will have a realistic goal on which to focus.

A second approach is at two or three points in the season to ask a number of students to observe one team or group. They can be asked to take note of whose voice is dominant in the group, who makes the decisions, who helps to get the tasks done, who contributes to the success of the group and how and what might help the team be more effective focusing on the positive attributes. The feedback should allow individual students to gain a picture of how they behave in groups and how they might change some behaviours to maximise their own and/or others' contribution to the success of the group.

Issue 3: Resignation of minimal involvement with peers

There is a general appreciation that there will be disparities in participation and achievement of students during group work relative to student status. In this study, economic level, attractiveness, athletic involvement and personality defined student status on group interactions and decisions. Consequently, this affected whose opinions were acknowledged and which students were silenced. While the authors qualify that status is specific to the environment and defined by the student culture, it is likely that regardless of environment and school culture there will always be those students who are resigned to never having the required status to be actively involved in the dynamics of group work. It is these students that we consider here with respect to how we can best create an environment that enables and encourages equitable interaction and participation. While Don Hellison's (2011) work on teaching personal and social responsibility provides numerous instructional strategies that can be used to encourage equitable interaction and participation, we choose not to focus on this here as they have already been highlighted in our response to the Hastie and Curtner-Smith (2006) study.

Lund and Tannehill (2010) encourage teachers to find out what is most meaningful and worthwhile to students, being careful to note that they are not suggesting that a curriculum be based solely on what students want to do. They report the work of Sagor (2002), who suggests that we all possess five needs (the need to feel competent, that we belong, useful, potent and optimistic) and the inherent desire to satisfy them. It is believed that satisfying these needs will result in a full commitment to the activity.

Not all students will have the physical capacity to feel they are contributing adequately to a physical education lesson. Not denying that they should continue to be physically involved in the lesson, teachers can enquire into other ways in which the student may be able to increase their perceived value in the class and to their peers. One potential avenue would be to encourage those who are interested and convey a talent in media/photography or writing to undertake associated roles in physical education classes. This could entail being responsible for taking photographs that would contribute to team portfolios and/or posters or compiling short sound bites on events throughout a lesson. In instances where students have acquired a low status through the complement of physical activities on the curriculum, the teacher could explore alternative physical activities that the individual is committed to and have them share and teach the activity to their peers. Either opportunity could potentially fulfil the five needs listed by Sagor (2002) above for the particular students.

While there may be some merit in stating that it is not necessary for all students to be overtly active in group work, there is some evidence that students' social interaction rates during group work are strong predictors of learning. This encourages us as teachers to attempt to find ways in which students, with a disposition/status that does not allow them to be pro-active in contributing to the work of the group, are not excluded from opportunities to learn. The apparent learned behaviour of the low-status students in doing what the high-status students tell them questions the extent to which low-status students are either (1) not concerned with the actions of those conveying high status and consequently choose to disengage or (2) are concerned with the actions of the high-status students but resigned to not having an opportunity to contribute. Scenario (1) is less upsetting if the student has made a conscious choice to disengage in this instance but has the capability of re-engaging and being pro-active in instances that are more important to them. Scenario (2) is worrying if the student continues to have their low status reinforced through numerous activities, believing that there are no instances in which they can meaningfully contribute. Teachers are therefore obliged to consider ways in which they can assist young people in appropriately dealing with inequalities that arise.

13

INFLUENCE OF A HYBRID SPORT EDUCATION–TEACHING GAMES FOR UNDERSTANDING UNIT ON ONE TEACHER AND HIS STUDENTS

 The study

Hastie, P.A. and Curtner-Smith, M.D. (2006). **Physical Education and Sport Pedagogy, 11(1), pp. 1–27.**

This paper presents a hybrid Sport Education–Teaching Games for Understanding (SE–TGfU) unit with an interest in identifying innovative ways of teaching and learning that may arise in collating the two models – that is, the collation of the structure of SE (i.e., seasons, formal competition and student roles) with the approach of TGfU (i.e., skills and tactics being taught using problem solving and guided discovery approaches).

Participants

Twenty-nine Australian sixth-grade students (aged 11 to 12 years, 11 boys and 18 girls), who had no prior experience of SE or TGfU, met daily for 30 minutes over a five-week period. The first author was the primary teacher of the unit and had significant experience in the teacher-as-researcher role with regard to SE, though not TGfU.

Design and method

The design followed that of a 'teaching experiment' where the researchers (one of them the teacher in the study) worked to develop a curriculum and study their teaching of and the students' responses to the curriculum. A 22-lesson season of batting and fielding games where the organisational structure of the unit was SE and the main pedagogical style was TGfU was designed and delivered. Data was collected from students through the recording of critical incidents, tactical quizzes, game design forms and team interviews on completion of the season. The critical incidents were analysed by sorting data into thoughts and perceptions, before being coded and placed in a series of emerging categories and subcategories. The analysis of tactical quiz responses involved determining the number of students who were successful in identifying the correct solution to the tactical problems presented. Game design forms were analysed with a view to identifying commonalities across and unique components within the games. Thoughts and perceptions recorded from team interviews were sorted into two themes, (i) the process of game intervention and (ii) explaining how another team might be taught to play the game.

Results

At the conclusion of the unit students were able to understand and execute a number of batting, bowling/pitching, and fielding tactics and strategies. Students also understood the overarching principles, rules and structures of batting/fielding games and were able to transfer them from one game to another. The authors were particularly impressed with the students' ability to include risk/reward strategies and avoid problematic skills in the games they invented. Combining SE and TGfU placed a heightened emphasis on the teacher and was therefore more labour-intensive, with a necessity to possess superior content and pedagogical content knowledge.

 Research perspective

Students were encouraged to design their own small-sided and modified games based on the knowledge they had acquired in the unit. Time was allocated to allow each team to present its game to the other teams and students voted for the game they wished to play for the final mini-tournament. This allowed students to not only demonstrate transfer of batting, bowling/pitching, and fielding tactics and strategies but also the overarching principles, rules and structures of such games. The success of the game design activity was further supported by the authors identifying that the three consistent features were inclusion, incorporation of risk/reward strategies and the avoidance of problematic skills.

The authors' use of the word 'pure' when discussing that the structure of the unit was 'pure SE' and that the main pedagogical style employed was 'pure TGfU' is interesting but somewhat contentious. It is not clear if, in using such a preface, the authors are deliberately attempting to convey that they are maintaining the 'fidelity' of both models – that is, that the SE processes and TGfU principles were reliably used as intended for the delivery of the full experience associated with each. This point is revisited in the section below.

In reading the abstract of the paper the first author, who was also the teacher in this study, is not listed as a participant. There is no hint in the abstract of this dual role and little in the paper about the challenges that arise in the teacher-as-researcher role. It would have been insightful for the first author to position himself in the study and provide more context to the expertise that they brought with him. Familiarity with models is critically linked with a teacher's/researcher's awareness of their own values and how those comply with the models. It would have been interesting and informative to have read the first author's positioning. We are told that the first author was a content expert in SE, which raises the question on the extent to which the hybrid unit could be replicated by teachers, who may, depending on countries, be generalist primary teachers and not physical education specialists. Is the first author/teacher positioning a limitation of the study or is the intention to have specialist physical education teachers delivering a hybrid unit to primary-aged students?

The paper conveys a strong example of a multi-method design that clarifies the study procedures. The paper also shares an unusual but welcomed level of detailed results in denoting the eight major categories and 45 subcategories that arose from the critical incident reflective sheets, the inclusion of students' thoughts and perceptions on game invention/design and on how to play their games well/win. Unfortunately, the researcher's reflective log and notes receive minimal attention under 'data collection' and is not mentioned at all under 'data analysis' or 'results'. While we are introduced to some of the issues, problems and challenges that emerged during the course of the unit from the perspective of the teacher/first author, these observations are not acknowledged as arising in the researcher's reflective log and notes. As a consequence, we have no information on at what point these issues, problems and challenges arose throughout the unit.

Teacher educator response

We began our discussion of this research paper at the same time one of us was engaged in assisting pre-service teachers with understanding and implementing several physical education curriculum and instruction models. It was interesting that the researchers in this study used SE as a curriculum model and TGfU as an instructional model, yet did not discuss SE as an instructional model or TGfU as a curriculum model. This is a bit like comparing apples and oranges and thus caused us a bit of confusion in interpreting the study for application in our teacher education classrooms or the teaching taking place in primary and post-primary gymnasia and on playing fields.

Curriculum models are focused, theme-based and reflect a specific philosophy. Each curriculum model intends to define a clear focus around the content, and aims toward specific, relevant and challenging outcomes. Once a curriculum model has been selected, it is up to the teachers to develop and promote the type of learning intended for students to experience through determining which instructional models will guide learning. The instructional model organises instruction and how students will interact with, and practice, content. An instructional model includes a number of strategies, methods, styles and skills that are used to plan, design and implement a unit of instruction. Often curriculum models are most effectively delivered using a specific instructional model.

If you accept our differentiation between curriculum *and* instruction models, then you will see why we suggest that both SE and TGfU are curriculum and instruction models. SE as a curriculum model strives to assist students in becoming competent, literate and enthusiastic sport persons by experiencing key elements of authentic sport through seasons, affiliation, playing performing and non-performing roles, taking part in a competitive season with a culminating event and records kept in what is a festive environment. The instructional models that are most effective in SE are small group strategies, peer teaching and problem solving as participants work together to achieve success as a team. TGfU is a curriculum model in that it classifies games based on the transfer between like games. In other words, many games share common tactical problems and, although they may be solved differently due to skill requirements or implements, there is much that can transfer among them. Thus, the classification system includes invasion games, net/wall games, target games, and striking and fielding games. The most effective instructional models used in TGfU are teaching through questions and problem solving as participants attempt to solve tactical problems related to game play that include determining what to do, when to do it, why to do it and how to do it.

As we discussed the study, we began to question if this was a true hybrid if it combined only pieces of the two models, and combined two different aspects of the models. Would it have made a difference if the researchers had combined all aspects of the two curriculum models, or the instructional models rather than to select one or two aspects from both the curriculum and the instruction model of each? Some research has explored SE being taught first, then TGfU before developing a hybrid as the final model, in this case a full hybrid. Perhaps the question needs to be considered relative to the reality of how teachers actually employ the two models. Do they teach SE and TGfU separately or together? Do they teach either SE or TGfU depending on where they feel most confident? This of course then pushes us to consider if this choice would limit and narrow the scope of the curriculum. Fidelity of the two models is important from our perspective and we feel more clarification from the researchers would assist us in interpreting their work.

When teaching SE, the teacher plans ahead of time and develops teaching aides and instructional materials that guide both the teaching (by peers and teacher) and student learning. In TGfU, the teacher plans and sets the stage for the lesson yet responds to the learners as the lesson unfolds. So, in SE the teacher is more of a facilitator as the lesson progresses and the TGfU teacher is more on stage guiding and formally teaching and responding to the students. With no games background TGfU is more difficult to teach as tactics are difficult to understand

and break down to teach if you do not know the game. In the moment of games making, if you do not have the background or conceptual understanding, you as a teacher will struggle. Two different kinds of teachers emerge; those who prompted by SE can plan ahead of time and then in class be willing to let go and give the lead to students or those who stay at centre stage but do so through responding to student responses, such as required by TGfU.

 ## Primary response

Working within a primary setting the approach described in this paper provides food for thought related to issues such as the increasing possibility for teachers to incorporate work on numeracy and literacy in physical education lessons. As physical education struggles to gain more time within the school day, increasing attention is being paid to the concept of learning *through* physical education. Integration across subject areas is generally regarded as a positive principle and it seems that the hybrid model described in this paper provides many opportunities for development of children's literacy skills in particular. This emphasis need not detract from the general aim of both models (SE and TGfU), which is described by the authors as being centred on providing democratic pedagogies and providing sporting experiences that allow students to learn how to play well. They suggest that a coalition of the two might lead to some real pedagogical breakthroughs. Perhaps the potential for development of numeracy and literacy skills might represent a further 'breakthrough' for a primary teacher.

This paper would seem to point towards the scope for development of literacy skills in particular. How might this development work out in practice? It is worthwhile examining the data collection methodologies: recording critical incidents, completing tactical quizzes, recording game design forms and team interviews. As children are challenged to complete a critical incident sheet they are in practice being asked to reflect on an experience that they have just had and are provided with prompts: did the incident make you excited, bored or worried? Did you learn something really new? These are challenging questions for many young children to answer and indeed for some young children describing the critical incident using these probes would engage them in real learning in terms of their oral language development. As children present their thoughts in writing they are engaging at another level and are completing a written record of an incident as well as providing a rationale – that is, trying to explain why it was important. Self-/peer- or teacher assessment of this written account could provide scope for children to critically examine their writing using techniques that they are learning to use as part of their writing skills programmes.

The completion of tactical quizzes is another opportunity for children to read a functional piece: the written scenario. They are then challenged to solve questions related to the scenario by drawing diagrams or providing a written answer. While the *quantity* of writing may not be significant, the *quality* of the writing will be key to presenting a clear rationale for their tactical decisions. Indeed, their responses might be recorded using digital technology, hence, contributing to their digital literacy.

There are a myriad of oral language possibilities as children discuss their game designs: they will be likely to debate the merits of allocation of particular space for their game, the equipment they might use and the tactics that might be used including the scoring strategy. They are then required to represent this game in a written format perhaps using diagrams to help communicate the real meaning of their game.

While the team interviews undertaken as part of this study were conducted by the researchers, this work could be undertaken by children themselves as part of a literacy module. Each team could be interviewed by a 'class reporter' and challenged to describe their motivation for and rationale behind the games they had invented. Why did you choose to use a bat? How did you decide on the space used for the game? Did the game change in any way as you played it? Why? This practice would provide useful experience for the child related to the development of oral competency within the literacy programme in primary schools.

The results section of the paper provides evidence of links with other aspects of curricula too: children's references to teamwork and cooperating for example, children's references to aspects not being fair or the few comments about winning. These are the seeds of potentially wonderful work within social and personal development programmes and they are based on children's lived experiences. A formal space can be created within school programmes to allow for meaningful discussion of these issues.

Understanding the cross-curricular approach as practised by many primary teachers could provide insight into another positive outcome of using this approach. The authors of this paper highlight time for instruction as a constraint in the discussion section of this paper. If the true potential of this hybrid approach is realised, it is clear that the classroom teacher at primary level can be teaching other subjects through physical education resulting in the alleviation of the time constraint on their teaching. By teaching in this integrated way, time dedicated to literacy teaching and to teaching of physical education can be combined in such a way that the child is a 'winner' in both spheres.

 ## Post-primary response

One of the fundamental aims of physical education is to develop each student's potential to have the confidence and competence to participate in physical activity and sport. Working with student-centred curriculum models such as SE and TGfU supports and encourages the engagement of students of very different abilities in physical education class. Both of these models are truly student centred, allowing the teacher the flexibility to plan the learning in a meaningful way starting from where the particular group of students is in terms of skill, aptitude, attitude and experience.

Both models place a premium on students being actively involved in their learning as they engage in problem solving, decision making and organisational tasks. Both models encourage students to apply what they have learned in creative ways, be it in response to a challenge in a modified game context (TGfU) or in the design of a culminating event (SE). All the time, students are working with, and learning from, their peers, which we know to be important for student's learning in physical education. While some of my teaching experience has been with using these models as discrete entities, this article has prompted me to look again at the strengths of including them separately and the potential benefits for combining them.

SE aims to provide students with a range of learning experiences that mirror all that is positive about real sport. It provides me with a clear, worthwhile and tangible aim of developing my students' potential to become competent, literate and enthusiastic sports people. It gives me a meaningful structure to organise my students' learning as I plan for each of the 'non-negotiables', including providing for seasons, affiliation, playing and non-playing roles and festivity.

The model allows me to plan for the authentic experience of the activity at a level that is suitable for the group of students. Each experience linked to SE can be made sufficiently demanding without being beyond the reach of the students. The potential for differentiated learning within a class group is also there. The activity itself can be structured and modified in a way that will support participation. A growing sense of affiliation, if it happens for students, can be a powerful catalyst for students to want to improve their skill, technique and tactical knowledge so they can contribute to their team's success. Improving their game/their role begins to matter in a way that it seldom matters in an ordinary games class.

The problem arises for me as a teacher when I feel the need to be more directly involved in supporting students' efforts to improve their performance. My experience has been that SE provides a scaffolding for an authentic experience of sport for many students who may not otherwise ever have known what it is like to be part of a team and a group. Because these students often do not have a well-established pattern of physical activity participation, they often lack in skill and a basic understanding of fundamental tactics, for example, switching from defence to attack, making space, defending space. Subsequently, the student coach or captain in the different groups in SE cannot always provide the kinds of focused learning experiences that address these deficits. This is why the hybrid model in this article appeals to me.

The TGfU approach moves beyond the more traditional teacher centred model of games teaching where the skilled performance is the benchmark and this is beyond the reach of many students. TGfU requires that the teacher plans to provide developmentally appropriate games experiences for the students. The games are generally small sided and can have modified rules and/or equipment. They are designed to start where the students are in terms of their ability and understanding. The main focus is on developing tactical understanding. The possibilities are endless in terms of making the activities incrementally more challenging as students' tactical understanding improves. The chances are that as their understanding improves students' participation will be more effective and their experience of the game more rewarding. They are more likely to want to build their skill set so as to be even more effective in their play.

Unlike SE, in TGfU the teaching style is more teacher-led. The teacher sets up the challenge in the modified game and uses carefully chosen questioning to draw out the students' understanding of what they are doing and how they might improve. As students' tactical awareness is developed, their experience in the activity improves – that is, they are free to receive a pass, they call at the right time, they stay between the attacker and the target. From a student's point of view, what better way to consolidate and authenticate learning than to go back into the SE season. They can participate now with a better understanding about what is required of me as a player, an improved ability to give meaningful encouragement and advice to their team mates as a captain, or be better able to organise different modified games in my role as a coach.

The challenge for the physical education teacher is to have a sufficiently developed understanding of both models. In SE, the teacher requires the ability to act as a facilitator of an authentic experience of the activity, including the capacity to allow the students to really experience the flow of a series of games. In TGfU, the reverse is needed. The teacher needs to be much more hands on, being able to adapt and modify the game as the need arises and then crucially, to be able to articulate the kinds of questions that will clarify students' understanding about how they can become better players. Essentially, there are two very different skills sets but both equally worthwhile.

14

MEASURING STUDENTS' PERCEPTIONS OF PERSONAL AND SOCIAL RESPONSIBILITY AND THE RELATIONSHIP TO INTRINSIC MOTIVATION IN URBAN PHYSICAL EDUCATION

 The study

Li, W., Wright, P.M., Rukavina, P.R. and Pickering, M. (2008).
Journal of Teaching in Physical Education, 27, pp. 167–178.

This study focuses on testing the validity and reliability of a Personal and Social Responsibility Questionnaire (PSRQ) consisting of two factors: personal responsibility and social responsibility. The study sought to examine the relationships between perceptions of personal and social responsibility and intrinsic motivation in physical education.

Participants

Participants consisted of 253 middle school students in the southern United States who completed the questionnaires. Their ages ranged from 9–15 years.

Design and method

The questionnaire used to measure personal and social responsibility was a modification of the Contextual Self-Responsibility Questionnaire developed in an earlier study. It was validated by a panel of Teaching Personal and Social Responsibility (TPSR) experts including the developer of the model and those with expertise in the fields of education, physical education and sport psychology. A four-item intrinsic regulation subscale of the Behavioural Regulation in Exercise Questionnaire (BREQ-2) was used to assess participants' intrinsic motivation in physical education. Participants were asked to complete both questionnaires, which took them approximately 15 minutes to complete.

Analysis of the data included:

a   checking the validity of the two-factor PSRQ model;
b   checking internal consistency reliability for all subscales from the PSRQ and intrinsic motivation;
c   examining relationships between participants' perceptions of personal and social responsibility and their intrinsic motivation in physical education.

Results

Perceptions of personal responsibility were positively related to perceptions of social responsibility and intrinsic motivation. Perceptions of social responsibility were also positively associated with intrinsic motivation. Participants who worked hard and had clear goals in physical education were likely to respect their peers and teachers and care for them. Those who exhibited higher levels of personal and social responsibilities were likely to enjoy physical education more. The results of the study suggest the two-factor PSRQ is valid and reliable for assessing students' perceptions of personal and social responsibility in physical education. The PSRQ may represent a useful tool for evaluating and improving programmes of TPSR designed to directly address personal and social responsibility, although it does not measure the transfer of responsibility outside the physical activity setting. It is important that while this instrument may assess students' self-reported responsibility, it does not address TPSR implementation. However, it could be used to measure levels of personal and social responsibility in any programme regardless of instructional style. It is argued that the PSRQ can contribute to the examination of some of the core TPSR assumptions using a quantitative instrument that has not been available before now.

 ## Research perspective

This paper provided the reader with a valid and reliable assessment tool for assessing students' perceptions of personal and social responsibility in physical education. The necessity for the validation and reliability of a PSRQ is made on the basis that quantitative evaluation studies in the area of teaching personal and social responsibility remain underrepresented. For readers less familiar with this type of paper, it is important to acknowledge that a number of scholars build their careers on the validation and reliability of measurement and assessment instruments in the same way that other scholars may build their careers on exploring and reporting students' perceptions towards physical education.

It is disappointing and frustrating to read that 'Many students do not enjoy physical education and there is no sign that this trend is slowing down' (p. 170).

There is a tendency for (physical education) researchers to focus on the minority of students who report disliking, or having trouble accessing, physical education. This subsequently results in the accumulation of a significant body of literature that targets populations who are less likely to enjoy or access physical education. Interesting, however, are the results from studies focused on the delivery and associated experiences of particular curriculum and instructional models that consistently report that the majority of students do enjoy their physical education experiences. We need to acknowledge the evidence we have to support the extent to which most young people do enjoy physical education and also continue to investigate what structures and pedagogies enhance such experiences.

The study hypothesises that participants who exhibited high levels of personal and social responsibility would report greater intrinsic motivation in physical education. This is confirmed as being true when reporting the questionnaire results, allowing the authors to state that the results suggest that the PSRQ is valid and reliable for assessing students' perceptions of personal and social responsibility in physical education. It is important to note that data collected through the PSRQ assesses students' self-reported responsibility regardless of the presence of TPSR implementation. It is not clear however, in admitting that the validated instrument addresses only selected aspects of TPSR and that the first four TPSR levels are represented by only a few items each, to what extent the instrument accurately measures the exposure to all aspects of TPSR.

Shared response

One of the reasons we initially chose this article for inclusion in the book came from reviewing the abstract where the authors note:

> An important implication for teaching practice is that, to encourage all individuals to be intrinsically motivated to participate in physical education, physical education teachers need to empower students with choices and voices, focus them on effort and self-direction in physical education, and create a respectful and caring learning environment.
>
> (p. 167)

As we progressed through the article we read about the importance of focusing young people on effort and skill mastery, creating a caring learning environment, and use of empowerment strategies that give young people ownership of their own physical education programme. However, we found no suggestions, ideas or recommendations on how to do this, how teachers might develop creative and innovative ways to increase students' intrinsic motivation and their willingness to increase participation in physical education. What the article did achieve was to push us into discussion on the teaching pedagogies that might be employed to impact student motivation to participate, especially those promoted within Hellison's TPSR curriculum and instruction model.

Empowerment instructional strategies

Don Hellison (2011) believes that the teacher-student relationship is the most important aspect of teaching. He identifies four student characteristics that teachers must recognise, understand and respect if they are to develop a positive relationship with students. These include:

- Students have both strengths and deficiencies. Rather than focusing on, and becoming frustrated with their deficiencies, helping students to recognise and build on their strengths generally allows them to strive toward improving deficiencies progressively.
- Students want to be recognised for who they are as both individuals as well as members of a group. He reminds us to focus on the individual, not the behaviour, teach students not content, and teach individuals not the group.
- Students know what they know and believe what they believe. In other words, all students have the right to share their opinions and beliefs and for those to be heard by teachers and their peers. Helping young people to share those feelings and insights appropriately is critical.
- Students each have the ability to take responsibility for themselves, their own learning and to make decisions. However, they need to be allowed to take responsibility, to have practice making decisions and to be aided in reflecting on and determining how to do each better.

Several pedagogical strategies can be employed in developing teacher-student relationships. Hellison (2009) encourages teachers to employ many of these strategies as they come to know and understand their individual students and assist each of them in feeling empowered in their own learning. Two strategies we have found most effective when working with young people include counselling time and participation by invitation.

Counselling time

Counselling time is when a teacher spends one-on-one time with students with the intent of getting to know them, letting them know you care about them, acknowledging their voice, and focusing on their involvement both in and outside of physical education. It might be as simple as asking, 'How was your weekend?', 'How did you feel after last week's game?', or telling them, 'I appreciate how much effort you have been putting into class the past few weeks'. The key of course is to truly care about each student and their growth and development as they will see right through you if your interactions are insincere.

Participation by invitation

Participation by invitation, sometimes referred to as 'challenge by choice', is intended to provide all learners a place to begin where they feel comfortable.

Self-paced challenges encouraging participation with physical activity tasks that have specific goals, that allow each individual to determine their starting point and the amount of effort they are willing to put in, can help to motivate or assist students who are not confident. The challenge might be to try to do better than they did yesterday on a given task, attempt an activity every day for a week before deciding it is not worthwhile, or choose which of three activities will be the focus of their participation for the day. The key is to have students reflect upon and judge their level of participation and involvement at the end of each lesson so they can modify their tasks and challenge themselves appropriately.

Strategies for assessing PSR in the classroom

Students bring varying degrees of intrinsic motivation to physical education based on a variety of factors including their perceived levels of competence in physical activity and their prior personal and social experiences in physical activity and physical education settings. This article reminds us that in order to build an individual's intrinsic motivation to participate in physical education, physical education teachers must focus equally on building effort and skill mastery in physical education and creating a respectful and caring learning environment. Building intrinsic motivation to participate in physical education and physical activity now and into the future is a fundamental part of a physical education teacher's role. There are a number of strategies that we propose for creating a supportive environment in physical education class.

Hellison (2011), in foregrounding the importance of the teacher-student relationship in support of students' learning in physical education, reminds us to focus on the individual, not the behaviour, teach students not content and teach individuals not the group. In physical education class, how can you, as the teacher, recognise in a meaningful and manageable way that students learn as individuals and individuals learn in different ways? How will individual students experience the class that you are planning to teach?

At the outset, it is important that the teacher relates to individual students on a regular basis. In practice, we realise there is often a pattern to our own interactions with students in class. We can relate disproportionately with those students who can support the class plan and to those who are interfering with the smooth running of the class. In the 'moment', the interaction can be more about 'fire-fighting' with the latter group and building the leadership capacity of the former. An alternative strategy could be to consider the lesson through the eyes of a different five students each day. Consider making a particular effort to greet these five students by name, give them feedback on their participation and effort, identify tasks that they might be willing to undertake and check in with them at the end of class about how they are feeling after the class. In checking in at the end of class, the teacher can use strategies including thumbs up, sideways or down to indicate the extent to which students felt they engaged in relation to respecting the rights and feelings of others, making an effort, being self-directed and/or behaving in a caring and helpful way in class. Teachers can use wall charts/totem poles for each of the behaviours that they are hoping to encourage in an effort to build a caring and respectful learning environment.

By focusing on only five students, the teacher has a manageable opportunity to talk to these students about their self-assessment, and to reflect with them on their reflection of their experiences in the lesson. This conversation not only facilitates the building of a relationship with the student, it also supports future goal setting and allows the student to feel 'recognised' by the teacher, which we know from other research is important for students' enjoyment of, and investment in school.

Physical education class is a busy space. Unless the teacher consciously adopts such a plan, they can tend to gravitate towards students who are already enthusiastic, involved and who make the class idea happen. If as the teacher, we bring different students to mind when planning and teaching, we are reminded that individual students are just that – individuals who deserve to be considered.

In planning a lesson(s), the physical education teacher is advised to consider the full potential of activities to provide students with opportunities to build successful social relationships with their peers. By taking account of the social aspect of learning, teachers can further support students' enjoyable engagement in physical education. Much of what we know from the research suggests that there is a hierarchy among students in group work (see Brock Rovegno and Oliver, 2009, in this section). Depending on what is valued by the group (i.e., sporting competence, attractiveness, being wealthy, belonging to the 'right' social group), different students will be afforded varying degrees of status within the group thereby affecting their participation and positive experience in the group activity. Planning group work activities must take this into account. In planning group activities, it is important therefore to change groups around and to design the tasks so that different individuals are given the opportunity to lead and to undertake different tasks. It is also worthwhile to reflect with students on how they participated in the group, how they facilitated others' participation, what supports and hinders their participation and what would help them to be more involved. Unless we, as physical education teachers, can understand more about how individual students experience what we plan to be an inclusive, enjoyable and worthwhile engagement in physical education, we will continue, despite our best efforts, to compound, what can be for some students, a negative experience in physical education class.

Physical education class provides multiple opportunities for building students' intrinsic motivation to participate in class. Positive relationships with peers and the teacher is a fundamental pre-requisite to this. In planning opportunities to develop skill and mastery in physical education, such activities must be planned with careful consideration of the possibilities that the different activities offer for a positive interpersonal experience for students in physical education.

15

THE ROLE OF VARIOUS CURRICULUM MODELS ON PHYSICAL ACTIVITY LEVELS

 The study

Culpepper, D.O., Tarr, S.J. and Killion, L.E. (2011).
The Physical Educator, *Fall, pp. 163–171.*

The study investigated the impact of three curriculum models (Fitness, Game/ Sport and Skill Theme) on physical activity by measuring the amount of total steps accumulated during physical education lessons taught over three months.

Participants

Teachers across primary and post-primary in the mid-west and southern regions of the US were sent emails at the start of the school year with definitions of the three curriculum models (Fitness, Game/Sport and Skill Theme) that the researchers deemed were most frequently used to increase the physical activity levels of students. Teachers who used any of the three models in teaching their programmes were asked to describe their curriculum focus and a class session. The teachers who either did not use one of the curriculum models or whose curricular focus did not match the chosen curriculum model were eliminated. A total of 1,111 students in selected teachers' typical primary and post-primary classes were identified as participants in the study.

Design and method

All classes were taught by physical education specialists with a minimum of five years of teaching experience. The content in each class varied according to the curriculum model. The Fitness Model included aerobics and fitness games, the Skill Themes Model consisted of activities that developed and promoted fundamental skills, and the Games/Sport Model consisted of team activities. Class time varied across the different schools. Pedometers were used to assess physical activity levels for each class. The physical education teachers conducted their lessons as planned and the researchers oversaw the class as it was being taught. Pedometers were collected by the researchers at the end of each class to allow for the recording of the total number of steps accrued by each student.

Results

It was reported that students in the Game/Sport Model obtained the highest number of steps and that the biggest contributor to the total number of steps accrued during physical education was class time. More steps were accrued in the shorter primary class periods than in the longer post-primary class periods and males obtained more steps than females. The researchers observed extended periods of low activity across the three curriculum models and grade levels, concluding that a curriculum model does not guarantee higher activity. They subsequently suggest that the teacher should strive to create and implement lessons that provide increased time for movement or activity for all children.

 Research perspective

It is perhaps not surprising to read that the Fitness Model does not guarantee higher activity levels, especially when components of the model tend not to rely solely on students being physically active to understand the model, for example, teaching strategies and learning experiences that explore the concepts of fitness and how to gain fitness. In fact, any curriculum model does not guarantee higher physical activity levels, with most curriculum models encouraging low activity levels at particular times in a lesson due to the associated teaching strategies, for example, the debrief in Adventure Education and the questioning and decision-making strategies of Teaching Games for Understanding. The take home message from the study appears to be that the physical education teacher should strive to create and implement lessons that provide increased time for movement or activity for all children. This has perhaps always been the main tenant of what physical education is about and it is not clear in what way the study has contributed to enhancing such a well-established aim of physical education. It appears that the main conclusion from the study was always going to arise, as it is not necessarily a particular curriculum model per se that increases physical activity levels in a physical education class but rather the instructional strategies through which you deliver the model and how you best utilise the time allocated to the physical education lesson. The argument could be made that it is not necessarily more time that is required to deliver an effective physical education curriculum in schools but rather how we more efficiently use the time that is allocated to providing a worthwhile, relevant and meaningful physical education student experience.

The selection procedures for schools involved in the study could be mis-construed as being contradictory to observing and commenting on the reality of teaching curriculum models in school physical education. Many potential schools were eliminated from the sample due to not being deemed to fulfil the 'operational definitions' of the identified models. Even for those schools that were deemed to be appropriate for the study, the focus remained on the 'accuracy' of the model and the activity used. If the researchers believed that a particular class did not confirm the accuracy of the model and activity used, the data was not included in the analysis.

The admittance by the authors that increasing the amount of steps should not be the guiding force in any physical education lesson, nor should one particular curriculum model be assumed to provide the benefits for student learning, somewhat deflates the rationale behind the study being conducted in the first place. It is perhaps obvious to those involved in the delivery of physical education that the guiding force of our practice is to first consider instructional strategies to develop physical activity levels before considering which curriculum model would best accommodate such instructional strategies.

 ## Teacher educator response

Often we see pre-service teachers relying solely on their content knowledge and experiences to inform their decisions when designing lessons. A teacher's content knowledge should not drive choice of curriculum and instruction models but rather what it is that students are intended to achieve. As noted in the 'Researcher perspective', a teacher's choice of curriculum model does not guarantee high rates of physical activity. The curriculum model provides the framework through which content is delivered to students. Any curriculum model could frame a focus on physical activity, and even fitness. Fitness concepts and principles can be taught through activity, numerous learning experiences and/or assorted instructional models and teaching strategies. Once a focused theme-based curriculum model is selected, the instructional models and teaching strategies the teacher will employ to deliver that model and chosen content are selected. The instructional model organises the lesson and determines how students will interact with and practice the content. Regardless of the chosen curriculum model, not all lessons will be characterised by high activity. Is this due to lack of planning, student inability to participate at a higher level or poor management strategies? Is this due to teacher choice to emphasise a point, review a concept, or provide application of a principle, or is it merely a transition to students' taking responsibility for their own participation?

When working with pre-service teachers, we remind them that before they choose a curriculum model and subsequently the aligned instructional models for lesson delivery, they must first determine what it is they intend for students to learn and achieve. If our goal for post-primary students in their first or second year of post-primary is to understand components of fitness and how they can contribute to an active lifestyle we might choose to teach different fitness principles to match the content with which they are most closely aligned using a curriculum model that can provide a suitable framework for each. For example, flexibility and coordination might be taught through a Sport Education season of gymnastics where students are striving to become competent gymnasts. The instructional models selected to deliver this might include cooperative learning where all team trainers are challenged to collectively develop a flexibility warm-up to increase flexibility around the larger joints in the body and subsequently teach the routine to their own teams. Cardiovascular fitness (aerobic fitness) could be taught through Outdoor Education that concludes with a culminating event of students hiking into a campsite in a rough outdoor setting. Instructional models might include peer teaching as students help one another learn to take and record heart rate and determine their training heart rate zone.

Active teaching could help students in learning to set goals and monitor their achievement, and task teaching might lead them through an understanding of pacing while hill walking. Muscular endurance might be delivered through athletics utilising the Teaching Personal and Social Responsibility model to assist young people in taking responsibility for their own involvement and learning. Using station teaching, students could work with a partner to safely spot one another as they rotate through a series of strength training exercises designed to develop their power and endurance. Each of these selected curriculum models could be used to frame the content and expected learning, yet all require the teacher to make effective choices on how to deliver the content through exciting, challenging and well-designed learning experiences using selected instructional models. In other words, it is critical that pre-service teachers understand that the instructional models selected to impact learning can reside within any curriculum model and are the means by which students engage with the content.

 Primary response

Two factors emerged from this study as significant, regardless of the curriculum model selected. The first significant factor is time allocated to physical education. It could be argued that this is not a new issue, as time allocation has been a contentious issue internationally in many teaching contexts. Other responses in this book have dwelt on the importance of effective planning and organisation of lessons in maximising learning time within physical education. However, there is another angle worth examining other than the planning of individual lessons and units of work, that of whole school planning at the primary level.

If time allocated to physical education at primary level is as little as one hour per week, it indicates to us that at the school level we need to make some policy decisions about how that hour might be used. While at first this might seem a paltry allocation of time some schools have approached the issue in a positive light. Their approach has focussed on school planning to inform planning by individual teachers and they have got the 'blueprint' right. They acknowledge that particularly with younger classes children move 'in short bursts'. Hence, they split the one hour allocation in two half-hour periods and critically examine what can be achieved within that time. The answer is often 'a lot!'

First, the school can plan at a whole-school level so that strands or topics are taught at particular times of the year. Equipment is shared so that equipment taken out can be used by a number of classes in succession throughout the day. The children enter the play area and the teacher uses well selected management strategies to ensure smooth transitions and that activities flow seamlessly from one to the next. Time for physical activity, as well as other important aspects of physical education such as discussion, questioning and feedback, is maximised. These schools have frequently tested a single one hour period and found that especially with the younger classes, energy and concentration levels of children wane over a one hour period. Subsequently, younger children gain more from a shorter lesson and have a second physical education lesson to benefit from.

Other strategies that schools consider as they engage in whole school planning centre on timetabling physical education for the younger classes immediately after their break time, particularly where a break lasts for short time periods. Where the physical education class is conducted immediately after break time in the playground, no time is lost in moving directly into a lesson where opportunities are provided for physical activity that might not be possible if children have to return to class and file along later for a physical education class. Another strategy that some schools have explored is inviting post-primary students to support primary teachers as they teach physical education. This may be useful where school subjects at post-primary level are focussed on providing students with learning experiences in various workplaces. Such students can provide real support to primary teachers ensuring that transition times within and between lessons are reduced and children can be more active. This might mean that a student plays a parachute game with one group, another student might work on leading a striking game such as mini-rounders with another group, while the primary teacher focuses on organising running games for other groups.

The second significant factor to emerge from this paper was the link between physical activity levels and gender. As females obtained fewer steps than males, the challenge cited by the authors of the paper was for teachers to provide the necessary incentives, opportunities and activities to motivate females to be active. They also referred to the importance of critically looking at 'what' is being taught in physical education classes. One focus for this thinking might be to listen to what girls say about what they like in physical education classes, appreciating that this is the area that will likely provide them with the most opportunities to be physically active. Another important point to consider is the amount of positive feedback we provide to young girls, especially in contexts where both girls and boys are taking part together. Is there sometimes a reason for grouping by gender according to the dynamics of the particular class? It may be that girls require more time 'on the ball' and in particular classes are struggling to get that time if the boys in the group are dominating. This strategy has to be employed carefully – it should not become the norm at primary level. Are girls provided with the same opportunities to discuss and see female role models who engage in physical activity? Some schools invite sportswomen and women who regularly engage in recreational physical activity to talk to, or work with, young girls in physical education classes. Expectations of teachers are important and simple indicators of expectations might include teachers using the same tone of voice to provide affirmation to boys and girls as they undertake an activity that is physically challenging? The authors of the paper challenge us to move beyond having children who are merely 'busy, happy and good' and this might be a good starting point for discussions at staff level about the physical activity levels of girls physical education classes.

Cognisant of some of the arguments presented in the post-primary response, I will focus on two different elements that are related to this. The first is the role of play for the young child. The post-primary response questions why we should be examining physical activity levels within physical education, proposing that there are much more significant factors to be examined such as the motivation of the young person to engage in physical activity. In the same way I prefer to see the spotlight on another focus in the primary physical education lesson: the role of play for the young child. Primary schools need to emphasise physically active play that is fun and enjoyable. This is not a new proposal, with worldwide programmes being designed to emphasise active play by children (e.g., Active sport, Kiwisport, SPARK). However, within existing curricular frameworks simple play activities are possible too. The findings of this study that the Fitness Model was weak in promoting physical activity prompted me to consider this issue again. In many countries primary physical education is highlighted as the subject where outcomes related to physical 'fitness' or 'skill development' should be measured. We need to present very strong arguments for the other purposes of physical education to be remembered (i.e., the importance of 'hooking' children into some form of physical activity early). What better way than to offer them as many opportunities within physical education to perform natural movements of running, jumping, skipping and hopping?

We must caution against an over emphasis on teaching these fundamental movement skills in isolation. Many children merely need freedom to practise and intervention by the teacher must be judicious. A more positive way of intervening might be to move outside the often limited environment of the school to the local park or playground and let children play. I recently played with a nine year-old boy who had been engrossed with a video game. He asked to be taught the cartwheel. Between each effort he ran a lap of the grass area without any prompt and dived to the ground before re-commencing his effort. Does physical education class provide this freedom to move? It is probably not possible for a teacher to replicate this provision of one-on-one tuition but what they can do is reflect on providing as many opportunities as possible for children in and outside of physical education to run, spin, dive jump or even walk. Moderate to vigorous activity is the target but sometimes if we let children play it is a lot easier to achieve with young children than we think.

Another area that deserves attention is the capacity of playground games in promoting physical activity within primary physical education lessons. More importantly, play as described above and playground games can be effective not just in promoting physical activity but also in motivating children to enjoy physical activity and in developing good relationships with others. Selecting games that are age appropriate and adapting them to suit the group are key to enjoyment. Tag games and games that involve 'active make believe' can often be the springboard for young children to enjoy physical activity. A final thought . . . multi-activity programmes are often criticised as they fail to provide adequate opportunities for children to engage to any great depth with any one activity. However, they can provide children with exposure to many activities where one might be their chosen lifelong activity. It is worthwhile considering each of the elements raised above and deciding which aspects we can fit into our primary physical education programmes so that we provide children with some valuable physical activity but, more importantly, provide them with multiple opportunities to discover how much they can enjoy it! As the authors of the study remind us, the focus on fitness within the Fitness Model does not provide us with the solution for the multi-faceted problem of increasing physical activity levels. Is it worth considering a return to a focus on play, playground games and lots of choice of activities in our quest to hook children into physical activity through appropriate play related to their age and stage of development?

 ## Post-primary response

We have always felt that it was disingenuous of the physical education community to claim that they held the key to the solution of the obesity problem – that is, 'if only students could have more physical education classes, all would be solved'. It is equally disingenuous for legislators and politicians to divest themselves of their responsibility to make the healthy choice the easier choice. Addressing the obesity problem is a complex and multi-faceted task and it requires that the many partners and agencies look realistically at the contribution that each can make.

One of the main aims of physical education is that students, as a result of their learning, would choose to participate in regular health enhancing physical activity and/or sport because they enjoy it and they believe that their lives are better because they are physically active. The challenge is to decide the realistic contribution that physical education can make to this aim while also acknowledging the central role that other partners play in building a more supportive environment for physical activity within and beyond the school.

Coincidently, at the same time we were reading this article, I came across the work of *New York Times* bestselling author, Dan Buettner, www.bluezones.com/about/dan-buettner. Buettner has spent many years studying the secrets of the best practices in health, longevity and happiness – outcomes we hope for all of our students. Having travelled the globe in an effort to identify the best strategies for longevity and happiness, he eventually zoned in on four regions where people have the greatest life expectancy and where more people reach age 100 than anywhere else. These regions share nine common denominators, which he calls 'Power 9™', and yes, regular physical activity is one of them. Interestingly, these communities engage in low to moderate physical activity and live in physical and 'built' environments that support regular physical activity including active commuting – that is, walking and cycling. The focus was not on the levels of intensity and duration that we often hold up as the ideal when we teach the Health-Related Activity Model or the Fitness Model as was the case in this study. These people set up their lives so that they are constantly nudged into physical activity. They live in tall houses with stairs, for example, and trips to shop, to pray and to socialise all involve an active commute. Physical activity is first and foremost in the service of their daily lives, is sociable, and benefits everybody. What then are the lessons for physical education and teaching health related activity?

Weekly physical education classes cannot provide the levels and frequency of physical activity required for health and wellbeing. The messages about the importance of regular physical activity cannot happen in a vacuum. They need to resonate meaningfully when the student leaves the physical education class where they are met with social modelling of regular physical activity by significant others. For this to happen, the physical activity environment within and beyond the school should be supportive – that is, attractive, safe and accessible for a variety of physical activities. Physical education can provide enjoyable experiences through which young people can learn about the principles of health related physical activity, grow in their appreciation about the importance of physical activity and experience low, moderate and high levels of intensity in a variety of enjoyable physical activities. It can only do so much in providing the kind of supportive environment that supports regular physical activity beyond physical education class.

At another level, the use of other curriculum models such as Teaching Personal and Social Responsibility and Sport Education can provide learning experiences through physical activity that build the kinds of personal and social skills that, Buettner's research has established, support people in living longer, happier and more connected lives. In my opinion, physical education can provide the kinds of learning experiences that will support students' long-term commitment to, and enthusiasm for, regular physical activity. However, I am now convinced that this requires a lot more than planning for moderate to high levels of physical activity in physical education classes.

It is naïve to believe that physical education teachers can simply plan for moderate to high levels of physical activity in every class given the range of fitness and skills levels possessed by students as well as their different degrees of motivation and willingness to participate. A variety of approaches are necessary (e.g., approaches such as challenge by choice should be explored) and, sometimes, it is about accepting that it may involve negotiating with some students about the extent of their engagement with the planned activity.

In physical education, let's focus on what we can achieve. Let's work to develop our students' confidence and competence to participate in a range of enjoyable, accessible activities. Let's teach them about physical activity – the different types and benefits. Let's encourage them to become advocates for a healthier and more supportive 'built' environment for physical activity. Let's encourage them to participate in regular activity and let's not impose an unspoken hierarchy of activities where the less skilful students feel they don't measure up because they want to walk as their activity. Let's focus on making the 5 km radius around our schools more 'physical activity' friendly. Let's get our students interested in making our parks safer and cleaner. Let's aim to make the active option the easy option for all the school community.

Perhaps we are most likely to develop lifetime physical activity habits in our students by helping them to appreciate the multitude of ways that they can be physically active in their daily lives and to realise that the individual is not solely responsible. Those who hold the purse strings must also engage in building supportive environments including free or reasonably priced easily accessible opportunities for physical activity and sport. Buettner uses the analogy that there is no one silver bullet when it comes to providing the best conditions for living a long and healthy life. He suggests that it is more about silver buckshot! When it comes to promoting regular physical activity, it is a lot more complex than planning to include it in physical education class. Providing a wider supportive environment is at least as important.

16

INFLUENCE OF OCCUPATIONAL SOCIALISATION ON TWO PRE-SERVICE TEACHERS' INTERPRETATION AND DELIVERY OF THE SPORT EDUCATION MODEL

 The study

Stran, M. and Curtner-Smith, M. (2009). **Journal of Teaching in Physical Education, *28*, pp. 38–53.**

Stran and Curtner-Smith acknowledge the impact of the extensive implementation of Sport Education (SE) internationally on student learning in physical education. They review the limited literature investigating how pre-service and practicing teachers learn, interpret and deliver the SE curriculum and instruction model. Within this review, they cite a plethora of examples from those that suggest SE is compatible with their beliefs about physical education to those that recognise SE advantages over more traditional models, and from those that suggest pre-service teachers struggle teaching skills and tactics within SE game play practice sessions to those that report the problems students have appreciating all aspects of the SE model. They share a recent Curtner-Smith *et al.* study highlighting three ways SE tends to be delivered by beginning teachers (full version, watered down and 'cafeteria' style) with occupational socialisation cited as accounting for the choice of delivery method. The authors report having clear knowledge of how to teach pre-service teachers to teach SE and what has an impact on their implementation of it when they begin teaching, yet they are less clear on what it looks like in teaching practice. The purpose of this study is therefore twofold:

1   To examine how two pre-service teachers (PSTs) interpreted and delivered the SE curriculum and instruction model during their student teaching placement.
2   To determine factors that led to their interpretation and delivery of SE.

The occupational socialisation literature is used to help understand why pre-service teachers choose to teach SE as they do.

Participants

Two pre-service teachers in the final semester of their physical education teacher education programme at a US research institution in the southwest served as participants in this study. Enrolled in their final teaching placement, these two 23-year-old pre-service teachers were selected as a result of strong performance in earlier coursework, suggesting their potential as quality physical education teachers. Both participants were noted for having a strong coaching orientations.

Design and methods

The two pre-service teachers taught in the same middle school for eight weeks during the study. Numerous qualitative data collection techniques were used to indicate how the pre-service teachers' interpreted and delivered SE and how their professional socialisation influenced their interpretation and delivery of the model. For each pre-service teacher data collection included:

1   nonparticipant observation with extensive notes once a week;
2   1-hour semi-structured formal interviews were conducted at the beginning, middle, and on completion of teaching practice;
3   informal interviews whenever the opportunity arose with notes being made immediately after;
4   two 50-minute stimulated recall interviews using video of the pre-service teacher teaching SE;
5   document analysis of teaching portfolios, pupil evaluations and teaching materials;
6   a weekly submission of reflective electronic journal entries and critical incident reports.

Data was read, analysed and coded using the 2002 QSR computer programme. Researchers identified how pre-service teachers interpreted and delivered SE and how their occupational socialisation influenced both their interpretation and delivery. Data types were divided into themes, categories and subcategories using a combination of Goetz and LeCompte's (1984) analytic induction and constant comparison techniques.

Results

Student portfolios examined at the conclusion of the study revealed that pre-service teachers met all of the benchmarks identified by Metzler (2000) for delivering a full version of a SE season. In congruence with the literature, both pre-service teachers had chosen to teach physical education due to their interest in sport, and their experiences in physical education were influential in impacting their development once in the teacher education programme.

Results also indicated that commitment to SE, and ability to teach the full version (whether teaching-orientated or moderately coaching-orientated) was facilitated by an effective physical education teacher education programme. Pre-service teachers noted the strong impact of their cooperating teachers, university supervisors, the young people they taught and being held accountable for teaching the SE model. The researchers concluded that the critical aspects of the teacher education programme influencing this commitment and teaching competence was a result of taking part in mini-seasons of SE prior to teaching practice. In addition, a number of teacher education faculty characteristics linked to the socialisation literature were also presented.

 ## Research perspective

It is reported from an earlier study referenced in the paper that newly qualified in-service teachers interpreted and delivered SE in one of three ways. The 'full' version of the model is deemed to be when units of SE are taught using all components of the model. The 'watered down' version of the model entails SE being construed as formal game play. A 'cafeteria' approach entails the selection of components of SE that are employed within more traditional instruction units, for example, team affiliation within a multi-activity curriculum. There appears to be little sympathy in this paper for appreciating that there will be different extents to which PSTs and teachers enact SE (or any curriculum model) in school physical education, with an apparent bias to favouring the delivery of the 'full' version at the expense of understanding the realities of why such delivery may not be feasible in some schools.

Indeed, the authors' decision to not include 'organisational socialisation' on the basis that they define this to be the influence of the workplace on in-service teachers and not PSTs, appears to be a crucial oversight in understating the extent to which the school culture can impact the 'version' of SE that is delivered. The omission also contradicts the literature that reports the extent to which school culture does impact the type of SE delivered. It is therefore more acceptable to present the school context in which PSTs are teaching to appreciate and understand instances where is it not possible to teach the 'full version' of SE but rather the 'watered down' or 'cafeteria' version. It is not until we are conscious of the school culture (including the support for SE from other physical education teachers, students' skills, abilities and behaviours and their experiences and views of sport) that it is possible to imply that one version of SE is deemed to be more appropriate than another. The concern here is with encouraging PSTs to explore SE through the 'watered down' or 'cafeteria' versions where the 'full' version is not a viable option. The notion noted in the paper that being selective about which elements of SE to use and which elements to ignore misinterprets the model is another instance where such a comment is difficult to accept without a school context. In addition, PSTs should be encouraged to 'start small' and select SE components that best fit them and their school setting, adding what they can and what they want in subsequent SE units.

It appears that while the authors chose not to interrogate organisational socialisation they are forced not to ignore the impact of the cooperating teacher and the nature of the students PSTs encountered on the delivery of SE. Indeed the authors conclude:

> . . . the conditions encountered by PTs in their culminating teaching practice would appear to be crucial in terms of both learning and gaining the confidence to teach using the SE model.
>
> (p. 50)

It would be remiss of us as a profession to hold PSTs accountable from teaching SE in its 'full' for when the school culture does not support this, which in turn could lead to PSTs choosing not to teach any components of SE in the event that they are accused of delivering a 'watered down' or 'cafeteria' version.

 ## Shared response

In our response to this paper we, as a group of physical education teachers in various settings including teacher education, primary and post-primary, have chosen to build on the feelings and perceptions shared by the first of us to respond.

Many years ago, I decided I wanted to become a physical education teacher. I enjoyed all things about physical activity and had opportunities to participate in a modest range of sports in a low key kind of way. I really looked up to my physical education teacher who worked hard to make classes interesting, enjoyable and above all, inclusive. With this prior experience, I headed off to college. I soon discovered that some of my classmates had similar experiences of physical education while others had come from a more competitive and higher level performance background, which they had received either in school or in clubs or both. All of us belonged somewhere on that continuum. Being honest, sometimes I struggled with my suitability to be a physical education teacher because I could see that I did not compare in terms of achievement and performance level to other students. Yet I wanted to teach physical education because I wanted to give back something of the great experience that I had in physical education.

This article has been important for me because it has given me the academic language and theory to understand my own personal experience and its impact on the teacher that I became. It has also allowed me to look again at the variety of dispositions that my different classmates brought to their study of physical education, and the importance of these dispositions for the ways that we thought about, and went on to teach, physical education. I now know that my prior experience of physical education in school was a process of 'occupational socialisation'. In common with all of my classmates, before we came to college, our values and beliefs about physical education had been shaped by key people – that is, physical education teachers and/or coaches, contexts and cultures. This shaping process is known as 'acculturation'. In our formative years, our physical education experience probably fell into a number of categories. For some, the experience was mainly centred on a strong extra-curricular sports programme. For others, they experienced possibly a fairly weak or perhaps a meaningful physical education programme. Reflecting on this range of physical education experiences, we realise that pre-service primary and pre-service physical education teachers are affected by both their primary and post-primary experiences of physical education. For pre-service physical education students, it is likely that they would have participated regularly in whatever physical education/physical activity programme there was in place in their schools. In some cases, pre-service primary teachers may have chosen to simply opt out because the programme offered had little relevance for them and was not a positive experience.

In acknowledging the impact of our earlier experiences of physical education, we appreciate now that pre-service teachers mainly bring one of two dispositions to their learning in physical education – that is, a coaching orientation or a teaching orientation. For pre-service primary teachers, there may be an additional group – those who fail to appreciate the value of physical education and yet will be expected to provide a physical education experience as part of their role as primary teachers. Whatever our earlier experiences of physical education, they were significant because they fundamentally affected how we went on to think about physical education and how we saw ourselves as teachers of physical education. And therein lies the challenge for pre-service teacher education for physical education.

Physical education as a subject has so much to offer young people's learning throughout their years in formal education. Its potential can only be fully exploited by the full engagement, commitment and professionalism of the teacher of physical education. Teachers provide the key to a worthwhile experience and yet it so often suffers in the hands of some teachers. We all know that the experience of physical education continues to reflect practices that are easily recognisable as belonging to teaching or coaching orientations or where the teacher has little interest in, or commitment to, physical education. For those students whose teacher clearly subscribes to a coaching orientation, they may find that physical education class period is used as a coaching session for 'the team'. They may find that only the more talented students seem to be noticed and that they don't learn much or enjoy physical education class. Yet their teacher may work extremely hard, often giving freely of their own time to provide some students with a rich sporting experience.

Unfortunately there is a whole other group of pre-service teachers whose experiences of physical education in either primary or post-primary have been in the hands of teachers who showed little interest, enthusiasm or commitment to physical education.

And so it will go on. Students will continue to have these experiences unless we grapple with this challenge. In pre-service education, students should be given guidance to reflect on their 'occupational socialisation'. This could be done in a number of ways. Biographical timelines much favoured in the Cultural Studies curriculum model could provide one approach, where students identify significant others and events on their physical education journey. In comparing their journey with classmates, they can identify similarities, differences and the impact of these on their thinking about how they want to teach physical education. The use of case studies might also be considered where students would be encouraged to problematise the teaching and coaching orientations exemplified from the perspectives of a variety of students, particularly because both coaching and teaching orientations can have both positive and negative outcomes. It just depends on whose perspective you are considering – that is, the talented, competitive child or the child who is not so disposed. These case studies could also be used to highlight the impact of physical education experiences that are offered by teachers who have little interest in what they are doing.

Another strategy might be considered in initial teacher education. In the primary setting, a natural way might be to prompt students to reflect on their own, and listen to others reflect on, experiences in physical education. In any group of pre-service primary teachers, there will be a wide range of experiences reflecting those dispositions/orientations described above. In pre-service physical education, the same strategy could see undergraduates from another faculty talking about their experience of physical education and why they think it was/was not important for them in their education. It can often be interesting, following this type of reflective process, to write your epitaph about how you would like to be remembered by your students when you retire from teaching and then to plot back and identify what might be the characteristics of your practice in support of this epitaph.

Teaching practice is another valuable learning site. When students go on teaching practice, part of their reflection should be in relation to the orientations/dispositions that they see being modelled by the cooperating or classroom teachers and the impact that this has on the physical education programme. Students should also be encouraged to reflect on their own comfort zones in terms of orientation and what this means for their role as teachers of physical education. Where pre-service teachers who show little interest in physical education become aware of this through the reflective process, it is important that these 'beginning' teachers are supported in taking on board every child's entitlement to physical education. After all, we should, as professionals, continually reflect on what our moral purpose is – is it to coach or is it to teach all students physical education in a way that is meaningful for them? While creating time for reflection may be challenging, the use of the student portfolio as a tool for enhancing reflection might be considered. This may prompt pre-service teachers to read about socialisation, to reflect on its meaning for them and how these experiences impact on them personally and professionally. This reflection can be carried out with particular reference to their teaching practice experience and working with teachers from a variety of dispositions.

The reflective process could also involve pre-service teachers considering to what extent they are open to change. What will change require of them? For those with a strong teaching orientation, it is likely that they will be readily open to change. Those with a coaching orientation will need to be given ample space to discuss the implications of this orientation. Many implications will be positive and will transfer readily into their teaching of physical education, for example, their understanding of the importance of preparation of classes will likely reflect their approach to preparation of coaching sessions. However, some of the implication of a coaching disposition will require teasing out. To what extent, for example, is an element such as 'student voice' or 'student choice' compatible with their view of teaching? Traditionally, their coaching practice probably hasn't factored in an element such as this. Another challenge might be that their proficiency in the area that was the focus of their coaching experience might pull them very strongly in that direction. Are they open to the demands that will be required to up-skill them for teaching other areas of physical education focusing more on the *teaching* element rather than the performance element? Whatever the outcomes of such reflection, we need to ensure that young people who want to become teachers of physical education do so in full awareness of the dispositions that will serve them, and those that they will need to guard against, if they are to provide a positive physical education experience for their students.

17

ADVENTURE-BASED LEARNING AND REFLECTION

The journey of one cohort of teacher candidates

 The study

Sutherland, S., Ressler, J. and Stuhr, P.T. (2011). International Journal of Human Movement Science, 5(2), pp. 5–24.

The paper explores how pre-service teachers learned to incorporate a meaningful debrief (reflection) in a five-day Adventure-Based Learning (ABL) unit. A clear and thorough explanation of the debrief aspect of ABL is shared, emphasising the importance of guided reflection before discussing how the most widely used debriefing strategy is based upon the Experiential Learning Cycle. That is, 'What?' questions guide the students through questions that allow them to reflect on the activity, the 'So what?' questions extend the reflection to consider generalisations about what happened in the activity and what they learned from the activity, and the 'Now what?' questions extend the reflection further by considering how to transfer learning to other life situations.

Participants

The participants included 11 pre-service teachers (five males and six females) ranging in age from 21–28 years. The group was undertaking a Physical Education Teacher Education programme and had completed the same ABL course at a Midwestern US university prior to delivering the ABL unit while on teaching placement.

Design and method

Data were collected through three sources. Observations involved videotaping each pre-service teacher twice during the unit, from which field notes were taken.

In addition, a university supervisor observed each lesson delivered by the pre-service teachers and observation notes were kept by the supervisor. Interviews were conducted with all participants prior to and at the end of the ABL unit. In addition, informal conversations were audio taped where possible. Daily reflections were shared in small groups of pre-service teachers and these were audio taped. Data generated from all three sources was analysed using line by line coding and constant comparison, meaning that each page of data was compared line by line before cross-checking with emerging themes from other pages of data.

Results

Two themes emerged from exploring how pre-service teachers learned to incorporate a meaningful debrief in a five day ABL unit. 'Technical vs. practical understanding' reported that while pre-service teachers began the five-day ABL unit with a good technical understanding of the debrief process, it was difficult for the pre-service teachers to put their knowledge of the debrief into practice during the unit. It also transpired that the quality of the questions asked during the unit were somewhat problematic, despite the pre-service teachers being able to understand the ordering of questions before the delivery of the unit. 'Learning to guide not teach' reported that at the start of the unit the debriefs were very pre-service teacher directed, heightened by the pre-service teachers sticking very closely to the questions they had prepared for the debrief. It was not until pre-service teachers learned to observe the students in the activity and use these experiences in the debrief that they transitioned from teaching to guiding in their debrief technique. The paper concludes with six clear and realistic recommendations for the effective teaching of meaningful debriefs.

 Research perspective

The study is a nice example of how isolating a component of a practice (in this case the ABL debrief) and interrogating it can allow for a worthwhile in-depth examination of how best to improve practice. The paper is clearly written and presents a theoretical component that is clearly applicable to the area of study – that is, how experiential learning (the theoretical component) helps us understand the incorporation of a meaningful debrief in ABL (area of study). The paper also concisely explains the different kinds of debrief and the case study design allowed for the thick description of eleven pre-service teachers' experiences.

The paper is a welcome addition to the literature for a number of reasons. The focus on the debriefing element of ABL tends to get overlooked and, through discussing this element, the paper engages with teachers as facilitators of learning. The paper also clearly articulates that debriefing is not the same as closure, explaining that there is more complexity around the debrief process. The difficulty in translating technical understanding into practice prompts us to suggest that teachers may 'know' something but do not necessarily understand until they attempt to put it into practice. Much has been written on the potential disjuncture between content knowledge and pedagogical content knowledge, although we acknowledge, as the authors do, that the pedagogical content knowledge necessary for ABL debrief is different from the more typical kinds of pedagogical content knowledge utilised in physical education.

Another interesting reference point is where the authors discuss learning to debrief 'in the moment', where what happens in the actual activity plays a more important role in the debrief than the prepared questions. Transferring this to teaching more generally, it is a very skilful part of teaching to be able to think on the spot and use questioning that has evolved from the class context rather than to rely on pre-determined questions.

The debrief strategy associated with the Experiential Learning Cycle incorporates the questions shared above in the summary of this paper. However, while the 'Now what?' question is most likely to be the most important part of the cycle, it does not appear to be explored in the paper. That is, in what way can interpersonal and intrapersonal relationships have a positive influence on all areas of life, not just within physical education?

It would have been interesting to hear how the pre-service teachers believed they had learned from their own experience of being involved in debriefing as a pre-service teacher. As they had been involved in debriefing previously, from the perspective of a pre-service teacher being taught by a teacher educator, this was likely to have affected their understanding, buy-in and delivery of debriefing. Had the pre-service teachers been prompted to reflect on the debriefing they undertook as a pre-service teacher? While the study did establish that the pre-service teachers began the five day ABL unit with a good technical understanding of the debrief process, it would have been interesting to know the dispositions they brought with them to the study as regards the debrief.

 ## Teacher educator response

What?

Reading this paper was a learning experience brought about by our own reflection on the paper, its content and its application to our own practice. We thoroughly enjoyed this paper, the questions it prompted, the learning we gained, and how it pushed us to consider how we prepare pre-service teachers to use the debrief in Adventure Education.

So what?

Reading and discussing this paper reinforced for us, the one point that is so critical for pre-service teachers to learn about the activities utilised in adventure education. That is, an activity is just an activity until it is debriefed and students recognise both what and why they have learned. For example, the theme for a lesson may be 'building trust' and a set of progressive activities are designed and used to build trust (holding hands, elevator simulation, back-to-back stand-up, trust walk, one-on-one trust fall, group trust fall, spider web, log roll, advanced trust fall). A result of participating in these activities may be student development of some semblance of trust in one another, but do they recognise it or what behaviours enhanced this trust or deterred from it? In other words, following one or more of the trust building activities, these young people need to experience a debrief where they begin to recognise what happened in the activity, what it means to development of trust and how to move forward in the next activity to strengthen this trust. They need to understand what they may have done that was detrimental to someone developing trust (laughing at them, teasing them that you might not catch them) and what was perceived as helpful (congratulating someone on effort, thanking a peer for their help, being constantly alert and on task).

Now what?

So, how do we move forward in helping pre-service teachers develop their skill in conducting a debrief with and for their students? The six recommendations provided by the authors were useful in stimulating our options. While we do model the debrief process and give PSTs opportunities to practice the debrief themselves, this paper helped us to realise that we tend to stop there, we do not discuss issues with the debrief, how it might be conducted more effectively, or even reflect on whether the debrief achieved its goal. After spending so much time planning the activity progressions for the various adventure themes (communication, cooperating, building trust, etc.) we need to spend as much time building learning progressions for the debrief process. When addressing the first recommendation proposed by the authors as providing pre-service teachers multiple opportunities to experience, practice and lead the debrief process, a learning progression for pre-service teachers might look something like this:

1 Observe and evaluate several teacher delivered debriefs using various methodologies and tools.
2 Observe and evaluate several teacher-delivered 'in the moment' debriefs.
3 Lead debrief following teacher led activity choosing (a) 'in the moment', (b) pre-planned or (c) assisted debrief.
4 Plan and teach a set of activities leading a debrief with the activities.
5 Conduct a debrief 'in the moment' following a peer's or teacher's lesson.
6 Written assignment of designing a set of activities and ideas on how to conduct a planned debrief or identification of considerations to look for in planning an 'in the moment' debrief.

An example of an assisted debrief might be for the pre-service teacher to be given a task card to guide their debrief. In one case, the card might be as noted below.

Debrief task:

Have pupils draw a picture of their progress during a lesson focused on a specific theme. For example, a student may choose to draw in stages- at the beginning, how did they feel and emotions that accompanied this. The second picture may show how they improved or developed, and again how they felt. A final picture might display how they felt at the end of the lesson about what they learned. Students may choose to share these with the entire class to stimulate group discussion.

 Primary response

What?

This was the article that brought one of the key messages of our publication home 'to roost': research should be read and applied to practice! I realised one further important element that is linked to this message: that reflection emanating from reading research can be unsettling. Let me explain. In spite of my working with young children in Adventure-Based Learning and subsequently with pre-service teachers during initial teacher education, I acknowledge that I have not fully embraced the rationale for debriefing. This article presented a powerful argument about the importance of the 'debrief' process, and I found the link to experiential learning particularly useful. When I read this article for the first time, clear and explicit in its discussion of debrief, I concluded without hesitation that I had got it (at least almost) all wrong. I fell into the trap time and time again of failing to truly realise the significance of the debrief. Hence, my description of this article as 'powerful', it helped me to realise what has been noted in the teacher educator response to this paper, 'an activity is just an activity until it has been debriefed'.

So what?

I now engage with what I concluded about student and teacher learning after reflecting on this paper. The research undertaken and described in this article made the process that the teacher candidates (TCs) were undergoing abundantly clear to me. It seemed that they were grappling with a very difficult concept: given that this was their first attempt at teaching ABL it was quite a challenge for them to reflect *in the moment* and allow students' responses to guide discussion. However, I believe that they are not unique in finding this aspect of their work difficult.

How might the process be simplified for the TC or indeed the teacher? Sometimes, at primary level in particular, aspects of the process might prove to be less challenging than we think. Discussion is often uninhibited, the young child blurts out how they feel and this can often be a useful starting point for the work of the teacher. We may take a simple blindfold activity as an example where one child (sighted) is leading her partner (blindfolded) as they undertake the 'feel a tree' activity. As the blindfold child returns to locate the particular tree, now sighted, she often chats to her partner in a spontaneous way describing somewhat randomly what she felt (rough, slimy, furry moss) as well as how she felt (confused, a little dizzy, scared she would trip or bump). In some ways children are already engaging in the beginning of the student-centred discussion. This initial reaction is an important part of the more in-depth discussion that centres on the issue of trust, the underpinning theme that the teacher desires as the focus. The teacher might just need to add a small element to this already established practice by prompting children to reflect: reflect on the trust element. A teacher might, through listening to the child, pick up on her reflections on trusting a partner. A simple comment such as 'I was afraid I was going to trip' could be used to prompt reflection on trusting someone to lead you in an outdoor setting. With experience the primary teacher becomes proficient at learning to debrief 'in the moment' throughout many classes in different subject areas. However, it seems to me that this ability to debrief 'in the moment' could be gained more readily through experience if the beginning teacher is aware that this is an important element of their teaching.

Now what?

So how can I apply what I have learned? This paper underlined the importance of the element of debrief for me providing a sound rationale for engaging in this processing of the experience. In addition, the recommendations so clearly outlined in the concluding paragraph of the paper provided me with a wonderful step-by-step process as a means of working through debrief. I can begin by providing opportunities for student teachers to experience, practise and lead the debrief process right through to allocating plenty of time to conduct a student-centred debrief. Indeed, the final sentence of the paper referring to the importance of a student-lead closure to a lesson was probably where my thinking was jolted to the greatest extent. My reflection on this point led me to concluding that it was an aspect of teaching that I rarely applied: either with children or with student teachers. My typical teacher directed closure needs to be questioned as there are merits in the student-centred closure that I need to explore.

The other issue that I need to reflect on is the allocation of time necessary to undertake the debrief. Like many practitioners, I am overly concerned about physical activity levels within lessons, particularly when working with children who want to skip, spin, turn, run and jump. The implication of this dual demand (for activity and debrief time) leads me to conclude that if I am convinced that the debrief is important I will consider ways of ensuring that it happens.

 Post-primary response

What?

This research article provides a very clear picture of the 'rich' added value that a skilfully led debrief offers to the students' learning experience in Adventure Education. The different technical components that underpin the debrief are clearly articulated as the research process unfolds but more importantly, we begin to see clearly that while this technical 'know how' is important, it is not in itself, enough. The teacher is required to play a significant 'in the moment role' as facilitator of the debrief. This article really highlighted the powerful nature of the learning for both the teacher and the students when this happens.

So what?

We are reminded once again that every group of students will respond differently to learning experiences in physical education as happened here in researching Adventure Education classes. We are reminded that we teach students physical education and not the other way around, and therefore in any given class, we require the skills, the flexibility and creativity to respond in a meaningful way to the learning that is happening before us. While the student teachers in this case had been well prepared in relation to the technical 'know how' and rationale for the debrief, it was that 'in the moment' ability to customise what has been planned in a meaningful way, to what actually happened in the class, that really enriched the debriefing experience.

As teachers, we can learn to plan an appropriate debriefing process. However, it is the practical experience of knowing what to use from the plan and how to use it that makes the real difference. A significant advantage in Adventure Education is that the teacher will have had the opportunity to observe the students as they participate in the different activities. The debrief can be customised to focus on the actual learning experience that unfolded in a class. The debrief works best when it can facilitate students in capturing and reflecting on what happened, their role in it, what the experience was like for themselves and others and how that will inform their thinking and behaviours in the future.

It is not an insignificant task. It does require the technical debriefing toolkit and the 'know how' to use it and adapt it in multiple ways in response to the class that has happened and not the one that you were counting on happening. Deciding on the actual debrief to be used will happen in the busyness of facilitating the Adventure Education class and the teacher's ability to do this can only come with practice, experience and reflection.

I also believe that teachers' personal commitment and belief in the debrief process will be required to sustain their engagement with fine tuning the debriefing process in Adventure Education. At a professional level, am I, as a physical education teacher, convinced of the worthwhile nature of the debriefing process? How high up do I rate it as part of my role as a physical education teacher? Do I believe that physical education offers a valuable opportunity for social and emotional learning? Am I convinced that students can really develop an understanding of themselves, and themselves in relation to others, as a result of engaging in a series of 'trust building activities'? Am I prepared to act as a facilitator for their reflections and allow my students to come to conclusions that may be other than I had planned for the class? Without this personal and professional conviction, my sense is that the debriefing process might not happen in an authentic way and students will quickly pick up that the debrief is a 'tag on', a 'going through the motions' exercise. My belief is that physical education teachers' commitment to, and engagement with, the debriefing process can be best supported by the kinds of reflective processes documented in this research paper.

Now what?

Having reflected on this research piece, I am now convinced of a number of things. First, I believe that it is important that I have opportunities to experience adventure activities including the variety of debriefing approaches. Second, it is by reflecting on my own learning in the adventure activities, and how it allows me to develop a picture of myself and how I behave and perform/participate in particular situations, that I can come to see how students might also benefit from similar experiences. Third, there is a place for reflecting on the debriefing experience itself, how it was designed, managed/facilitated and what might have improved it. This could happen both from a participants' perspective but also by watching a debrief being done by others. The latter approach provides the time and space to reflect on what is happening as it is happening because it allows me the luxury of being outside the demands of the moment. By observing a range of debriefing styles, I have an opportunity to critique them, identify the strengths, weaknesses and the skills exhibited in the various approaches.

Would it not be interesting also to set up an adventure education class that teachers could observe, then leave before the debrief takes place and be asked to design and discuss a debrief for the class that they have just witnessed?

These are ideas that might be provided by continuing professional development providers and while they are potentially valuable learning experiences, it will be in the sustained engagement with debriefing process and reflecting by oneself, or preferable with a colleague, that real progress can be made. It is always challenging to recall with any great accuracy what I have has just done in a class and feedback from a second source is invaluable.

The feedback from one's students should also be considered, not only in relation to their own personal learning but also about how they experienced the debriefing process. By consulting students, we can learn, for example, if we are falling into the trap of telling students the significance of their learning because we witnessed the class therefore we believe that we know best what they learned! Again, I believe if as teachers we are given the opportunity to experience this type of debrief, we will become re-acquainted with how frustrating this experience can be.

I like to think about the skills required for debriefing being on a continuum. At one end, I have the technical skills, I have planned the debrief and I am fully in control right down to being prepared to set my students straight about what they have learned even if they don't see it themselves. At the other end of the continuum, the debrief is facilitated completely by students. They are willing and able to carry it out and they are able to articulate what they have learned and how their learning might be applied beyond the adventure education setting. As with all professional development learning, becoming an expert facilitator of the debriefing process takes time, professional and personal commitment and conviction. The dividends are rich, however, because as we engage with others in reflection, we also learn so much ourselves.

SECTION IV

Continuing professional development

Deborah Tannehill, Ann MacPhail,
Ger Halbert and Frances Murphy

The five papers in this section support each other in and through a number of continuing professional development (CPD) concepts that include:

1   the necessity for teachers to be positively disposed to enhancing their own professional development;
2   CPD opportunities acknowledging 'teachers as learners';
3   CPD provision that works 'with' teachers rather than 'to' them;
4   CPD across the continuum of initial teacher education, induction and in-service;
5   an acknowledgement that the personalities of individual teachers will in some instances enhance, and in other instances limit, professional development opportunities.

A number of the papers also prompt discussion on the definition and subsequent use of 'professional learning' rather than 'professional development'.

Parker, Patton, Madden and Sinclair (2010) examine the factors that facilitated the creation and maintenance of a community of practice through the process of curriculum development for four primary teachers and a curriculum coordinator. The shared response to the paper is based on the importance of being a professional at all levels within our field and how teacher professional development is inherent in that professionalism.

Sinelnikov (2009) examines the effectiveness of a school-based development programme for primary physical education teachers as they learned to teach Sport Education (SE). While the reported programme focused on the content of SE more than pedagogical practices that could be transferred across a number of physical education teaching contexts, the teacher education, primary and post-primary responses to the paper engage with the relationships necessary to accommodate cooperative learning and how best to encourage and consider CPD opportunities as opportunities for changes in practice.

Keay (2006) presents collaborative learning as an effective form of professional development that provides an alternative to professional development offered through structured courses. In her study, Keay focuses on the experiences of newly qualified post-primary teachers. Two clear distinctions are posed ('professional development and professional learning' and 'collaborative learning and collegiality') and are revisited throughout the responses to this paper and to some extent in response to other papers in the section. Responses to the paper are provided from the perspective of teacher education, administrators and principals, and veteran physical education teachers. Each engages to differing extents with cooperation, collaboration, collegiality and professional learning.

Armour and Yelling's (2004) paper is one of the first papers to focus on the issue of CPD in physical education. The authors examine traditional forms of physical education professional development experienced by qualified physical education teachers and provide suggestions on alternative forms of delivery. The responses to the paper consider professional learning as part of your 'job' (as a teacher) and bridge the gap between professional development and professional learning for experienced physical education teachers.

Petrie and McGee (2012) explore the design and delivery of a professional development programme for teaching primary physical education and the extent to which the programme supported teachers as learners. Some of the findings are not dissimilar to those shared in the Armour and Yelling (2004) paper and therefore reinforce what constitutes effective professional development. In attempting to address how we can meet the criteria for effective professional development, responses include interrogation of the teacher as learner and a teacher education perspective that engages with suggested practices that may encourage pre-service teachers to pursue professional learning.

18

FROM COMMITTEE TO COMMUNITY

The development and maintenance of a community of practice

 The study

Parker, M., Patton, K., Madden, M. and Sinclair, C. (2010).
Journal of Teaching in Physical Education, 29(4), pp. 337–357.

The purpose of the study was to follow a group of primary physical education teachers whose objective was to develop and disseminate a district-wide primary physical education curriculum. The study examined the factors that facilitated the creation and maintenance of a community of practice (CoP) through the process of curriculum development. A CoP is distinguished from other groups and communities as a community that shares a domain of interest and interacts over a sustained period of time to pursue that interest. Trust and respect among members of a CoP encourage a safe and supportive environment for teachers to challenge current practices.

Participants

Four female primary physical education specialists and the district curriculum coordinator from a school district in Arizona constituted the CoP. The teachers knew each other previously, but they had not had the opportunity to work together and had no curriculum development experience. While the district curriculum coordinator had limited knowledge about physical education, she supported primary physical education and acted as the administrative participant. The three facilitators (three of the four authors) of the CoP were participant observers with varying previous experiences in professional development and physical education.

Design and methods

Data was collected over a two-year period and included:

1 interviews with the teachers, the district coordinator and lead facilitator;
2 researcher field notes from observations of curriculum retreats and follow-up meetings;
3 artefacts such as working papers, videotapes of CoP sessions, emails and voice messages.

Open coding was used to analyse interview transcripts, field notes and artefacts throughout the study, leading to the development of categories and their relationship to each other.

Results

Five main themes were identified as facilitating the development and maintenance of a CoP for this group. First, three events acted as a catalyst to initiate the work of the group. These included financial support and content specific leadership available through a grant award, a nucleus of highly motivated teachers willing to challenge the current curriculum, and a change in district administration. Second, over time, teachers conveyed their purpose as directing other teachers to their work and gaining support of the teachers in the district, and by association, impacting all students. Third, support from university faculty and the school district was essential for teachers who had not learned how to develop a curriculum of this magnitude. Fourth, positive personal and professional connections among the teachers and facilitators were critical factors in the initiation and maintenance of this community of practice. Fifth, empowerment was the most prominent theme identified as a result of this community of practice. Empowerment arose not only in teachers' realisation of the ownership they exercised over the creation of what was to constitute knowledge but also in generating commitment of other teachers to the developed curriculum.

 Research perspective

In setting the context for the study, the authors state that:

> ... teachers need opportunities for active hands-on learning which is intensive and sustained over time, built into the school day, connected to comprehensive change, organised around collaborative problem solving, and facilitated with care.

(p. 338)

In addressing this philosophy towards encouraging a community of practice, there is some evidence that the study surpassed expectations. Teachers grew a sense of responsibility to attend to the needs of other primary physical education teachers in the district, increasing in confidence to take on leadership and advocacy roles. The fact that teachers saw their work as meaningful and contributing to a significant goal of curriculum development is impressive. This instils confidence in those of us who work to encourage practicing and pre-service teachers to become involved in a leadership and advocacy role for the teaching of physical education. The study provides some direction on how to do this in such a way that allows teachers to be empowered. However, the bottom line of the success of the CoP appears to be attributed to the extent to which the four teachers had a genuine interest in being involved in curriculum development. That is, if we wish to encourage effective CoP, we need to allow exploration of what the teachers identify as meaningful, purposeful and authentic learning tasks for them as a group of teachers. The longitudinal nature of the teachers contributing to curriculum development appeared to act as an incentive for teachers to continually invest on a regular basis to a CoP.

 ## Shared response

We have chosen to tackle this paper with one response from a teacher educator, primary and post-primary perspective based on our view on the importance of being a professional at all levels within our field, and how teacher professional development is inherent in that professionalism. While not intended to define communities of practice, the diagram below represents our effort to pull together the key points that emerged from our discussions and which we highlight in our response.

Teacher professional development is important. It is a central part of what it is to be a professional. It can sustain us in our practice through our engagement in, and reflection about, what it is that we do as physical education teachers. But most importantly, it can enhance students' learning in physical education. Teacher professional development happens in many different ways throughout our teaching lives. Sometimes it is about curriculum or system change. Other times, it may resemble a 'lucky dip' where we attend a workshop about the 'latest craze' in physical activity, whetting our appetites about its potential but not learning enough to sustain a worthwhile engagement with the activity. The format of teacher professional development can often be something that is 'done' to teachers rather than 'with' them. But sometimes we can get it right. In this paper, we can see the possibility for deep and meaningful learning when teachers learn together, and from each other, in a CoP. Such professional development opportunities can serve to deepen our learning about what it is that we do in physical education, how we do it and how we can improve our own practice and encourage others to do so. The level of engagement required of participants is more demanding

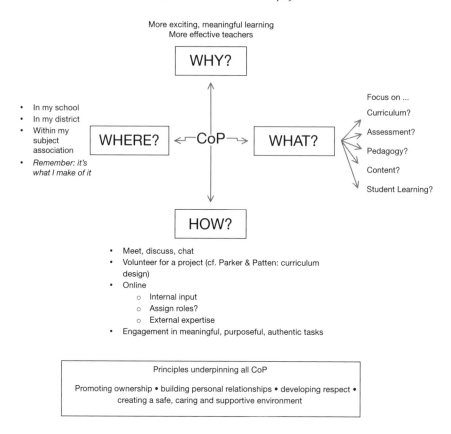

FIGURE 18.1 Communities of practice

but the rewards are significant. So what can we learn from this research about setting up and maintaining an effective CoP?

First, a CoP is about more than a 'one off' course. It is about teachers sharing a domain of interest over a sustained period of time. This shared interest could be either externally driven or internally brokered among the group members. At a local level, the group could look outwards to see what might be worth engaging in to support their practice in physical education. Is there a particular initiative happening in physical education? Is there a source of funding available that might be targeted for a particular project? Is there expertise available locally, perhaps through a third-level college, that might be of interest? Equally, teachers might decide to focus on themselves, sharing ideas, planning collaboratively and reflecting on practice. Both approaches are equally legitimate, but what is important is that shared moment where members of the group identify what it is they want from this group at this point in time. It is about meaningful, purposeful engagement based on authentic tasks drawn from the reality of teaching physical education.

So how does the CoP work? It works essentially by teachers learning together and from each other. In the initial stages, it is important to build trust and respect in the group so that each member is comfortable talking openly about their work and the challenges they face. This takes time and effort on everyone's part but it is time well spent. The research tells us that effective, CoP interact over sustained periods of time. Teachers are less likely to stay involved unless they have a strong feeling of ownership of the group and that it is a safe and supportive environment where they can be honest and open about their current practice. As teachers get to know each other through sharing their professional experiences, they will also forge personal relationships. In times of low motivation or other demands on time and energy, it can often be these informal ties to the group that will sustain the individual teacher's involvement and commitment to the process.

While agreed interest, or a project may dictate the parameters of the work, group members will need lots of opportunities for 'hands on learning' and time to reframe their thinking and planning. While no one person's agenda should have precedence, it is important, that the process is facilitated with care. The group can support itself by, for example, different group members assuming different roles and/or the group agreeing to a way of organising itself that will benefit all of the group. The group can also be supported externally by calling on outside sources of content or expertise in the areas of teaching and learning. These sources of alternative input have the potential to bring new ideas into the group and invigorate the process.

Finally, as the CoP becomes established, participants should experience a greater passion for, and commitment to, their work as physical education teachers. This new sense of empowerment will often result in CoP teachers wanting to spread the word about what it is they have achieved.

Every physical education teacher can be part of a CoP. It may mean setting it up yourself with a few like-minded physical education teachers in your community. It may mean putting your hand up when the call goes out about a new project in physical education. It may mean becoming involved in an online community. The possibilities for engagement are there and the potential for your learning in physical education are significant. For example, what might a CoP with a focus on primary physical education look like? You as a teacher might begin by chatting with the teachers in your lower primary setting. You might adopt the 'subject leader' role but only in so far as you suggest a way to begin, and then facilitate the various meetings of the group. It might be wise to foster that safe and supportive setting by beginning with an invitation to chat about the aspects of practice that are going well and those that are challenging. The course the group might take could be determined by drawing on input among the group, external expertise or assigning roles within the CoP. Could different members look into some aspect of practice that could be shared, one that requires input to improve – for example, that we prompt good discussion by children within games lessons where children are involved in creating games, whereas our work in gymnastics is dominated by teacher voice and we want to increase the input of the child in our gymnastics lessons. How best might we achieve this? Could it be through a staff member sharing his/her work within the games unit by describing a typical class or recording it for viewing by the CoP or could it require that a person with expertise in teaching gymnastics be asked to work with the group with a focus on pupil involvement in discussion? The CoP might then allow time for practice to become embedded before meeting again. The focus might be related to the original theme or might extend into a new domain.

What is the catalyst for teachers choosing to be lifelong learners and become involved in professional development opportunities? For some it is personal and about helping them to become more effective teachers, while for others it is about the students and how to make learning more exciting and meaningful for them. As we interact with young teachers it is critical to help them gain a sense of professional commitment, to value professional colleagues and to engage with one another as critical friends in order to impact what happens in the name of physical education and its impact on children and youth. A pre-service teacher once asked, 'What will I gain from being a member of the professional organisation?' She seemed oblivious to the fact that we, physical educators, are the professional organisation; it is what we make it. Involvement in the professional organisation, its initiatives, policies and events might serve as the first step in teachers' professional development. Modelling this involvement – and taking responsibility for promoting our work with young people in physical activity settings – helps us grow as teachers, has an impact on the experiences that young people have in our programmes, is enjoyable and is also contagious, encouraging others to become involved.

19

SPORT EDUCATION FOR TEACHERS

Professional development when introducing a novel curriculum model

 The study

Sinelnikov, O. (2009). **European Physical Education Review,** *15(1), pp. 91–114.*

This study examines the effectiveness of a school-based professional development programme for physical education teachers as they learned to teach Sport Education (SE). SE is an instructional and curriculum model designed to provide an authentic approach to teaching sport by encompassing its essential characteristics, for example, team affiliation and a culminating event.

Participants

The school where the study was conducted was a small public school in a rural Russian community with approximately 600 students in the first through eleventh grades. Participants were two physical education teachers and their respective sixth grade (11- to 12-year olds) physical education classes. These two teachers were assigned as either the *expert* or *advanced beginner* using the Dreyfus and Dreyfus (1986) skill acquisition model. The author/researcher was the professional responsible for delivering the professional development. The *expert* teacher had 27 years of teaching experience and was recognised for his ability as an effective teacher. The *advanced beginner* teacher had three years of teaching experience and was currently a graduate student at a local university.

Design and method

The professional development programme was designed for physical education teachers unfamiliar with SE. It was delivered in three steps with the intent of the teachers using the resources provided to implement the model in their own classroom. In Step 1 printed materials on benefits, main features and detailed explanations on how to implement SE were given to the teachers. Step 2 entailed a two-day SE workshop that provided experience in specific features of the model. During this step, teachers then designed a SE season outline and wrote sample lesson plans. Step 3 was a time intensive effort designed to make the link between SE theory and practice. It involved the researcher observing weekly physical education lessons and briefing and debriefing with the teachers using the Tsangaridou and O'Sullivan (1994) Reflective Framework for Teaching in Physical Education.

The teachers and researcher communicated through email throughout this investigation as well as taking part in both informal discussions and interviews. The data sources included the researcher's log (of any and all communications with the teachers), informal discussions, briefing/debriefing sessions (twice a week), semi-structured interviews (prior to implementation of SE and weekly throughout its delivery), telephone conversations (prior to implementing SE) and document analysis (lesson and season plans). Thematic coding was employed for analysing all data and identifying common themes. Patterns were identified, all data related to the patterns were identified or a new pattern created, patterns and subthemes were then noted and themes to define patterns were developed. This analysis was ongoing throughout the investigation with the Ko, Sohn and Lee (2006) modified SE benchmark observational instrument used to confirm the existence or not of SE benchmarks in lesson and season plans.

Results

Both teachers exhibited the majority of the SE specific pedagogical behaviours. Teachers acknowledged the need to observe the actual teaching of SE. They required assistance in identifying how to effectively allow students to take responsibility in organisation tasks and in introducing student roles in addition to that of a physically active participant. Teachers requested the need for constant validation of the accuracy of their teaching and implementation of SE. They also reported initially experiencing difficulty in relinquishing control of the gym to promote student responsibility, particularly when delegating class management and teaching episodes to students. However, as the SE season continued, both teachers reported that teaching became easier when students became more involved and responsible for some of the instructional and managerial decisions within the lesson. The teachers appreciated the time they spent working cooperatively, including the devising of season and lesson plans, observing each other teach and discussing the model and their teaching practices.

Research perspective

The central focus of this study was to establish the effectiveness of a school-based professional development programme for physical education teachers, with SE providing the medium through which the programme was delivered. Perhaps unfortunately, the programme in this instance focused on the content of SE more than pedagogical practices that could be transferable across a number of physical education teaching contexts. Teachers' request to observe the researcher teach a SE lesson heightens the importance of teachers viewing delivery in practice. The provision of resources complements such observation and do not appear to be sufficient on their own. The extensive on-site presence of a person delivering professional development to train, observe and assist in curriculum implementation appears critical to teachers' initial training in the instructional principles and curriculum design of a model. While the teachers requested the need for constant validation of the accuracy of their teaching of SE, we would caution against enforcing that, to be seen as successfully implementing SE, teachers need to deliver all facets of the model. It is also interesting to note the importance that teachers attribute to working cooperatively and this is particularly important for physical education teachers who may find themselves working in a school as the only physical education teacher. As alluded to by the author, further research is needed to investigate the extent of permanency of teachers' changes in teaching practice as a result of the professional development programme. Further research is also necessary to establish the extent to which the teachers' delivery of SE remains true to the principles of the SE model.

Teacher educator response

The paper encourages a relationship between teachers in schools and pre-service teachers (PSTs) and researchers/faculty members in physical education teacher education (PETE) programmes in a number of ways. Teachers requested to observe a researcher teach a SE lesson in which students take leadership roles. If the researcher is attached to a PETE programme where SE is an integral part of the programme, teachers could be invited to observe how PETE faculty deliver a SE season on a weekly basis. In this instance the PSTs would represent the leadership roles that the teachers would encourage students to undertake in a school physical education SE unit. This would encourage a more meaningful relationship between the teacher and researcher/PETE faculty member. If the teachers were able to attend on a weekly basis they could be a member of a SE team and this would encourage a relationship between teachers and PSTs. In PETE programmes where PSTs are expected to be familiar with, and articulate in, delivering SE there is the potential for PSTs to provide professional development opportunities for teachers less familiar with SE. In this instance, PSTs could deliver a SE workshop that illustrates what SE 'looks like'.

The cooperative learning that took place is another opportunity to develop meaningful relationships between teachers and PETE programmes. The two teachers spent a considerable amount of time working cooperatively. This could be extended to incorporate a learning environment that encouraged cooperative learning between teachers, the researcher/PETE faculty member and PSTs. Such a learning environment could entail PSTs undertaking their formalised teaching placement in a school that is keen to pursue SE, with the agreement that they, along with the teacher, would explore further the delivery of SE. This would encourage cooperative learning between the teacher and PST, keep teachers active in their own professional development and reinforce to PSTs the importance of cooperative learning in improving one's own professional learning. If through such cooperative learning PSTs can experience the development of collegiality, then there is a hope that PETE programmes can successfully encourage PSTs to sustain their notion of collegiality into a time when they are qualified teachers. At this point it is hoped that they would then be confident to contribute to established communities of physical education teachers.

 ## Primary response

The findings of this study prompted me to consider if primary teachers reflect on the significance of their role as mentors of PSTs. One aspect of the support they provide might focus on highlighting the importance of the PSTs availing of every opportunity to gain an understanding of physical education content knowledge as they engage with programmes of physical education in their undergraduate programmes. The researcher in this article makes it clear that teachers receive little support related to content knowledge in any continuing professional development provision. This is a feature of many systems. There is often an assumption by PSTs that their physical education content knowledge will be reinforced and enhanced as they gain experience teaching the subject. Indeed it could be argued that there are gains but little in terms of formal support.

As the researcher in this study debates teacher change it might be useful for primary teachers or those beginning teaching to consider how to 'position' themselves to be open to change. Can reading or CPD courses prepare you for change? Sometimes setting aside time to think how you might change your teaching of physical education may be sufficient. Or might it be outside events, for example, observing children participate in sporting events, that prompt you to change how you teach as you observe provision for children in sport. Sometimes it may be a spectator reaction to children's efforts in a sporting context that encourages thinking about how you might change a particular emphasis in your teaching. This might prompt discussion with colleagues on how, as primary teachers, we overtly display respect for all children during our teaching of physical education.

The understanding developed by both teachers in the study led to 'a sense of shared professional culture'. This strikes us as a wonderful stage of professional development for a teacher. Therein lies a challenge for all subject or curriculum leaders within primary school, (a) how to propose and design programmes of CPD for teachers in a particular staff who may not yet 'share' a professional culture and (b) how to create a climate of change. One possible solution is proposed given that teacher change is a gradual process underpinning the actions. The researcher argues that significant changes in teacher beliefs and attitudes occur after teachers see improvements in student learning. It is important then that a subject leader is sufficiently patient with the process so that there is meaningful opportunity to allow professional development to take place over time.

This study and others suggest that CPD should be school based and contextualised. These conditions for effective CPD may challenge CPD systems and indeed the teacher. On the other hand, these principles may serve to guide the subject leader. What CPD support can be identified that will be continuous, school based and contextualised? Often, it may be the subject leader who is in the best position to offer this form of support to colleagues: on-site and continuous. However, I believe a key quality of the subject leader could be defined as patience ... allowing time for improvement in learning of children to prompt teacher change. In so many instances we believe teachers are interested in 'exploring changes to their teaching practices', but they will change more readily if they see gains in learning. It is imperative that the subject leader plans CPD carefully to ensure that this enthusiasm for change is not harmed by either an overzealous approach by the subject leader (failing to allow time for change to occur) or poor planning of content (disregarding research findings such as those cited in this article that provide a blueprint for effective CPD).

 ## Post-primary response

There are two types of CPD available to physical education teachers, the 'one off' course where teachers are provided with a taster of a new physical activity or an approach to teaching an activity. The latter, an alternative and less commonly available CPD, is designed to support teachers over time to improve their practice with a group of like-minded professionals. Of the two CPD approaches, I have found the second form of engagement more beneficial and sustaining. The important decision for professionals is to commit to locating, accessing and engaging in regular CPD. This engagement is usually in addition to the demands of the 'day job' so it is worth reflecting on what is available and how the different possibilities might best develop professional practice.

When we participate in CPD, we are required to make conceptual and practical leaps between what is envisaged in the particular initiative (or adoption of curriculum model) and the reality of our own professional practice, our students and the particular school setting. Teachers' professional lives are littered with good intentions to embrace wholeheartedly new ideas and approaches that engagement in CPD offers them. Too often however, CPD happens as a 'one off' event in an 'out of school' setting with little opportunity for the sustained engagement necessary to allow change to become effectively assimilated into practice. The author suggests that CPD should ideally happen on site, in the school and include expert demonstrations of what the practice resembles as well as provide opportunities and support for teachers as they try to incorporate the new approach into practice. Opportunities for briefing and de-briefing about how the change is progressing were also found to be significant supports for teachers. CPD is something that should be done with teachers rather than to them. It really is worthwhile reflecting on the CPD opportunities available and critiquing them in relation to the principles of good practice proposed.

This paper also highlights the importance of the 'process' in CPD – that is, working with teachers and schools in a purposeful, developmental way over time. The principles highlighted by The Center for the Future of Teaching and Learning at WestEd (2002) in this regard suggests the following guidelines for the design of CPD. First, it is important to remember that teachers are central to student learning, therefore what works for teachers must be a central consideration. Second, CPD should support collegial and organisation improvement in order to support teachers in their 'change role'. In order to do this, teachers should be encouraged and supported in building professional and supportive relationships. Again, it is worth considering, will CPD offer this support?

Real change takes time and is driven by a long term plan. CPD in support of real change should include consideration for how the effectiveness of the CPD provided will be measured. Ultimately, well thought out CPD should build in ways in which effectiveness will be measured in terms of more effective teaching practice and improved student learning. If the CPD you are considering includes ways in which the process and outcomes will be evaluated and reflected upon, then it will have ticked a number of important boxes.

There will always be a struggle in CPD design between the demand by teachers for new content and new ideas and providing CPD which focuses on generic pedagogical skills and curriculum models which require a more sustained engagement by teachers. Yet it is through sustained engagement in CPD that we can develop the skills and dispositions that are central to being a professional. These skills and dispositions include having a good subject knowledge which is always being developed throughout one's career, a commitment to ongoing CPD and a sense of pride and ownership of one's work, always striving for high standards in teaching and learning. How can we, therefore, encourage teachers to participate in CPD regularly over the duration of their professional life? In my opinion, this journey has to start in undergraduate teacher education.

In undergraduate teacher education, every opportunity should be taken to encourage students to work with each other, to learn from each other, to share resources and skills and to reflect on their own, and others', work. Cooperative learning is at the heart of effective CPD, therefore students ought to be completing their teaching programme with a real sense of its worth. Personal traits including an openness and willingness to share practice and to learn from each other will continue to support teachers throughout their professional lives. If we can build these dispositions in pre-service teachers and continue to provide them with similar learning opportunities for professional development once they have completed college, perhaps we can be more optimistic about the quality of physical education into the future.

20

COLLABORATIVE LEARNING IN PHYSICAL EDUCATION TEACHERS' EARLY-CAREER PROFESSIONAL DEVELOPMENT

 **The study**

Keay, J. (2006). **Physical Education and Sport Pedagogy,** *11(3), pp. 285–305.*

This paper acknowledges that professional development is a crucial element of professional practice and presents collaborative learning as an effective form of professional development that provides an alternative to professional development offered through structured courses. The paper uses the four criteria of relationships, commitment, culture and reflective practice to examine examples of what could be considered as collaborative learning opportunities.

Participants

Participants comprised four cohorts of newly qualified physical education teachers (41 in total) undertaking their induction in post-primary schools in England.

Design and method

The research was conducted in three stages. Data was collected from all participants in stage one by questionnaires that were administered to three successive cohorts of newly qualified physical education teachers. The questionnaires focused on issues related to professional learning. 'Professional life histories' were also constructed for each participant and sought information on personal details (age, sex), education, qualifications, degree and training application. To explore professional development opportunities throughout the induction year, case study methodology using semi-structured interviews and 'personal life histories' were utilised in stage two with eight teachers. A card check system was adopted in stage three, the teachers' second year of teaching, to confirm or reject the researcher's interpretation of their experiences. Data from stage one was entered into Excel tables while data from stages two and three was analysed using a qualitative data analysis package.

Results

The study found that if the school culture is collaborative and individuals recognise opportunities to further their learning in a collaborative way, any form of professional development can lead to collaborative professional learning.

 Research perspective

The paper provides two clear distinctions that are useful reference points when discussing professional development and related concepts. The first distinction is between 'professional development' and 'professional learning'. Professional development opportunities tend to be experiences through different forms of school-based and off-site events while professional learning is a process that takes time to become part of a teacher's practice. The second distinction is between 'collaborative learning' and 'collegiality'. Similar to the definition for professional learning, collaborative learning is a process that not only promotes professional learning but can also provide the means by which learning is embedded into practice. Collegiality is seen to sit in the middle of a continuum between cooperation and collaboration, noting that there is a distinction between a collaborative school culture that encourages professional development and that which merely expects collegiality.

The paper makes one consider the extent to which the criteria listed for collaborative learning (the ability to get on with one another at a personal level, a similar philosophical stance and mutual professional respect) is very much reliant on the personalities of the people involved. Subsequently, the challenge is how to include more people in collaborative learning and sustain their engagement. As teachers, we need to be reflective practitioners as well as examine the extent of collaboration in the school/university department. In planning for collaboration, we should each be encouraged to plan for collaboration, considering the context of the department and what we each can bring to it as a teacher. One way to develop collaboration would be for teachers to support each other's potential to encourage the most effective platform for professional learning and development. This would include learning collaboratively from each other, whether it is qualified teachers learning from pre-service teachers or beginning teachers learning from qualified teachers.

The three-stage research design shared in the paper had potential to provide a rich evidence base. However, in drawing on the new teachers' professional development experiences (categorised as working together, teacher influences, developmental groups and community acceptance) and comparing them with the criteria identified as necessary for effective collaborative learning to take place (relationships, commitment, culture and reflective practice), there is minimal reporting of data from the particular data sources – that is, questionnaires, semi-structured interviews, personal life histories and the card check system.

 ## Shared response

We have chosen to respond to a beginning teacher's critical incident from the perspective of administrators and principals, veteran teachers in school and teacher education.

Critical incident: Isolation as a (un)welcomed form of autonomy

There is no other physical education teacher in the school so effectively I am the Physical Education Department. I found it difficult to adapt to the level of responsibility being directed towards me. With regard to physical education, I must admit I am alone (...) my teaching has not been interfered with during the course of the year. The other teachers have not questioned how I am getting on. They have not offered advice either on how to teach different aspects of each syllabus. There has been no physical education-focused support system for me and there has been no-one that I could turn to during the year with physical education questions (...) There is nobody to tell you, 'This is how you teach' ... Once I was gone, that was it. It was a shock being the only physical education teacher. Suddenly I was responsible for all the plans, timetabling, pupils, everything ... You have a lot of things being thrown at you. At the start there was a sense of panic. You find yourself fighting your own corner when you are on your own.

(John, beginning teacher, Prompt Sheet 1, 6/11/2009;
Prompt Sheet 4, 14/05/2010; Interview, 03/06/2010,
in MacPhail and Tannehill, 2012)

Administration and principals

Keay's study on collaborative learning prompted us to think about collaborative learning in the context of the primary school. She described the subject department in the post-primary school as having the potential to be the context for rich professional development if managed appropriately and if the teachers are committed to the process of collaborative learning. Within the primary school we thought about who might encourage collaborative learning related to physical education. It often falls to a member of staff who perhaps attends a course and shares their learning with others on returning to the school. Keay argued that this can lead to collaborative learning particularly if the collaboration is valued and extended into a learning network.

Perhaps, however, we need to consider a more formalised structure to ensure that physical education becomes a focus for collaborative learning in a primary school. Could the school principal ascertain if the conditions that Keay outlines as important for collaborative learning pertain to their school? That is:

1   the ability to get on with one another at a personal level;
2   sharing a similar philosophical stance;
3   the ability to create an atmosphere where constructive criticism can flourish;
4   mutual professional respect and time commitment to plan, evaluate, reflect and speculate.

The time commitment to plan, evaluate, reflect and speculate is probably the key aspect that the principal of a school needs to control, provided the other criteria are features of their school. Once this is addressed, collaborative learning as a process can be nurtured.

We are familiar with a school-university partnership where a rural primary school and a college of education worked well together to drive forward learning through engagement in outdoor and adventure activities. The teachers had undertaken some adventure activities with the children in each class. They identified a lack of cohesion in what they were doing and the principal approached the college of education seeking assistance. The principal was the key to creating the space for the collaboration between the school and the college to occur. The college of education facilitated the exploration of content and subject knowledge but the key to learning by the staff was their collaborative engagement. While the professional experience was varied this did not appear significant in the process of collaboration. In fact, the collaboration was perhaps richer because of the diversity of professional experience within the group. The teachers in the school engaged with the content, with a focus on the spiral nature of the learning and how elements needed to be taught and revisited to ensure progression. The sequencing of activities was a real challenge. They taught further elements of content and discussed their teaching, at times informally at the usual coffee break but subsequently discussed their teaching and children's responses during set times where the principal had blocked time devoted to this collaborative learning. Teachers shared the resources and most importantly they shared their experiences of teaching in this new way. The school plan from which the teachers worked was then re-designed, informed by the most recent experience the teachers had when teaching the content. This appeared to be a clear case where the principal promoted and developed an appropriate culture ensuring that professional development was carefully planned and where she valued the contribution of others, those on her staff and those from the college partnership. The practice in this particular setting matches Keay's description of settings where effective collaborative learning happens evident.

Another primary school worked collaboratively on preparing a whole school plan for physical education. The principal blocked time for meaningful discussion between teachers at each grade level and drew up a revised plan for physical education for each grade level. The work involved learning through discussion and experience of some of the activities. The principal built on this model subsequently extending it where other subject areas were the focus. Such collaborative learning in the primary school context is probably more frequently undertaken in priority areas such as literacy. The benefits of extending the opportunities for collaborative learning to an area such as physical education could be significant.

It is arguable that the culture of collaborative learning could be stronger in the primary school context where there tends to be shared responsibility for subject areas and where no teacher has a specialist background in areas such as physical education. Other papers discussed in this publication focus on areas such as SE within primary schools. A principal might use this topic as an example of an aspect of physical education that could be explored by staff who are committed to working collaboratively to improve their games teaching. Hence, having committed the time for collaborative learning focused on a particular curriculum and instructional model, a principal might be well advised to be aware of the opportunities for real collaborative learning to take place. Who might investigate the model? Who might help prepare a presentation to staff linked to exploration of the model? When might initial discussion on implementation of the model take place? Who might support teachers as they implement the model? When might evaluation of the model take place?

Keay's study suggests that changes need to be made to induction practice to ensure that the voices of new teachers are valued in any such collaborations. She argued that newly qualified teachers are a particularly important group to highlight and the findings of her study should send a strong reminder to principals to reflect on this aspect of collaborative learning. This is particularly important where a young teacher can raise some aspect for discussion that s/he is particularly able to present but that might involve change of practice by more experienced teachers on the staff. We listened recently to a discussion on the sports day for a primary school where a young teacher was presenting a format underpinned by a philosophy that was shared by staff but where practice related to their particular sports day did not match the philosophy. The principal facilitated discussion and collaborative learning with the staff over a number of sessions so that at least some change could occur. Keay referred to the success that is possible where 'collaborative learning is effective if members are attributed the same level of respect' (p. 297). This was the key challenge in the case described where the inexperienced teacher was recognised as someone who 'has something to offer in the process and that all can learn'. While the focus on our responses to research have generally been directed at teachers, it is important to remember that within primary schools time for such collaborative learning needs to be created. This is a key responsibility for principals. The time to engage in this learning can be identified by principals, sometimes the time has been mandated by local educational authorities and schools are provided with the authority to use it in whatever way they deem best fits their context. Collaborative learning in physical education could be one means of fostering real and meaningful professional development within schools where individual teachers can feel overwhelmed by the need to learn when the onus is on the individual working alone.

Veteran teachers in one department

Ongoing engagement in professional learning is a key characteristic of a teaching professional. In this response, we are choosing to use the term 'professional learning' in preference to professional development. We equate 'professional development' with something that is done 'to' teachers rather than 'with' them or 'by' them. The term 'professional development' conjures up images of activities for teachers that are often expert led and takes the form of 'once or twice off' engagements, usually away from the teacher's school. They seldom include enough time or emphasis on teachers customising what they have learned for their particular setting. There is often no follow up to ascertain it the course has had any impact on the teaching practice for those who attended. Once back in the busyness of school, the learning is often quickly lost as teachers revert to their familiar practice unless there is a real effort to embed the new learning in one's practice

Professional learning is about a more sustained and collaborative engagement with learning about how to improve teaching practice so that students have better learning experiences in physical education. It is about ensuring that new knowledge and understanding does become embedded in practice. The 'top down' model of professional development has failed us miserably in terms of its impact on supporting teachers to improve their practice. On the other hand, there are so many examples of the successful outcomes achieved as a result of sustained collaborative engagement by groups of teachers in working to improve their practice in a whole variety of ways. More often than not however, these teachers are drawn from a number of schools and it is seldom that whole subject departments either want to or can attend. The challenge for all of us as professionals is to focus on building collaborative professional learning environments in each of our schools in support of professional learning.

The foundations of these professional learning environments require that we recognise the importance of cooperation in the first instance – simply getting along with our colleagues, building and working to maintain personal connections that will in time build mutual respect and trust. Once established, the next step is about working to establish a shared goal about what the department hopes to achieve in physical education for all students. At its most basic, building collegiality can be about working out schedules and agreeing how facilities and equipment will be shared. It can also involve addressing more challenging areas such as programme planning, student reporting and how students might be encouraged to participate in physical education. Collegiality represents a big step up from cooperation. Collegiality does not ensure professional learning however. It requires the extra step of actively engaging in thinking about and wanting to improve the physical education programme. As a group of teachers begin to move towards a collaborative working environment, such practices as sharing and discussing teaching and learning ideas, team teaching, openness to constructive criticism and preparedness to give time and effort to planning and reflection, will become more common practices.

Creating and maintaining a collaborative learning culture is the responsibility of every teacher. It is in our interests that we belong to a group of teachers who work collaboratively and are committed to ongoing professional learning. Each of us can contribute to the creation and maintenance of such a community particularly when we understand what is required. If you are a practicing teacher, how would you describe the culture of your department, cooperative, collegial or collaborative? How do you know? How do you contribute to that? What would be required to move to the next level? What one/two things could you do to make this happen? What would be good about this for you professionally and personally? If you were to begin to work collaboratively, what would be the first thing you would like to focus on and why? If you are a collaborative learning community, who is the most important contributor to this culture? What do they do that is so important? If there was one thing that you could learn from this person, what would it be?

If your subject department is a difficult place to work, then you may be part of the problem and you are definitely part of the solution. If you were asked to explain what is important for your colleagues in physical education, could you? Do you share ideas or resources with them? Do you respect their opinions even if you do not agree with them? If you subscribe to a different vision for physical education, are you prepared to discuss how this might be managed? Building these stepping stones requires that each of us is prepared to listen and consider if there are issues on which you are prepared to compromise.

If you are a new beginning teacher reading this, know that it is time well spent getting to know and build relationships with your new physical education colleagues. Be prepared to share good ideas and resources. Be open to constructive feedback about your teaching. You, too, can lead by example. Be seen to plan your classes carefully and be prepared to talk about successes and challenges. If you are the sole physical education practitioner in your school, seek out a like-minded teacher in another subject department. Good practice is good practice irrespective of subject area.

Finally, if you are involved in school management, you have an important role to play in encouraging collaborative professional learning. It will make all the difference to the quality of teaching and learning in your school. Make planning for teaching and learning an explicit priority. Provide for a whole school planning initiative where teachers can learn about the different practices we can use to support each other in becoming better teachers. Where you see good practice happening, 'showcase' it for other members of staff. Encourage professional learning between subject departments. Make professional learning a recurring theme in conversations with your staff. Be as interested in teaching and learning as you are in the practical issues that often can become the main reason for communicating with subject departments. If your school culture is collaborative, it can lead to and support collaborative professional learning. In the coming years, effective schools will foster and support professional learning. We all have a role to play in this.

 ## Teacher educator response

This paper was useful in clarifying the difference between cooperation, collegiality and collaboration. Our understanding is that cooperation involves getting along and working together, collegiality represents the respect that is displayed as colleagues who share a common purpose or goal work together, and collaboration is working together to achieve a common goal and, as noted by Keay, requires both cooperation and collegiality.

Reading and discussing this paper also reminded us that teacher professional development can take place in the workplace, with teachers themselves taking control of their development as they learn with and from one another, both individually and as a group. Workplace development in a school setting can encourage teachers to practice what they are learning and allow access to regroup for discussions on their development. Workplace learning prompts us to consider that while there is certainly a place for the outside expert to provide guidance in teacher professional development, it is not always necessary.

During our discussions of this paper, we began to consider the response of teachers across all stages of their careers to the notion of professional development and perhaps more importantly in this case, collaboration and what it means to their teacher learning and development. This paper and the critical incident of the novice teacher noted above certainly challenged us to consider how to help pre-service teachers begin their careers cooperating as colleagues and collaborating in the best interest of students as well as their own learning and growth. Not only must we help pre-service teachers choose to collaborate with one another, we must provide them the space and tools with which to conduct this collaboration. Perhaps the first step is to encourage cooperation among a cohort of pre-service teachers, then assist them in recognising themselves as colleagues in the physical education teaching profession before finally engaging them in collaborative activity that is embedded in the teaching programme and requires accessing knowledge and in-depth discussion. It is hoped that this type of progression will give pre-service teachers the confidence once they are in school settings as full-fledged teachers to facilitate their own learning with colleagues. The progression might look like this . . .

Cooperation

Whether in an activity pedagogy module or theoretical lecture, everyday pre-service teachers are challenged to cooperate with one another. For example, in one of our modules pre-service teachers must come to class with what we have labelled a 'ticket to class', which is a response to a reading they were assigned to prepare them for class discussion. When pre-service teachers enter the class they may be asked to share with the person next to them the essence of their response, in small groups determine similarities among their responses, or to come up with points they need clarified from the day's upcoming discussions. These tasks encourage pre-service teachers to get to know one another and to work together on introductory tasks.

Collegiallity

As a means of coming to terms with their own beliefs about teaching and learning and what it means to be a physical education teacher, pre-service teachers are given the following teaching metaphor assignment during their first year of teacher education and then revisit it several times through peer discussion and challenges. They come to understand the perspectives of their teaching peers, what motivated them to become a physical education teacher, and how they can learn and grow from one another.

Teaching metaphor assignment

Write a metaphor of yourself as a teacher. Begin by visualising your ideal classroom: what are you doing, what are the pupils doing, what is the climate, how does it feel, what kinds of learning do you see, and what is your role? Jot down your thoughts after you visualise, read through it, and see if some image comes to mind. As these images evolve, attempt to articulate them in the form of a metaphor. You will share your teaching metaphors with a peer who will then be invited to challenge you, question you and attempt to understand if the metaphor reflects your beliefs about teaching and learning.

Collaboration

In their final year of teacher education, our pre-service teachers are assigned a project (see assignment on page 167) that requires them to work collaboratively to reach success. The response from these pre-service teachers is that it requires them to share discussions, take responsibility for various aspects of the project, interact with administrators and teachers outside of physical education and put their growing knowledge to work in an applied and exciting way.

Outdoor Adventure Education project

Self-selected teaching teams of five will choose a post-primary school class that fits all of your timetables.

Your task: Design a scheme of work/unit plan to align with the points below:

- An exciting and challenging outdoor education culminating event (e.g., orienteering, hill walking, overnight camping trip).
- Assign individual roles to each teaching team member and define the responsibilities for each role (e.g., school liaison officer, event coordinator, photographer).
- Design a set of five classes to prepare pupils for the culminating event.
- Design a set of formative and summative assessment(s) to determine if pupils learned and achieved learning goals.
- Reflect on and analyse daily lessons, pupil learning, and culminating event.
- Submit an evidence-based reflective work sample to document planning, delivering, teaching and learning.

21

PROFESSIONAL DEVELOPMENT AND PROFESSIONAL LEARNING: BRIDGING THE GAP FOR EXPERIENCED PHYSICAL EDUCATION TEACHERS

 The study

Armour, K.M. and Yelling, M. (2004). **European Physical Education Review, *10*, pp. 71–93.**

The authors argue that new thinking is required if continuing professional development (CPD) is to achieve all that it suggests in name. They examine traditional forms of professional development as delivered in physical education and they provide suggestions for alternative forms of delivery. Focusing on the CPD profiles of experienced physical education teachers, the authors sought to understand issues physical educators face accessing and engaging in CPD and factors that have an impact on teachers' practices and student learning.

Design and method/participants

Data was collected in a structured, interlinking and sequential fashion using interviews, a profile questionnaire and detailed case studies. Interviews were used to inform design of the profile questionnaire with case study teachers identified from the questionnaire data. In-depth, semi-structured interviews took place in a preparation phase with 20 experienced physical educators from 12 schools in England. Data reporting CPD experiences and their effectiveness were analysed collectively and as individual cases seeking patterns and recurring themes. Open-ended profile questionnaires were developed from the interview data as a means of allowing teachers to reflect on their experiences and add depth to their developing profiles through their personal CPD history and its relationship to their beliefs and values about teaching. Copies of the questionnaire were sent to 56 post-primary schools of varied type and location in the midlands of England and most with connections with a university programme. Respondents included 65 physical educators (37 men, 28 women) with between 6 and 29 years of experience teaching physical education and undertaking varied roles within the school. Respondents were asked details of CPD experiences (i.e., effectiveness, future plans, advice to providers and outcomes in their own programmes). As with the interviews, questionnaire data were analysed individually and collectively resulting in identification of key issues or themes.

Results

Interview data revealed a small and limited range of issues from a widely diverse (age, years teaching) group of teachers, suggesting that CPD tends:

1   to be minimally challenging;
2   to be basic giving-of-information meetings with little value;
3   to be sport-update courses that might be effective if action-orientated and provided by an effective moderator;
4   to provide little coherence of learning.

Four key issues and themes were revealed in the profiles from the questionnaires. The first issue identified the key outcomes that teachers held for students in physical education: (a) health, fitness and lifelong activity, (b) competence, knowledge and understanding in/of sports and (c) elements of personal, social and emotional education. Issue two involved the type of CPD teachers experienced. The authors suggested that teachers had little coherence or progression in their learning and that the majority of CPD was provided in one-day courses delivered away from the teachers' school settings. The third issue revealed that effective CPD experiences were practical, relevant and applicable, capable of providing ideas and practices, delivered by effective presenter, challenging and thought provoking, and offered time for reflection and collaboration. The fourth issue provided advice to CPD policy-makers and included course funding, cost and quality of substitutes, time and teacher workload, location and type of activity, and entitlement.

 ## Research perspective

The research design of the study is an interesting departure from the usual practice of survey data informing interview protocols. Thirty-four hours of in-depth interviews were conducted prior to the time-intensive profile questionnaires to help the authors understand the types of CPD opportunities experienced by physical educators. Data from the interviews guided development of questionnaires which sought to extend what participants' gained from CPD. The questionnaires were then used to inform the detailed case studies and teacher profiles that provide the main results and issues drawn from this work.

This paper is one of the first to investigate CPD in physical education, and subsequently is one of the most widely referenced in the physical education literature on CPD. As researchers, we are often reminded to go back to our primary sources rather than counting on another scholar's interpretations of the findings, and this paper provides us the opportunity to revisit such a primary source.

 ## Shared response

This paper prompted us to consider in what way, and to what extent physical education CPD has developed since its publication. We identified three issues related to CPD in physical education:

1 *Professional learning as part of your 'job'/profession.*
2 *Professional development and professional learning: bridging the gap for experienced physical education teachers.*
3 *What is effective CPD – what we know, but what else?*

Professional learning as part of your 'job'/profession

In responding to the Keay (2009) paper, we discussed the definitions of professional learning and professional development. It is worth reiterating that 'professional learning' in this paper refers to the dynamics of the day-to-day, school-based professional learning, while 'professional development' is conveyed as an 'add on' to the work of the teacher. It is this shift from the previously popular term of 'professional development' to 'professional learning' that encourages teachers to pursue the point made in the paper that a small number of teachers reported that they had undertaken or were currently pursuing, 'academic and professional' courses, such as higher degrees. We propose that if teachers are able to accumulate professional learning opportunities as part of their daily teaching, this would reduce the need for professional development opportunities that tend to be perceived as 'taking teachers outside of the school day'.

One practice that allows PSTs to experience enhanced professional learning opportunities, while gaining their teaching qualification is Master's-level Post Graduate Certificate of Education (PGCE) programmes in England. In such instances, Master's-level credits, which may contribute towards a full Master's, are offered within the programme (denoted as PGCE/M). This initiative is a precursor to teaching in England becoming a Master's-level profession. In establishing the PGCE/M, the argument was made that, first, there is a fundamental link between the required professional attributes of teachers and the requirements of Master's-level study and, second, Master's-level study has the potential to become a more effective approach in relation to helping pre-service teachers bridge the gap between theory and practice. The initiative also acknowledges the change in school culture towards the importance of CPD. The way in which the Master's-level work is incorporated into the PGCE programme means that it is not perceived as an 'add on' but rather a way in which to enrich the consideration of what it is be a professional teacher. That is, there is an acknowledgement of an additional amount of investment if a PST wishes to strive to produce Master's-level work, although many PGCE programmes at Master's-level integrate the M-level work within the day-to-day programme. One would hope that such a provision would instil in prospective teachers the feasibility of enhancing their professional learning through tasks that they are required to successfully complete in order to achieve qualified teacher status and that this would positively dispose them to pursue opportunities for heightened professional learning as a practicing teacher. The government has also introduced a Master's degree in Teaching and Learning (MTL), anticipating that such a structure would, in the first instance, build on initial teacher education and induction, encouraging teachers in their first few years of teaching to pursue further professional development work at M level to achieve a Master's qualification. Teachers studying for the MTL are to have the support of a tutor from a higher education institution and an in-school coach. The MTL is also practice-based, allowing teachers to incorporate their professional learning into their day in areas such as curriculum development, inclusion and subject knowledge for teaching. The PGCE/M opportunity and the availability of the MTL are an example of how PSTs can be encouraged to increase their professional learning opportunities as a student teacher and sustain an appreciation of professional learning through completion of a Master's qualification.

Professional development and professional learning: bridging the gap for experienced physical education teachers

Over my professional career, I have participated in many and varied professional development events. Some addressed areas that were very much within my professional comfort zone while others did make greater demands on me personally and professionally. For example, not having come from a dance background, in the earlier part of my career, I rarely included dance in my physical education programme. My undergraduate learning experiences in dance had done little to address this deficit. If anything, I lost considerable ground in terms of feeling more competent and confident about my ability to teach dance. However, having undertaken one or two short dance courses that I really enjoyed, and at a time where I had a more secure sense of myself as a teacher, I undertook a two year diploma in dance. This CPD provided an opportunity to address my skill deficit, knowledge and understanding about dance in education. And, yes, I did go on to include dance as an integral part of the physical education programme, and, no, it never did get to be very easy for me, but I did learn to enjoy it and I am really glad that I tried.

So why this story? On reading this research article, I was very struck by the fact that what these teachers undertook in CPD only narrowly related to what they saw as being the 'point' of physical education. In my story, I am realising that when I undertook the dance diploma, it was one of the few times that I sought out a CPD opportunity specifically in an effort to support my desire to include dance as an integral part of the physical education programme because I believed it was part of what the 'point' of physical education was for me.

As teachers, each of us has a sense of what we consider the 'point' of physical education to be. Defining and refining what we see as the point is an important first step in guiding our decision making in relation to what CPD we undertake. Teaching is all about 'moral purpose' where the student is the central consideration.

> The central moral purpose consists of constantly improving student achievement and ensuring that achievement gaps, wherever they exist, are narrowed. In short, it's about raising the bar and narrowing the gap.
>
> Barber and Fullan (2005)

In the context of physical education, it is about constantly aiming to improve the achievement of every student, and this, I would suggest, can only be achieved by providing learning opportunities across the different physical activity areas. In this paper, although the teachers included health, fitness and lifelong activity and personal, social and emotional education as part of what they saw as the key outcomes for physical education, they nevertheless engaged in significantly more CPD in the third area – competence, knowledge and understanding in/of sports. This mismatch between what teachers saw as their moral purpose in physical education and how they choose to develop professionally is striking if not uncommon. How many of us stop to think, how does the CPD I am planning to undertake support what I see as my moral purpose as a physical education teacher? Or do we tend to go with whatever CPD opportunities are readily available?

There are a number of useful steps that each of us could take to ensure that the CPD we choose to undertake supports the best possible outcomes for all students' achievement in our physical education programme:

- Take the time to identify what you consider to be the 'point' or the key outcomes for physical education. What is you moral purpose?
- Critique what you have identified with a colleague(s) to ensure that there is indeed breadth and depth of purpose in the key outcomes. It is important that the key outcomes should embrace all of the students in your physical education programme.
- Make a list of all the CPD you have attended in the recent past. Identify which key outcomes in your physical education programme that these CPD opportunities support. Which key outcomes tend to be over supported? Are there gaps? How might you address these gaps? What would be good about doing that? What would be challenging?

- Take the opportunity to discuss the outcomes of this CPD audit with a colleague to refine your thinking in this area.
- This individual process is a first important step in ensuring that the CPD that you undertake supports you in planning for an inclusive and worthwhile physical education programme.

Having completed this personal audit, however, and having identified where the gaps in CPD experiences are, you may then realise that the available CPD is itself unbalanced and does not provide for professional learning across a broad range of learning in physical education. Should this be the case, it is our responsibility to advocate for broader and/or different provision. It is not in our interests to remain passive recipients of whatever is deemed to be in our interests for professional development. It is rather our responsibility to seek out, or organise, for ourselves the range of CPD and professional engagement that will support the very best practice in teaching physical education.

What is effective CPD – what we know, but what else?

While this paper outlined what constituted effective CPD it might be useful to interrogate to what extent the criteria outlined might be applied to models of CPD. The quote from one participant in the study about 'interacting with new ideas and information' is probably particularly apt. Teachers will respond to different ways of exploring content. The onus on providers is to offer as many ways as possible of interacting with new ideas.

Take, for example, a school that is examining games within their programmes. A particular game or a category of games such as invasion games may be the focus. Some teachers may need to experience playing the game. Other teachers may have experience of exploring a game in practice and need to move on to examining how the game may be adapted to meet different levels of players. This may merit discussion or it may best be explored by using video clips of students playing the game and then discussing it. Other teachers will prefer to read material that explores the learning that children engage in to highlight how the game is contributing to the overall aims of physical education. A podcast presented by a teacher or consultant with expertise in the teaching of the game might prompt discussion by a group of teachers. Each of these different ways of engaging with content can encompass the five 'effective' aspects of CPD cited by the authors as noted in this example linked to invasion games:

- The practical element can be embraced: play an aspect of the games.
- 'Ideas' can emerge . . . adaptations or practices that can be recorded to guide the teacher as they embark on teaching the game.
- The presenter may well be from within the school or department (a physical education teacher or a primary curriculum leader).
- Practical exploration and discussion can be challenging if it embraces discussion on how the game can be adapted or developed or for example, become the basis for a unit within sport education.

- Time for reflection and collaboration can be built in at a time chosen by the teacher or agreed on by the principal or department head in collaboration with the staff.

The illustration above is merely an attempt at describing a school-based PD initiative that can lead to meaningful learning by the teacher embracing much of what the authors have described. Our challenge is to provide some 'external' input where a group of teachers would like to have an outside view . . . the podcast might be one example, another practitioner might provide a recorded teaching video clip that the group of teachers can view to prompt discussion. The use of digital technology in various ways is not new to physical education or indeed to PD. Good practice is already in the system, and some small supports may be all that is needed to provide structures for school-based PD in physical education to achieve the effectiveness outlined so clearly by the authors in 2004 and supported in much literature in the intervening years.

22

TEACHER PROFESSIONAL DEVELOPMENT: WHO IS THE LEARNER?

 The study

Petrie, K. and McGee, C. (2012). **Australian Journal of Teacher Education, 37(2), pp. 59–72.**

This paper explores (a) the design and delivery of a professional development (PD) programme that was part of the broader Physical Activity Initiative in New Zealand and (b) how the programme supported teachers as learners. The programme was government-funded and aimed to provide additional professional development to schools and teachers to improve outcomes for students through changes in teachers' practice. The focus in this paper is on supporting primary school teachers and examines what teachers learned about teaching physical education and how their learning had an impact on classroom practices.

Participants

Two sets of participants provided the data: PD providers (advisers) (n = 14) and teachers (n = 25), all of who were involved in the programme. Ten schools that varied in terms of socioeconomic status, ethnic make-up, enrolments and type were invited to participate. Purposeful sampling was used to ensure that the teacher responsible for leading the physical education PD was part of the sample. Ten leaders were chosen, and fifteen other teachers were drawn from their responses to an initial questionnaire seeking them to self-report their levels of competence and confidence in teaching physical education.

Design and method

The first phase of data collection involved three focus group interviews with advisers and the collection of documents from regional coordinators, Ministry of Education officials and other policy documents. Teachers completed a questionnaire and an initial interview, which provided baseline data with a focus on how they perceived the delivery of the PD programme and what it meant for their learning. They shared some of the documents that they had received or developed themselves. The second phase explored the advisers' impressions of the strengths and weaknesses of the design and delivery of the PD programme that they were providing to schools.

Results

The findings convey that there was standardised delivery of PD across all schools in spite of regional or local variations and that there was little regard for teacher background. In the delivery of PD teachers were encouraged to use student-centred approaches, but as learners they were not exposed to the same pedagogical understandings or approaches. Advisers reported that they had little time to engage in professional learning themselves and that they had few opportunities to develop knowledge of adult teacher learning. Teachers were positive about their active learning opportunities and reported that their learning 'by doing' enabled them to take it back to the classroom and deliver it. Advisers provided resources (model activities, games and full lessons) that did not reflect the different contexts, settings and needs of schools. The resources extended the teachers' repertoire of activities, but teachers became 'copiers' and seemed unable to innovate for themselves.

The findings demonstrate that teacher learning in PD needs to be challenged to explore how teacher learning is increased and how teachers best learn while also meeting outcomes related to student learning and achievement in specific classroom contexts. Professional developers believed that teachers would learn what was taught, and apply it in the classroom, in spite of their differences related to content knowledge, teaching approaches and capabilities. Developers of PD need adequate time and support for training the advisers and then allowing adequate time for advisers to develop and implement PD programmes responding to the unique needs of each school and teacher.

 Research perspective

The paper outlined clearly the background to the programme that is the focus of the study and left the reader very clear on the nature and extent of the intervention, providing insight comparable to an earlier paper by Armour and Yelling (2004) to which we responded. That is:

1   Effective PD needed to be contextualised, sustained and tailored to recognise differences between teachers.

2   Time should be provided for advisers to up-skill.
3   PD providers need to be helped to analyse the school and classroom context
    and plan learning experiences suited to particular contexts.

While suggesting that the model of PD in this study is ineffective in many ways,
the paper failed to interrogate these deficiencies in the programme. The authors
suggest that particular aspects of the PD programme are ineffective and that
alternative models need to be proposed but do not help us understand how to
develop more effective PD programmes.

We then grappled with the reality of meeting these criteria for effective PD.
Are there any programmes that can provide this 'ideal' PD? Perhaps the reality
is that this is not possible as a whole but that PD programmes can be underpinned
by this blueprint of best practice. An example of an Urban Schools Initiative
(Tannehill and Murphy, 2012) that drew together physical education teachers
to work together as a community of practice answered the need for contextualised
learning where student intake was similar across schools. Each element of any
PD programme (lecture, workshop, practical, discussions) should be structured to
allow for some work on contextualising learning or work on how we might bring
home some key messages and sustain learning.

A strong element to emerge from the paper for PD providers is hinted at in
the title, 'Who is the learner?' prompting the consideration of the teacher as
learner. This is significant as many PD programmes focus on student outcomes
expecting the teacher to be the passive receiver who will transmit learning to
students. It is acknowledged in the paper that the advisers in this programme had
few opportunities to develop content knowledge, pedagogical knowledge or
understandings about adult teacher learning.

 Shared response

*As we read this article, discussed its findings and the authors' interpretations, we asked
ourselves, 'After reading the paper what would each of us do differently to design and
deliver CPD?' Following are our responses to this question.*

Teacher professional development: who is the learner?

Professional learning must always be at the service of improving teaching, which
in turn should enhance the learner's experiences of, and achievement in, physical
education. We do not doubt that consideration of the teacher as learner is central
to this outcome. What helps teachers to learn? What supports their sustained
engagement in professional learning? This paper reminds us that there is no 'quick
fix' to any of these questions. A perfect storm is required where the various elements
necessary for effective professional learning come together in a coherent way. These
elements include a focus on the teacher as professional, good practice in the

design of CPD and the support of a 'learning school' environment. It is not possible, we suggest, to provide effective CPD without the active involvement and commitment of the individual teacher. When we look at the factors that are present when real change happens in the physical education class, chief among these will be the teacher's personal and professional commitment to, and engagement in, the change process. It requires that we, as teachers, are prepared to fully engage in professional learning.

Professional learning is not a linear process. It is cyclical and it requires that we are prepared to accept challenging goals, plan, reflect on their outcomes and construct our own understanding of the new learning. It requires that we are prepared to learn from others including being open to constructive feedback about our practice. Each of us can contribute to the kind of positive emotional climate that supports deep learning both for ourselves and for others. No matter how good the PD opportunity is, no matter how fancy the resources are, without the professionalism of the teacher, they are of little use. An ongoing commitment to continual professional learning is key for teachers managing to improve their practice throughout their professional lives.

The design of CPD opportunities can now draw on this and other research articles into what makes for effective professional learning experiences for teachers. Teachers should not be seen as little more than neutral intermediaries who can simply be primed to deliver the new ideas conceived by others as being worthwhile, no matter how well founded these ideas might be. Teachers are first and foremost learners who want to know more about the new ideas and how they might translate into their individual school context. As teachers are provided with a clear rationale for the proposed changes, they will require time to consider the new ideas and to decide how these can fit with their existing practice. Changing one's practice will cause teachers to reflect on their competence and their professional identity. There is therefore a need for opportunities to support teachers in building their confidence and belief in their own ability to introduce the change in their practice. Teachers are similar to other learners. They learn best by doing the activities and experiencing the different learning approaches. Teachers can grow in confidence when they have the necessary supports and resources to embed the new ideas into their practice, including the skills to adapt them in the variety of contexts that different class groups inevitable present. Good professional learning experiences can be designed to provide this.

These professional learning opportunities have for too long tended to reside beyond the school gates. We know from the research that change and improvement in practice is more likely to happen through sustained collaborative learning between colleagues in school. Many of our schools are designed as hierarchical structures where often the perceived wisdom and expertise is seen to reside with others including management and subject department leaders. More and more however, teachers are beginning to let go of the isolated nature of much of their practice and are increasingly open to learning from, and with, their teaching colleagues. Ideally, schools should critique how they organise their day-to-day business in terms of how it supports or works against teacher collaboration and professional learning. For example, is there a time in the week when all physical education teachers are not teaching? In after-school planning time, are there opportunities to meet to review practice? Is engagement in collaborative learning commended by management and/or shared with colleagues? Do end-of-year principal and teacher interviews include an opportunity to reflect on the quality of teaching and learning and what supports or resources might be considered to support improving practice? If the question is not asked, do you, the teacher, believe that you could bring it up?

Schools also have a responsibility to look beyond the four walls to learn from others and to draw on evidence-based practice to improve how the school goes about its business. In so doing, it indirectly validates those teachers who are also part of wider professional learning communities.

The teacher is the main agent for changing the quality of teaching and learning in physical education. However, the teacher requires the support of not only a well-conceived national or regional CPD programme based on good practice but also a school working environment that supports teachers working to provide quality learning experiences.

Initial teacher education response

One of the messages that arose in reading the paper is that, regardless of the CPD infrastructures that are put in place, teachers have to be inherently positively disposed and interested in extending their learning as a teacher for the CPD opportunities to be worthwhile and meaningful to the teacher. It is interesting that most studies concerning CPD in physical education, including this one, focus on qualified teachers' dispositions to CPD. Suggestions have been made that a more long-term development of teachers as learners requires initial teacher education programmes introducing, progressing and modelling the learning approach that teachers need to sustain an interest in professional learning throughout their careers (Armour, 2010; Loughran, 2006).

Consideration therefore has to be given to professional development and professional learning opportunities that can be introduced in initial teacher education programmes to not only help foster in PSTs a genuine desire for professional learning but also guide them as they become beginning teachers as regards the pursuit and maintenance of professional learning throughout their teaching career. That is, how do we best instil in PSTs the necessity to position themselves as career-long learners with an obligation to embrace and develop their own professional learning (MacPhail, 2012)? One example would be to encourage PSTs to develop a professional development plan to guide their first year of teaching. In compiling their professional development plan, PSTs could be asked to identify at least three areas in which they would like to improve during their first year of teaching, design at least one goal for each of these areas, identify strategies they intend to use to assist them in reaching each goal, and identify a timeline to achieve the goal. A second example to encourage and instil in PSTs the importance of professional learning is the opportunity for them to become part of a community of local/regional physical education teachers. This would expose PSTs to schools and teaching contexts, and associated class content and ideas, they will be introduced to as beginning teachers and allow them to begin identifying professional learning and development needs if they are to be effective teachers in such contexts. Paramount in promoting and encouraging PSTs' and beginning teachers' contribution to a community of physical education is exposure to, and attendance at, regional, state or national conferences, particularly those of the physical education professional association. Affording PSTs the opportunity to undertake such opportunities would hopefully heighten their understanding of what professional learning and development entails and how it benefits them in sustaining their learning as practicing teachers.

Collaborative reading and reflection

If we agree that CPD cannot solve all the problems teachers face in schools, cannot answer all teachers' questions related to teaching and learning and cannot provide teachers with the skills and 'know how' to deliver exciting and challenging learning experiences for students, then perhaps by viewing the school as a place of teacher learning we can find ways to assist teachers in helping one another grow and develop.

Book clubs and reading groups have grown in popularity in recent years in many communities across different cultures. It has been shown to be a great way to get a collection of people together to discuss a shared passion using a book or reading as a stimulus. Drawing on this idea, the Physical Education, Physical Activity and Youth Sport (PE-PAYS) Research Centre started an initiative four years ago called, 'Let's Talk Pedagogy'. We invited colleagues from across the multidiscipline, multi-university centre with the intent of fostering ongoing discussion focused on teacher education. Initially, a book was chosen to guide these discussions, *Developing a pedagogy of teacher education* (Loughran, 2006), with one chapter guiding each meeting, a facilitator chosen to guide us, and questions to encourage discussion. This was provocative, caused us to question our own practice, challenge one another's viewpoints and grow through a shared dialogue on best practice.

Why not initiate this same type of collaborative reading and discussion among a group of teachers in one school, in a single department, or who happen to share some of the same issues around teaching, and/or the learning of their students? Let's say that a number of teachers working within a primary school are struggling with the bullying behaviours of some pupils on the playground during lunch. Two or three teachers find an article about a school wide bullying prevention programme (e.g., Gibbone and Manson, 2010) and suggest that a group discussion around this article might provide them with ideas on how to proceed. On the other hand, a post-primary school may be attempting to develop new and innovative teaching practices in physical education and have heard a lot about inquiry-based teaching from other colleagues. They locate a Canadian website, *Heart health for senior high school physical education* (http://education.alberta.ca/media/618568/heart.pdf), that provides resources for inquiry-based learning to address the outcomes of physical education. It seems a perfect resource applying theory to practice that might serve to initiate discussions and planning for new strategies to be employed in their classes.

As we finish this section we had to laugh because in some ways the four of us relied on a book club mentality when writing this book, reading, discussing, brainstorming, learning from, and with, each other as we attempted to apply research to practice. What a challenging and growth-promoting journey it has been.

FINDING DIFFERENT WAYS TO MAKE RESEARCH SERVE TEACHING

Lawrence F. Locke and Dolly Lambdin

At this juncture, the authors have done their part. They have presented 22 studies in a reasonably accessible form, and they have tried to serve as a catalyst for your thinking by commenting on the studies and by providing the reactions of a teacher educator, and veteran practitioners (primary and post-primary). Our hope now is that you have become sufficiently intrigued to find yourself thinking about the next possible steps in the form of plans that will move you from reading to action. If you decide to use any of the valuables found in this book in your own teaching, you will become one of an elite group of teachers who have taken the long step to cross the gap between research and practice.

More than a century ago, the first American psychologist, William James, described such a gap between research and practice more succinctly than anything we ever could compose. He was lecturing to a class of future teachers when he observed that 'teaching is an art, and sciences never generate arts directly out of themselves. An intermediate, inventive mind must make the application, by using its originality' (James, 1983: 15). If you want to make something happen in your gym that will apply a valuable idea gleaned from research, that 'intermediate, inventive mind' must be yours.

Applying research

We can't tell you what will work in your school because we don't know your school. It may be a well-worn teachers' aphorism, but the following rule is true nonetheless. Every classroom and school is unique, and only the people who are there can determine what is needed and what is appropriate. It follows, then, that if research-based ideas are to be used to change and improve anything in your *classroom*, it is you who will have to determine what and how.

The process of making that determination is commonly called *research application*, but such a phrase is dangerously misleading. Its implication is that you simply take 'how to do it' off the pages of a book or journal, then insert the process into your daily practice. On rare occasions, that may happen, but far more often the process of fitting an idea or research finding to local conditions involves adapting rather than just applying. New teaching strategies inspired by research have to be stretched, shaped and tailored to meet the unique characteristics of your students, programme, school environment, resources, teaching style and educational objectives – which is exactly why James said that in inventing what to do with research, the educator's mind would have to 'use its originality'.

How teachers select studies for application

After many years of watching students and teachers rummage through stacks of research studies, we have acquired various observations about the application process that you may find useful. First, they are almost unfailingly able to *select* particular studies to serve as the basis for designing their own application to test in class. Those selections seem to fall into one of three broad categories:

- Studies with applications that reflect teachers' concerns about problems that are evident in their workplace, whether pedagogical, programmatic, political or social.
- Studies with applications that reflect teachers' desire to move students toward particular educational outcomes, whether physical, cognitive or affective.
- Studies with applications that reflect teachers' encounter with a topic they had not previously given attention, but about which they discover some special interest, curiosity or personal concern.

If you reflect for a moment on your responses to the studies annotated in this book, we are sure you will identify particular examples that reflect how your own responses fell into one or more of those categories. If those are some of the common reasons for deciding to try a research-based idea in the gym, what exactly is your next step? How do you go from an attractive-looking possibility to an actual application in action? There are too many answers to such a question to even begin a discussion in this limited space, but there is, however, a general pattern to a teacher's efforts to make use of research-based ideas – a pattern that might offer some guidance should you decide to take the next step yourself.

A model for common paths to application

At least in physical education, most efforts at research application seem to follow one of three well-defined paths. We have tried to describe them, and in doing so, we have labelled them simply as Paths A, B and C. In addition, we have provided a figure at the end of this chapter that diagrams the essential elements defining each route. You may want to consult that illustration as you consider the notion of alternative paths for application.

We caution you that, like all such diagrammatic representations, this one is a vast oversimplification. In the real world, the paths are not so nicely separated and linear, but are richly interconnected and full of branches. It is common for teachers to proceed along one and suddenly discover that they really need to be on an adjacent path. What makes the most practical sense is to start out by considering which path best fits the opportunity offered by a study. Avoid getting locked into a bad choice or failing to consider alternatives that are not even included in our figure. Diagrams are just abstractions about a world that is far too complicated to capture with little boxes and arrows.

Path A

Path A is the fast track to application. Research studies invariably turn up ideas for action that are simple, low cost, low risk and intuitively attractive. Remember not to make application into a big production – just make a simple plan for what you want to do and try it out on Monday morning. In this text, Chapter 2 – 'Physical education resources, class management and student physical activity levels' may fall into such a category for certain teachers.

The protocol for checking out a possible application follows the advice given in many of the responses (Teacher Education, Primary Response or Post-primary) of the preceding chapters. Keep it simple; start with just one class; use simple tools to economise time; prepare your pupils for any change in routine; watch for things that might improve a second try; and finally, don't expect to be perfect the first time around. Our own experience suggests that for most applications of this type, a recursive loop (not shown in the figure) often leads back to planning and thus to further trials.

The most common mistake in following this route is to fail to plan for some explicit method of deciding whether or how the application worked. In other words, how will you be able to tell if the application was successful or not? You do not need elaborate provisions for evaluation at the start, but you do need at least a simple strategy for noticing the consequences of change. With some evidence or impression of what the application actually produced, the decision about keeping, revising or discarding becomes simple.

Path B

This path leads first to collecting information, rather than some immediate effort at application. In the case of certain studies, their potential for application really cannot be assessed until you know exactly what is already going on in your classes. A perfect example in this book is provided by Chapter 9 – 'Student perception of caring teaching in physical education'. We have found that when prodded a bit, most teachers (ourselves included) will admit that they are not altogether sure of what constitutes caring teacher behaviour. The topic seems important and worthy of a teacher's inquiry. The first step, then, has to be determining what students identify as caring teacher behaviour – recognise me, help me learn and trust/respect me. This will then allow teachers to determine how to best demonstrate caring in their lessons and interactions with young people.

As Lambdin pointed out in the first edition of this text, the process of gathering data to establish a baseline need not be elaborate or costly, so long as you limit your effort to easily observed behaviours. In fact, the real problem is often forcing yourself to look at the findings of such preliminary self-assessment with honesty and a dispassionate eye. The outcomes of that first step are displayed within our figure as (in your judgment) either satisfactory or deficient in some regard. The latter, of course, may lead to the design of an intervention suggested by the study in question – in which case the full report of that investigation often can provide some useful leads.

In this text, likely candidates for Path B are Chapters 4 – 'Measuring secondary pupils' disruptive behaviours in physical education' and Chapter 12 – 'The influence of student status on student interactions and experiences during a sport education unit', both of which involve listening to what children have to say about various aspects of your teaching or programme. All of them require a certain degree of self-inspection before interventions can be considered. One of the common errors is mistaking a topic as appropriate for Path A (immediate action) when it really requires use of the Path B (see figure) strategy for establishing what is going on at present. In other words, if Path A is 'Leap!' then Path B is 'Look before you leap.' Although it is tempting to yell 'Geronimo!' and jump, many circumstances deem that you do a little investigation before diving headfirst into practical application.

Path C

This path is the route of caution, contemplation, consultation and collaboration. Some studies have implications that are unclear or complicated, and they call for careful reflection. In addition, as we have noted frequently throughout this text, they also call for consultation with colleagues who can help with understanding what the findings really mean and what might be involved in any effort to apply them in your school.

In other instances, the meaning of a study may be perfectly clear, but attempting any sort of application obviously requires an investment of resources, particularly time and energy (although money and political capital may ultimately be demanded as well). Simple prudence dictates that you proceed cautiously in contemplating research applications of that sort.

Finally, other studies simply yield no clear or immediate implication for where to take the findings. Selecting the target for application and devising the exact nature of what has to be done can present difficult problems that call for thought, creativity and, as always, the sharing of those burdens with others.

In this text, many of the chapters in Section III – 'Curriculum and instruction models' are among the logical candidates for treatment as Path C problems in application. This approach has rich potential for growing branches onto the other two paths. For example, some aspects of a study with complicated implications may require a period of self-assessment before serious collaborative planning can begin, while other aspects may permit an immediate trial run as a preliminary test before further investment.

Application as change

We would be remiss if we did not note that attempts to apply certain research findings can involve a measure of very real professional risk. At the least, the gamble of investing that most scarce commodity – time – is always without any guarantee of a reasonable payoff. Beyond that is the fact that any application of research-stimulated ideas will involve changing what already is happening, and as we all know, tinkering with existing regularities is not always welcome in the school workplace. Nor will every colleague immediately support every proposal for change – even when the *idea* appears to have a strong basis in research. At such points, application becomes a political problem as well as a pedagogical, or curricular, one. Resistance, however, is not always a fatal impediment, nor is it always inappropriate. A degree of respect for the feelings of others and a realistic anticipation of objections that might arise can serve to smooth the bumps along any of the three application paths.

The risks of unintended consequences

Finally, you too should be wary of the consequences that flow from change. The process of implementing research-based change in your gymnasium may be exciting, engrossing and empowering, and it can even be successful in producing exactly the desired effect. A particular rule, however, works in the midst of all that positive change, and it always must be observed. *Almost any change you introduce in the way you interact with students (or colleagues, administrators and parents) will produce at least some unintended consequences.* The world is simply too complicated to allow one change to produce one and only one effect.

Some of those unintended (and thus surprising) outcomes will be negligible or at least neutral; others will be as welcome as an unexpected bonus in your paycheque. A few, however, can be undesirable or, in rare instances, dangerous. The appropriate response to the rule of unintended consequences should be obvious. Keep your eyes and ears open; don't get romanced by what you hope will happen; and pay close attention to negative feedback – no matter what the source. With that kind of monitoring, we believe you will find that applications of research yield real benefits and a lot of fun and satisfaction along the path.

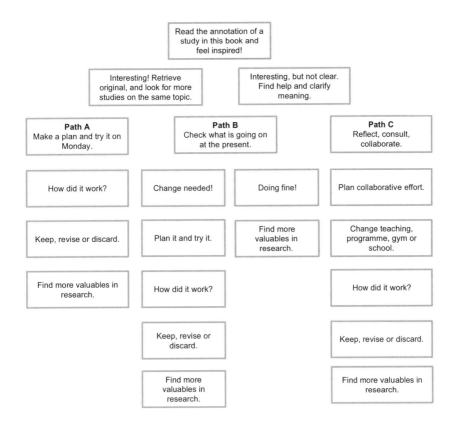

FIGURE A.1 Paths to the application of research in physical education

ANNOTATED LIST OF SELECTED JOURNALS

*Deborah Tannehill, Ann MacPhail,
Ger Halbert and Frances Murphy*

The impact factor of a journal is becoming more important in authors considering where to publish their work, and it is important that as a reader of research you appreciate what an impact factor is. The impact factor is a measure of the frequency with which the 'average article' in a journal has been cited in a particular year or period. The impact factor therefore clarifies the significance of total citation frequencies. The higher the impact factor for a journal, the more articles in that journal are likely to be cited than from another journal with a lower impact factor.

Education journals

Assessment in Education

Assessment in Education is the official journal of the International Association for Educational Assessment (IAEA). The focus of *Assessment in Education* is to provide a scholarly outlet for research in the field of assessment. The journal encourages contributions from a wide range of assessment systems and cultures with the intent of exploring both commonalities and differences in policy and practice.

British Educational Research Journal (BERJ)

The *British Educational Research Journal* is an international peer-reviewed journal focused on research in education and published by Taylor and Francis. It is the official journal of the British Educational Research Association (BERA) and includes research reports from a multitude of genres – case studies, experiments and surveys, discussions of conceptual and methodological issues, research in progress, and book reviews. *British Educational Research Journal* seeks original work that will interest and impact the educational research community internationally.

Journal of In-service Education

Journal of In-service Education is a peer-reviewed international journal published by Taylor and Francis. It is focused on continuing professional development; initial teacher education, induction, mentoring and coaching; professional learning; management and leadership of continuing professional development; the analysis of local, regional and national policies relating to CPD; and the work of higher education, advisory services and training and development organisations in supporting and promoting CPD. Although the main focus of articles is likely to be teacher education, contributions that discuss the policy and practice of CPD in other professions where the focus of the article is professional learning are welcome.

Teacher Education Advancement Network Journal

Teacher Education Advancement Network Journal is a recent online publication aimed specifically at teacher educators. It intends to advance research and scholarly activity across teacher education in all subject areas. The journal is published by the Teacher Education Advancement Network (TEAN) and is designed to be a journal whose contributors will offer examples from their own practice and activity.

Teaching and Teacher Education

Published by Elsevier, *Teaching and Teacher Education* is an international multidisciplinary journal focused on enhancing theory, research and practice on teachers, teaching and/or teacher education. It is intended for all who hold an interest in research on teaching. *Teaching and Teacher Education* includes empirical research using varied approaches and methodologies, theoretical and conceptual papers, and research.

Australian Journal of Teacher Education

Australian Journal of Teacher Education is a peer-reviewed journal that aims to enhance the quality of teacher education through the publication of research reports, learned points of view and commentaries. The various articles address the proposals for and descriptions of developments in the purpose, structure and methodology of teacher education; curriculum issues; changes in schools; or general social, ideological or political issues relating to teacher education. This journal can be freely accessed and is published six times a year by Edith Cowan

University. The Journal is rated A by the Australian Research Council 2010 (www.arc.gov.au/era/era_journal_list/htm).

Physical education related

European Physical Education Review

European Physical Education Review aims through its publication to stimulate scholarly enquiry in the broad field of physical education, including sport and leisure issues and research. The journal brings together articles from a variety of disciplines drawn from natural and social sciences and humanities. It occasionally devotes special issues to major topics and themes within the field. Contributions come from all over the world, promoting international communication among academics and professionals. This journal is a member of the Committee on Publication Ethics (COPE).

Journal of School Health

Journal of School Health is published monthly by the American School Health Association. The journal aims to provide information about the role of schools and their staffs in providing for the health and well-being of school-aged youth. Its readers include professionals working to provide young people with programmes, services and environments designed to support young people's good health and academic success. The journal addresses a wide range of youth health-related topics including articles about physical education, health services, nutrition services, counselling, psychological, and social services and healthy school environments.

Journal of Teaching in Physical Education (JTPE)

Journal of Teaching in Physical Education (JTPE) is an international peer-reviewed journal published by Human Kinetics. JTPE intends to publish international research related to physical activity in schools, communities and sport and that stimulates scholars to discuss, study and critique teaching, teacher education and curriculum. The nature of the work published in JTPE includes empirical studies in physical education, integrative reviews and analyses of educational and methodological issues in the field, and those that reflect a variety of methodological approaches.

Physical Education and Sport Pedagogy

Physical Education and Sport Pedagogy is the official peer-reviewed research journal of the Association for Physical Education. The journal publishes research that reports practice from a variety of contexts, including school physical education, cubs, sporting groups and physical activity programmes. Articles include research into a wide range of physical activities, including dance, outdoor and adventure activities, martial arts and different sports in a variety of contexts. The editors show a particular interest in articles that focus on the interaction between a variety of components, including knowledge and curriculum, learners and learning, and teachers and coaching.

Quest

Quest is the official journal of the National Association for Kinesiology and Physical Education in Higher Education. Its primary purpose is to publish articles that address issues and concerns relevant and meaningful to kinesiology and physical education in higher education, crossing disciplinary boundaries. Quest readers' include academicians, teachers and administrators, and it provides a public forum for scholarly and creative thought about the profession.

Research Quarterly Exercise and Sport

Research Quarterly Exercise and Sport offers the latest research in the art and science of human movement studies. It features articles and research notes covering a wide range of areas including biomechanics, epidemiology, motor behaviour, measurement and evaluation, physiology, pedagogy, psychology and history/philosophy/sociocultural foundations. This journal is a valuable resource for researchers and university students preparing for careers in exercise and sport science. The journal is published four times a year (March, June, September and December) and there is an annual online supplement containing approximately 250 abstracts of presentations from the Research Consortium Conference of the AAHPERD National Convention.

Sport, Education and Society

Sport, Education and Society is an international journal that focuses on the publication of social science research on pedagogy, policy and the body in society and the wide range of associated social, cultural, political and ethical issues in physical activity, sport and health. The journal draws on a wide range of research about the forms, contents and contexts of physical education, sport and health education found in schools, colleges and other sites of formal education, and on the pedagogies of play, callisthenics, gymnastics, sport and leisure found in familial contexts, various sports clubs, the leisure industry, private fitness and health studios, dance schools and rehabilitation centres.

The Physical Educator

The Physical Educator is one of the longest-standing journals designed to provide research-based articles relating to physical education, health, recreation and related areas. This journal aims to publish articles of interest to person's engaged in or pursuing careers in physical education, health, recreation, dance, human performance, exercise science, sports medicine and sports management.

REFERENCES

Alberta Education, Reading and Teaching Resource Branch. *Heart health for senior high school physical education*. Available at http://education.alberta.ca/media/618568/heart.pdf (accessed 7 June 2012).

Armour, K. (2010). Teachers, coaches and advanced pedagogies for lifelong engagement on physical education and sport. Symposium at the Congress of the International Association of Physical Education in Higher Education, La Coruna, Spain, 26–29 October.

Armour, K. and Yelling, M. (2004). Professional development and professional learning: Bridging the gap for experienced physical education teachers. *European Physical Education Review*, 10, pp. 71–93.

Barber, M. and Fullan, M. (2005). Tri Level Development: It's the system. Available at www.michaelfullan.ca/Articles_05/Tri-Level%20Dev't.htm (accessed 8 June 2012).

Bevans, K., Fitzpatrick, L.A., Sanchez, B. and Forrest, C.B. (2010). Individual and instructional determinants of student engagement in physical education. *Journal of Teaching in Physical Education*, 29, pp. 399–416.

Bevans, K.B., Fitzpatrick, L.A., Sanchez, B.M., Riley, A.W. and Forrest, C. (2010). Physical education resources, class management and student physical activity levels: A structure-process-outcome approach to evaluating physical education effectiveness. *Journal of School Health*, 8(12), pp. 573–580.

Black, P., Harrison, C., Lee, C., Marshall, B. and Wiliam, D. (2003). *Assessment for Learning: Putting it into practice*. Buckingham, UK: Open University Press.

Black, P. and Wiliam, D. (1998a). Assessment and classroom learning. *Assessment in Education*, 5(1), pp. 7–75.

Black, P. and Wiliam, D. (1998b). *Inside the black box: Raising standards through classroom assessment*. London: School of Education, King's College.

Bourdieu, P. and Passeron, J.C. (1977). *Reproduction in education, society and culture*. London: Sage Publications.

Broadfoot, P.M. (1996). *Education, assessment and society*. Buckingham, UK: Open University Press.

Brock, S.J., Rovegno, I. and Oliver, K.L. (2009). The influence of student status on student interactions and experiences during a sport education unit. *Physical Education and Sport Pedagogy*, 14(4), pp. 355–375.

Brown, D.H. and Rich, E. (2002). Gender positioning as pedagogical practice in learning to teach Physical Education, in D. Penney (ed.) *Gender and Physical Education*. London: Routledge, pp. 80–100.

Buettner, D. *Blue Zone: Secrets of a Long Life*. Available at: www.bluezones.com/about/dan-buettner/ (accessed 12 March 2012).

Casey, A. and Hastie, P.A. (2011). Students and teacher responses to a unit of student-designed games. *Physical Education and Sport Pedagogy*, 16(3), pp. 295–312.

Center for the Future of Teaching and Learning at WestEd (2002). *California's Teaching Force: Key Issues and Trends 2002*. Available at www.cftl.org/documents/KeyIssues2002.pdf (accessed 22 April 2012).

Cohen, E.G. (1994). *Designing groupwork: Strategies for the heterogeneous classroom* (2nd edition). New York: Teachers College Press.

Cooper, T., Nuyen, A. and Baturo, A. (2003). Integrating mathematics outcomes with Rich Tasks within a Productive Pedagogies framework report: An expert analysis of the Rich Tasks in relation to teaching mathematics Years 1–9. Available at: http://education.qld.gov.au/corporate/newbasics/pdfs/richtaskrep3-final-8.4.03.pdf (accessed 8 June 2012).

Culpepper, D.O., Tarr, S.J. and Killion, L.E. (2011). The role of various curriculum models on physical activity levels. *The Physical Educator*, Fall, pp. 163–171.

Denzin, N.K. and Lincoln, Y.S. (2003). Introduction: The discipline and practice of qualitative research, in N.K. Denzin and Y.S. Lincoln (eds), *Strategies of qualitative inquiry* (2nd edition). Thousand Oaks, CA: Sage, pp. 1–45.

Dillon, M. (2012) Understanding pre-service teachers' learning to teach: Influences and decisions during teaching practice. Unpublished Ph.D. thesis, University of Limerick.

Doyle, W. (1983). Academic work. *Review of Educational Research*, 53(3), pp. 159–199.

Dreyfus, H.L. and Dreyfus, S.E. (1986). *Mind over machine: The power of human intuition and expertise in the age of the computer*. Oxford: Basil Blackwell.

Duncombe, R. and Armour, K.M. (2004). Collaborative professional learning: From theory to practice. *Journal of In-service Education*, 30(1), pp. 141.

Elwood, J. and Klenowski, V. (2002). Creating communities of shared practice: The challenges of assessment use in learning and teaching. *Assessment and Evaluation in Higher Education*, 27, pp. 243–256.

Ennis, C.D. (2003). Using curriculum to enhance student learning, in S.J. Silverman and C.D. Ennis (eds) *Student Learning in Physical Education – Applying Research to Enhance Instruction* (2nd edition). Champaign, IL: Human Kinetics, pp. 109–127.

Gibbone, A. and Manson, M. (2010). Bullying: Proactive physical educators' contribution to school-wide prevention. *Journal of Physical Education, Recreation and Dance*, 81, pp. 20–24.

Goetz, J.P. and LeCompte, M.D. (1984). *Ethnography and qualitative design in educational research*. Orlando, FL: Academic Press.

Gorard, S. and See, B.H. (2011). How can we enhance enjoyment of secondary school? The student view. *British Educational Research Journal*, 37(4), pp. 671–690.

Hay, P.J. and Macdonald, D. (2010). The gendering of abilities in Senior PE. *Physical Education and Sport Pedagogy*, 15(3), pp. 271–285.

Hastie, P.A. and Curtner-Smith, M.D. (2006). Influence of a hybrid Sport Education–Teaching Games for Understanding unit on one teacher and his students. *Physical Education and Sport Pedagogy*, 11(1), pp. 1–27.

Hellison, D. (2011). *Teaching personal and social responsibility through physical activity* (3rd edition). Champaign, IL: Human Kinetics.

Hellison, D. (2003). *Teaching responsibility through physical activity* (2nd edition). Champaign, IL: Human Kinetics.

Hellison, D. (1995). *Teaching responsibility through physical activity*. Champaign, IL: Human Kinetics.

James, A.R., Griffin, L. and Dodds, P. (2009). Perceptions of middle school assessment: An ecological view. *Physical Education and Sport Pedagogy*, 14(3), pp. 323–334.

James, W. (1983). *Essays in psychology*. Cambridge, MA: Harvard University Press.

Keay, J. (2006). Collaborative learning in physical education teachers' early-career professional development. *Physical Education and Sport Pedagogy*, 11(3), pp. 285–305.

Ko, M.S., Sohn, C.T. and Lee, J.Y. (2003). Pedagogical content knowledge of elementary physical education specialists. DAEGU Universiade Conference, Yeungnam University, Korea.

Krech, P.R., Kulinna, P.H. and Cothran, D.J. (2010). Development of a short-form version of the Physical Education Classroom Instrument: Measuring secondary pupils' disruptive behaviours, *Physical Education and Sport Pedagogy*, 15, pp. 1–17.

Larson, A. (2006). Student perception of caring teaching in physical education. *Sport, Education and Society*, 11(4), pp. 337–352.

Li, W., Wright, P.M., Rukavina, P.R. and Pickering, M. (2008). Measuring students' perceptions of personal and social responsibility and the relationship to intrinsic motivation in urban physical education. *Journal of Teaching in Physical Education*, 27, pp. 167–178.

Locke, L.F., Silverman, S.J. and Spirduso, W.W. (2010). *Reading and understanding research* (3rd edition). Thousand Oaks, CA: Sage Publishers.

Loughran, J. (2006). *Developing a pedagogy of teacher education*. London: Routledge.

Luke, I.T. and Hardy, C.A. (1999). Metacognition and pupils learning, in C.A. Hardy and M. Mawer (eds) *Learning and teaching in physical education*. London: Falmer Press.

Lund, J. and Tannehill, D. (2010). *Standards-based physical education curriculum development* (2nd edition). Burlington, MA: Jones and Bartlett.

Macdonald, D., Hunter, L. and Tinning, R. (2007). Curriculum construction: A critical analysis of 'rich tasks' in the recontextualizing field. *Australian Journal of Education*, 51(2), pp. 112–128.

MacPhail, A. and Halbert, J. (2010). 'We had to do intelligent thinking during recent PE': Students' and teachers' experiences of assessment for learning in post-primary physical education. *Assessment in Education: Principles, Policy & Practice*, 17(1), pp. 23–39.

MacPhail, A. and Tannehill, D. (2012). Helping pre-service and beginning teachers examine and reframe assumptions about themselves as teachers and change agents: 'Who is going to listen to you anyway?'. *Quest*, 64(4) 299–312.

Markland, D., Ryan, R.M., Tobin, V.J. and Rollnick, S. (2005). Motivational interviewing and self-determination theory. *Journal of Social and Clinical Psychology*, 24(6), pp. 811–831.

Marzano, R.J. (2003). *What works in schools: Translating research into action*. Alexandria, VA: Association for Supervision and Curriculum Development.

McCroskey, C. (1992). *An introduction to communication in the classroom*. Edina, MN: Burgess International Group.

Metzler, M. (1990). Teaching during competitive games: Not just playin' around. *Journal of Physical Education, Recreation & Dance*, 61(8), pp. 57–61.

Metzler, M. (2000). *Instructional models for physical education*. Boston, MA: Allyn and Bacon.

Noddings, N. (2002). *Education moral people: a caring alternative to character education*. New York: Teachers College Press.

O'Sullivan, M. (2007). Teachers matter: A framework for professional development in physical education, in P. Heikinaro-Johansson, R. Telema and McEvoy, E. (eds) *The role of physical education in promoting physical activity and health*. Jyvaskyla, Finland: University of Jyvaskyla, pp. 45–59.

Parker, M., Patton, K., Madden, M. and Sinclair, C. (2010). From committee to community: The development and maintenance of a community of practice. *Journal of Teaching in Physical Education*, 29(4), pp. 337–357.

Petrie, K. and McGee, C. (2012). Teacher professional development: Who is the learner? *Australian Journal of Teacher Education*, 37(2), pp. 59–72.

Poekert, P. (2011). The pedagogy of facilitation: Teacher inquiry as professional development in a Florida elementary school. *Professional Development in Education*, 37(1), pp. 19–38.

Quennerstedt, M., Ohman, J. and Ohman, M. (2011). Investigating learning in physical education – a transactional approach. *Sport, Education and Society*, 16(2), pp. 159–177.

Reay, D. and Wiliam, D. (1999). I'll be a nothing: Structure, agency and the construction of identity through assessment. *British Educational Research Journal*, 25(3), pp. 343–354.

Redelius, K. and Hay, P. (2009). Defining, acquiring, and transacting cultural capital through assessment in physical education. *European Physical Education Review*, 15(3), pp. 275–294.

Richmond, V. P. and McCroskey, J. C. (1992). *Organizational Communication for Survival*. Englewood Cliffs, NJ: Prentice-Hall.

Rink, J. and Mitchell, M. (2003). State level assessment in physical education: the South Carolina experience. *Journal of Teaching in Physical Education*, 22(5), pp. 471–614.

Rovegno, I. and Bandhauer, D. (1994). Child-designed games: Experience changes teachers' conceptions, *Journal of Physical Education, Recreation and Dance* 60(3), pp. 60–63.

Ruiz, L.M., Graupera, J.L., Moreno, J.A. and Rico, I. (2010). Social preferences for learning among adolescents in secondary physical education. *Journal of Teaching in Physical Education*, 29, pp. 3–20.

Sagor, R. (2002). Lessons learned from skateboarders. *Educational Leadership*, 60, pp. 34–38.

Siedentop, D. (1991). *Developing Teaching Skills in Physical Education* (1st edition). Mountain View, CA: Mayfield Publishing Company.

Siedentop, D. and Tannehill, D. (2000). *Developing Teaching Skills in Physical Education*. Mountain View, CA: Mayfield Publishing Company.

Sinelnikov, O. (2009). Sport Education for teachers: Professional development when introducing a novel curriculum model. *European Physical Education Review*, 15(1): 91–114.

Strauss, A. and Corbin, J. (1998). *Basics of qualitative research techniques and procedures for developing grounded theory* (2nd edition). London: Sage Publications.

Stran, M. and Curtner-Smith, M. (2009). Influence of occupational socialization on two preservice teachers' interpretation and delivery of the Sport Education model. *Journal of Teaching in Physical Education*, 28, pp. 38–53.

Sutherland, S., Ressler, J. and Stuhr, P.T. (2011). Adventure-Based Learning and reflection: The journey of one cohort of teacher candidates. *International Journal of Human Movement Science*, 5(2), pp. 5–24.

Tannehill, D. and Murphy, G. (2012). Teacher empowerment through a community of practice: The urban school initiative. Paper presented at the 2012 annual AAHPERD Convention, Boston, MA.

Taylor, S.J. and Bogden, R. (1984). *Introduction to qualitative research methods: The search for meanings*. New York: Wiley-Interscience Education.

Tsangaridou, N. and O'Sullivan, M. (1994). Using pedagogical reflective strategies to enhance reflection among preservice physical education teachers. *Journal of Teaching in Physical Education*, 14(1), pp. 13–23.

Watson, D.L., Newton, M. and Kim, M. (2003). Recognition of values-based constructs in a summer physical activity program. *Urban Review*, 35, pp. 217–232.

INDEX

Please note that any references to Figures or Tables will be in *italics*.